Common Currents

Common Currents

Examining How We Manage the Ocean Commons

Edited by

H. Jordan Diamond, Holly Doremus and Hee Cheol Yang

TUTA SUB AEGIDE PALLAS · 1683 ·

BRILL
NIJHOFF

LEIDEN | BOSTON

The Library of Congress Cataloging-in-Publication Data is available online at https://catalog.loc.gov
LC record available at https://lccn.loc.gov/2022007709

Typeface for the Latin, Greek, and Cyrillic scripts: "Brill". See and download: brill.com/brill-typeface.

ISBN 978-90-04-51420-1 (hardback)
ISBN 978-90-04-51421-8 (e-book)

This book is printed on acid-free paper and produced in a sustainable manner.

This book is dedicated to Jane L. Scheiber – inspiring friend, selfless mentor, and tireless supporter of the law of the sea

Contents

Acknowledgments

This volume stems from a conference co-hosted by the Law of the Sea Institute at the University of California, Berkeley School of Law, the Ocean Law and Policy Institute at the Korea Institute of Ocean Science and Technology (KIOST), and Columbia Law School in September 2018. We wish to extend our gratitude in particular to Ms. Charity Lee and Joan Fargo for their collaboration on the conference, and to then-Berkeley Law students Charisa Gowen-Takahashi and Elizabeth Glusman for their research and drafting assistance. We also want to extend our heartfelt thanks to Autumn Bordner, who in addition to authoring the chapter on biodiversity in areas beyond national jurisdiction also contributed to the editing and compilation of this volume, and to now-retired KIOST Law of the Sea scholar Dr. Moon Sang Kwon for his tireless dedication to the peaceful manifestation of UN Convention on the Law of the Sea and strengthening development of the Law of the Sea Institute. Support for this effort was provided primarily through a KIOST project on Challenging Ocean Regime Conflicts and International Networking to Promote Securing Expanded Maritime Development Domain.

Figures

Notes on Contributors

1 Editors

H. Jordan Diamond

is the Co-Director of the Law of the Sea Institute (LOSI) and Executive Director of the Center for Law, Energy & the Environment (CLEE) at the School of Law, University of California, Berkeley. LOSI is an internationally recognized forum that facilitates in-depth, expert research and commentary on critical marine issues. CLEE develops pragmatic policy solutions to environmental and energy challenges in California and beyond. In both capacities, Jordan's work focuses on ensuring laws and policies are based on the best information available, developed through inclusive and transparent processes, and implemented through adaptive systems. Previously, Jordan co-directed the Ocean Program at the Environmental Law Institute. In 2013, Jordan received the ABA Section of Environment, Energy, and Resources *Distinguished Environmental Advocates: The Next Generation* award. In 2018, Governor Edmund G. Brown, Jr. appointed Jordan to the California Ocean Protection Council.

Holly Doremus

is the James H. House and Hiram H. Hurd Professor of Environmental Regulation at the University of California, Berkeley, Co-Director of the Law of the Sea Institute, and Co-Faculty Director of the University of California, Berkeley, Institute for Parks, People, and Biodiversity. She is an elected Fellow of the American Association for the Advancement of Science. She holds a B.S. in biology from Trinity College (Hartford, CT), Ph.D. in plant physiology from Cornell University, and J.D. from University of California, Berkeley. Her scholarship focuses on biodiversity protection, the intersection between property rights and environmental regulation, and the interrelationship of environmental law and science.

Hee Cheol Yang

is currently a Principal Research Scientist and Director General for the Ocean Law and Policy Institute at the Korea Institute of Ocean Science and Technology. He received his Ph.D in international law of the sea and Chinese law from the National Taiwan University in 2006. His specialties are maritime boundary delimitation, marine scientific research, deep seabed, and other issues relating to the ocean. He has been serving as an expert government consultant on various issues of marine affairs including issues relating to the law of the sea and maritime delimitation of Korea, ocean legal regimes and policy, and various marine science and technology policies and governances.

2 Authors

David Balton
served as the Deputy Assistant Secretary for Oceans and Fisheries in the Department of State, attaining the rank of Ambassador in 2006. He coordinated U.S. foreign policy concerning oceans and fisheries, as well as issues relating to the Arctic and Antarctica, and oversaw U.S. participation in international organizations dealing with these issues. Ambassador Balton functioned as the lead U.S. negotiator on a wide range of agreements and chaired numerous international meetings. During the U.S. Chairmanship of the Arctic Council (2015–2017), he served as Chair of the Senior Arctic Officials. He also co-chaired Arctic Council Task Forces that produced the 2011 Arctic Search and Rescue Agreement and the 2013 Arctic Oil Pollution Agreement. He separately chaired negotiations to produce an Arctic fisheries agreement. Ambassador Balton received an A.B. from Harvard College and a J.D. from Georgetown University. He appeared with the National Symphony Orchestra (juggling oranges).

Leonardo Bernard
is a Lecturer with the Australian National Centre for Ocean Resources and Security (ANCORS) at the University of Wollongong, Australia. Leo has written extensively on law of the sea issues such as the continental shelf; maritime boundary disputes; and on the application of historic rights under international law. Leo is the co-author of Promoting Compliance: The Role of Dispute Settlement and Monitoring Mechanisms in ASEAN Instruments (2016); as well as the co-editor for East China Sea: How to Build Confidence and Promote Cooperation (2018) and Beyond Territorial Disputes in the South China Sea: Legal Framework for the Joint Development of Hydrocarbon Resources. Leo is also a regular guest lecturer in maritime delimitation subjects and short-courses at the National University of Singapore, Law School.

Autumn Bordner
is an Interdisciplinary Researcher focused on empire and environmental justice in Oceania. She is the co-founder of the Allies for Micronesia Project, a non-profit organization working to address the unique justice challenges facing U.S.-affiliated islands in the Micronesian region. Autumn is an associate

at Blue Ocean Law, a Ph.D. student at the University of Melbourne investigating ways in which climate justice can be achieved within colonial legal systems, and a former Oceans Fellow at the Center for Law, Energy, and the Environment at the School of Law, University of California, Berkeley. She holds a J.D. from Stanford Law School, an M.S. from Stanford University, and a B.A. from Columbia University.

David Freestone
is a Professorial Lecturer and Visiting Scholar at George Washington University Law School, Washington, D.C. He is Co-rapporteur of the ILA Committee on Sea level Rise and International Law and the Executive Secretary of the Sargasso Sea Commission. He is founding Editor of the International Journal of Marine and Coastal Law (now in its 37th year). From 1996–2008 he worked at the World Bank in Washington, D.C., retiring in 2008 as Deputy General Counsel/ Senior Adviser. He is the 2007 Winner of the Elizabeth Haub Gold Medal for Environmental Law.

Seokwoo Lee
is Professor of International Law, Inha University Law School, Korea (2003-present). He was Chairman of the Foundation for the Development of International Law in Asia (DILA) (2012–2017). He is the Co-Editor-in-Chief of the Asia-Pacific Journal of Ocean Law and Policy (APJOLP) and Asian Yearbook of International Law (Asian YBIL), the Executive Editor of the Korean Journal of International and Comparative Law (KJICL), the Co-Series Editor of the book series entitled Maritime Cooperation in East Asia, and the Associate Editor of Brill Research Perspectives in the Law of the Sea, all published by Brill. He has authored more than 100 publications in English in addition to his more than 90 publications in Korean. His representative recent book publication in English is: The Making of International Law in Korea: From Colony to Asian Power (Brill/Nijhoff, 2016). He holds a D.Phil. (Oxford), LL.M.s (NYU, Minnesota, and Korea University), and LL.B. (Korea University).

Young Kil Park
is Director of the Law of the Sea Research Division at the Korea Maritime Institute (KMI) and leads the Yeosu Academy of the Law of the Sea. Previously he was a visiting scholar at the R.I. Transportation Research Center, University of Rhode Island and the Stockton Center for International Law, Naval War College. He has also served as Head for the Polar Policy Research Center and the Maritime Territory Research Center at the KMI. His academic interests cover the law of the sea, maritime security, and Arctic governance.

Harry N. Scheiber
is Chancellor's Distinguished Professor and Stefan Riesenfeld Professor of Law and History, Emeritus, at the School of Law, University of California, Berkeley. He brought the Law of the Sea Institute to University of California, Berkeley and co-directed it with David Caron from 2002–2013 and then directed it from 2013–2016. He is a Fellow of the American Academy of Arts and Sciences, honorary life fellow and former president of the American Society for Legal History, and twice a Guggenheim Fellow. He has published over 100 articles and is author or editor of twenty-eight books in the fields of ocean law, marine fisheries management, history of American constitutional law, and law and economic policy.

Clive Schofield
is Head of Research at the WMU-Sasakawa Global Ocean Institute, World Maritime University (WMU) in Malmö, Sweden and is a Professor with the Australian Centre for Ocean Resources and Security (ANCORS), University of Wollongong (UOW), Australia. He holds a Ph.D in Geography from the University of Durham, UK and an LLM in international law from the University of British Columbia. His research interests relate to international boundaries and particularly maritime boundary delimitation and marine jurisdictional issues. Clive is an Observer on the Advisory Board on the Law of the Sea (ABLOS) and is a member of the International Law Association's Committee on International Law and Sea Level Rise. He is a Distinguished Fellow of the Law of the Sea Institute at the School of Law, University of California, Berkeley, is a Global Associate, Centre for International Law (CIL), National University of Singapore and is a Fellow of the Royal Geographical Society. He has provided advice to governments engaged in boundary negotiations and in dispute settlement cases before the International Court of Justice (ICJ) and recently served as an independent expert witness in the international arbitration case between the Philippines and China.

Karen N. Scott
is a Professor of Law at the University of Canterbury in New Zealand, President of the Australian and New Zealand Society of International Law (ANZSIL) and Editor-in-Chief of *Ocean Development and International Law* (ODIL). Karen is on the board of seven journals including the *Brill Research Perspectives on the Law of the Sea* and the *Australian Yearbook of International Law*. She researches and teaches in the areas of public international law, law of the sea and international environmental law and has published over 100 edited books, journal articles and book chapters in these areas. Karen is a

University Proctor and she was Head of the School of Law at the University of Canterbury between 2015 and 2018. She previously taught at the University of Nottingham in the UK.

David L. VanderZwaag
is Professor of Law and Canada Research Chair in Ocean Law and Governance at the Marine & Environmental Law Institute, Schulich School of Law, Dalhousie University. He is a Member of the IUCN World Commission on Environmental Law (WCEL) and was co-chair of WCEL's Specialist Group on Oceans, Coasts and Coral Reefs (2004–2017). He has published over 150 papers in the marine and environmental law field. His most recent co-edited book publications include: Research Handbook on Ocean Acidification Law and Policy (Edward Elgar 2021); Research Handbook on Polar Law (Edward Elgar 2020); Aquaculture Law and Policy: Global, Regional and National Perspectives (Edward Elgar 2016); Routledge Handbook of National and Regional Ocean Policies (Routledge 2015); and Polar Oceans in an Era of Environmental Change (Edward Elgar 2014).

Introduction

H. Jordan Diamond and Holly Doremus

The world's oceans are both vast and mysterious.[1] They cover over 70 percent of the planet, and hold roughly 97 percent of its water. Measured by volume, they provide 99 percent of the living space on the planet. It is estimated that they remain more than 80 percent unexplored, unmapped, and indeed unknown,[2] and it is commonly accepted that although we have identified several hundred thousand marine species, that represents only a small proportion of the ocean's biodiversity.[3]

The oceans provide humanity with a staggering array of goods and services. They furnish protein to feed us, medicines to keep us healthy, shipping routes to connect us, fuel to power our cities, protection for our vulnerable coastal settlements, recreational opportunities to delight us, and wonders to inspire us.[4] For centuries, human ability to exploit ocean goods and services was limited to resources near shore and near the surface. In the last hundred years or so, however, technological advances have given us the ability to access and control distant and deep ocean resources.

But the ocean also faces the triple threats posed by climate change, extraction, and pollution. Greenhouse gas emissions cause both direct and indirect problems for ocean systems. The oceans have absorbed as much as

1 H. Jordan Diamond is the Executive Director of the Center for Law, Energy & the Environment and Co-Director of the Law of the Sea Institute at the University of California, Berkeley, and public member of the California Ocean Protection Council (2018–2022). Holly Doremus is the James H. House and Hiram H. Hurd Professor of Environmental Regulation, Co-Director of the Law of the Sea Institute, and Co-Faculty Director of the Institute for Parks, People, and Biodiversity at the University of California, Berkeley. The editors wish to thank Autumn Bordner for her assistance throughout the editing process, as well as her written contribution; and Charisa Gowen-Takahashi and Elizabeth Glusman, who were Berkeley Law students at the time of the conference, for their pre-conference research and post-conference drafting of summaries that supported this introduction. Most of all, the editors thank the speakers and participants from the 2018 conference leading to this volume for contributing their expertise to both the conference and this volume.

2 National Geographic Encyclopedia, *Ocean*, https://www.nationalgeographic.org/encyclopedia/ocean/. "A far greater percentage of the surfaces of the moon and the planet Mars has been mapped and studied than of our own ocean floor." Ibid.

3 Census of Marine Life, *Scientific Results to Support the Sustainable Use and Conservation of Marine Life—A Summary of the Census of Marine Life for Decision Makers* (2011), available at http://www.coml.org/comlfiles/policy/ENGLISH_Policy_Report_reduced.pdf.

4 Edward B. Barbier, "Marine Ecosystem Services," *Current Biology* 27 (2017): R431, June 5, 2017; *World Ocean Review: Living with the Oceans* (2010).

 | DOI:10.1163/9789004514218_002

40% of the anthropogenic carbon emissions since the late 1800s.[5] That absorptive capacity has helped at least temporarily buffer the globe against temperature increases,[6] but at the cost of significant increases in ocean acidity, which disrupt ocean ecosystems.[7] Rising global temperatures also affect the oceans, causing fish species to change their range,[8] bleaching corals,[9] reducing dissolved oxygen,[10] and intensifying harmful algal blooms.[11]

Climate change is a dire threat, but hardly the only anthropogenic problem ocean systems face. Human populations extract numerous resources from the ocean, from fish to marine genetic resources and from oil and gas to rare minerals, often in unsustainable or ecologically harmful ways.[12] And we emit staggering quantities of pollution into the marine environment, from land-based plastics that have formed a gyre of marine debris in the Pacific[13] to a steady flow of chemicals, medications, and more channeled through local wastewater systems.[14]

The range of current threats introduces new dimensions to an old dilemma: ocean governance. Governance of the oceans has long been a delicate balancing act between those wishing to exert individualized control over ocean resources and those who see the world's oceans as the paradigmatic shared resource. The oceans cannot be fenced. Pollution does not stay contained where it enters the seas. Highly migratory fish and mammals travel thousands of miles, without regard to jurisdictional boundaries. The oceans

---

5 *World Ocean Review*, 35.

6 Li-Qing Jiang et al., "Surface Ocean pH and Buffer Capacity: Past, Present and Future," *Nature: Scientific Reports* 9: 18624 (2019).

7 *World Ocean Review*, 36–45.

8 Ben Goldfarb, "Feeling the Heat: How Fish Are Migrating from Warming Waters," *Yale Environment 360* (June 15, 2017), https://e360.yale.edu/features/feeling-the-heat-warming-oceans-drive-fish-into-cooler-waters.

9 Terry Hughes et al., "Global Warming and Recurrent Mass Bleaching of Corals," *Nature* 543: 373 (2017).

10 Peter G. Brewer and Edward T. Peltzer, "Ocean chemistry, Ocean warming, and Emerging Hypoxia: Commentary," *Journal of Geophysical Research: Oceans* 121: 3659 (2016).

11 Christopher J. Gobler, "Climate Change and Harmful Algal Blooms," *Harmful Algae* 91: 101731 (2020).

12 *See, e.g.*, Jason S. Link and Reg A. Watson, "Global Ecosystem Overfishing: Clear Delineation Within Real Limits to Production," *Science Advances* 5: eaav0474 (2019).

13 National Oceanic and Atmospheric Administration, National Ocean Service, *What Is the Great Pacific Garbage Patch?*, last updated Feb. 26, 2021, https://oceanservice.noaa.gov/facts/garbagepatch.html.

14 Beth A. Polidoro et al., "Land-based Sources of Marine Pollution: Pesticides, PAHs and Phthalates in Coastal Stream Water, and Heavy Metals in Coastal Stream Sediments in American Samoa," *Marine Pollution Bulletin* 116: 501 (2017).

are inherently interconnected, and cannot be effectively managed piecemeal. Simultaneously, however, most every coastal nation seeks the maximum range of its sovereign jurisdiction so as to assert ownership, or at least control, of the living marine resources in the water column and the mineral resources of the seabed.

In 1967, then-Ambassador of Malta Arvid Pardo made a historic speech at the United Nations General Assembly proposing that the deep seabed should be considered the common heritage of mankind, and its benefits shared. This foundational concept was integrated into the UN Convention on the Law of the Sea (UNCLOS), which mandates conservation and optimal utilization of living resources within sovereign waters, but designates the seabed beyond national jurisdiction as the common heritage of mankind.[15]

In September 2018, we convened a gathering of experts in international ocean law, policy, and science to address this balancing, and evaluate how successful it has been. We asked if, when, and how the oceans remain effectively a global commons. Six expert panels explored various aspects of the commons dialogue, identifying points of agreement and areas of contention. The goal was to enhance understanding of the status quo, share lessons learned, and explore paths forward for strengthening future governance of the ocean commons. The unifying conclusion was that the tension between a global commons and nationally controlled resources continues to dominate ocean management. The oceans are both a commons and a collection of individuated resources, and sometimes the distinctions between those two are difficult to draw. Moreover, the areas that remain at least nominally commons are far from being open access. They are regulated in various ways by a variety of institutions. Allocating their resources, or the wealth those resources can produce, among the sovereign nations that wish to claim them remains a daunting problem. So does the paradigmatic commons management problem, protecting them against overexploitation.

Over the course of two days, we learned from a series of panel presentations, followed by robust discussion among our participants, many of whom are experts in their own right. Below, we briefly summarize the presentations and highlight some prominent areas of discussion. The rest of this volume then captures expert thinking on some of the key issues, questions, and lessons related to the ocean commons.[16]

---

15 David D. Caron, "Law of the Sea," in Nigel J. Young, ed., *Oxford International Encyclopedia of Peace* (Oxford: Oxford University Press, 2010).

16 The editors want to recognize that some of the specific details included in descriptions of the panel discussions as well as in the following chapters may not be fully up to date, given the gap between the conference and our publication of the written contributions.

1 The Area

UNCLOS[17] puts the majority of the ocean floor, the seabed beyond territorial seas, exclusive economic zones (EEZS), and extended continental shelves, outside the jurisdiction of coastal States. This portion of the ocean floor is known as "the Area."[18] Article 136 designates the Area and its resources as the "common heritage of mankind" (CHM), meaning it can be used exclusively for peaceful purposes, for the common benefit of all nations, and for both present and future generations.[19] Although the CHM principle might seem to call for preservation of the Area's natural resources, the seabed commons has historically been conceived of and managed under an extractive framework.

Deposits of high-grade metal ores were first discovered on the ocean floor in the 1860s.[20] Since then, we have only managed to explore about 5% of the ocean floor.[21] Commercial interests in the seabed revolve around three types of marine mineral deposits: polymetallic nodules, polymetallic sulfides, and cobalt-rich ferromanganese crusts. To date, the only mechanism developed for governing the seabed commons is a seabed mining regime.

We asked a panel of experts to discuss how the seabed commons is managed, and how successfully the CHM principle has been implemented. The panel was deftly moderated by Tullio Treves, former judge of the International Tribunal for the Law of the Sea. Gwenaelle Le Gurun of the International Seabed Authority spoke about the Authority's management regime for the Area, and the challenges it faces in developing a framework for environmental protection and equitable sharing of benefits. Seokwoo Lee of Inha University detailed Korea's development of a comprehensive legal framework for exploration and extraction of resources from the deep seabed, including regulation of its nationals working in the Area.[22] Clive Schofield of World Maritime University's Sasakawa Global Ocean Institute and Leonardo Bernard

---

But the fundamental lessons and learnings drawn from these examples, case studies, and analyses remain extremely salient as we contemplate the future of the oceans.

17 United Nations Convention on the Law of the Sea, *opened for signature* Dec. 10, 1982, 1833 U.N.T.S. 397 (entered into force Nov. 16, 1994).

18 UNCLOS Part XI, "The Area."

19 UNCLOS art. 136.

20 R.R. Churchill & A.V. Lowe, "The International Seabed Area," in *The Law of the Sea* (3rd ed. 1999).

21 Oishimaya Sen Nag, "How Much Of The Ocean Have We Explored?", *World Atlas* (Aug. 27, 2018), https://www.worldatlas.com/articles/how-much-of-the-ocean-is-still-unexplored.html.

22 This volume, Chapter 2.

of University of Wollongong's Australian National Centre for Ocean Resources & Security (ANCORS) explained the ambiguities and uncertainties in defining the geographic limits of the Area, and the continuing challenges to identifying the precise scope of the global ocean commons.[23]

The discussion following the panel presentations highlighted the importance of the Area in its own right as an embodiment of the concept of the common heritage of mankind—a key driver of Convention negotiation—rather than merely the residual left over from State claims. In fact, the granting of control of enormous EEZs to individual States, rather than reserving them for the global community, was the historically radical aspect of UNCLOS' jurisdictional innovations. Some concern was expressed that the Commission on the Limits of the Continental Shelf (CLCS) might be used as a forum for excessive sovereignty claims.

There was further discussion of the complications of implementing UNCLOS Article 82, which calls for the equitable distribution of benefits from activities in the Area. Many see a need for it to be activated more robustly and ambiguities clarified, although the ISA has been exploring the range of outstanding questions. The ISA contemplated developing a model contract with coastal States to provide uniformity across the international community regarding terms and benefit-sharing mechanisms; however, individual countries may need more exacting terms for benefit-sharing depending on their domestic legal traditions and government structure. The debate is still ongoing regarding how the ISA can administer benefit sharing, both cash payments and payments in kind, and exactly what the Authority's role should be. Finally, the lack of clear spatial definition of the Area may be less of an impediment to the ISA's work than it appears. The fact that, at least for now, most deep seabed activity occurs far from the margins of States' claims limits the practical implications of ambiguous jurisdictional lines.

2 The Polar Regions

To much of the world, the northern and southern Polar Regions are similar: frigid, marked by glacier dominated landscapes, and inhabited only by the most resilient creatures and people. However, besides the geologic fact one is characterized by a continent and the other an ocean, their governance is remarkably different.

23 This volume, Chapter 1.

Antarctica is international territory, governed by the Antarctic Treaty[24] and a myriad of international institutions and frameworks.[25] The Arctic, by contrast, is dominated by the claims of just eight Arctic countries comprising the primary members of the Arctic Council: Canada, Denmark, Finland, Iceland, Norway, the Russian Federation, Sweden and the United States.[26] These States claim exclusive sovereign rights in their territorial seas and EEZs.[27]

Climate change is impacting regional governance of the Arctic and Antarctic in vastly different ways. Melting glaciers and loss of land-based ice in the Antarctic are a major driver of sea-level rise, and therefore an existential threat to coastal populations around the world. Meanwhile, loss of Arctic sea ice has devastating impacts on Arctic ecosystems, communities, and livelihoods. Reduced sea ice may also bring some economic opportunities for both Arctic and non-Arctic States,[28] however, and the possibility of opened seaway passages and newly accessible energy resources is driving research and investment in the region.

We asked a panel of experts to discuss global approaches to governing the polar regions. Seokwoo Lee of Inha University School of Law chaired the panel. Karen Scott of University of Canterbury, New Zealand, articulated lessons learned from international management of the Antarctic through a "regime complex" of independent, but overlapping and interacting, institutions.[29]

---

24 The Antarctic Treaty, Dec. 1, 1959, 402 U.N.T.S. 71.

25 In addition to the Antarctic Treaty, many international agreements are in force in the Antarctic, including, for example, Convention on International Trade in Endangered Species of Wild Fauna and Flora, Mar. 3, 1973, 993 U.N.T.S. 243; Convention on the Conservation of Antarctic Marine Living Resources, May 20, 1980, 1329 U.N.T.S. 47; Convention on Biological Diversity, June 5, 1992, 1760 U.N.T.S. 79; and Agreement on the Conservation of Albatrosses and Petrels, Jun. 19, 2001, 2258 U.N.T.S. 257.

26 For more information on the permanent member states, see Arctic Council, *Member States*, https://arctic-council.org/index.php/en/about-us/member-states.

27 Six organizations representing indigenous peoples are also Permanent Participants, enabling the active participation and full consultation of Arctic indigenous peoples within the Council. For more information, see Arctic Council, *Permanent Participants*, https://arctic-council.org/index.php/en/about-us/permanent-participants. In addition, non-Arctic States, inter-governmental, inter-parliamentary, regional, and global non-governmental organizations can participate as Arctic Council Observers with the permission of the Council, primarily engaging in the Council's six Working Groups. For more information, see Arctic Council, *Working Groups*, https://arctic-council.org/index.php/en/about-us/working-groups.

28 *See, e.g.*, Stine Jacobsen, "Maersk Sends First Container Ship Through Arctic Route," *Reuters* (Aug. 24, 2018); James Stavridis, China Joins the Race for Arctic Dominance as Ice Caps Melt, *Washington Post* (Apr. 20, 2019).

29 This volume, Chapter 3.

Brian Israel of Planetary Resources spoke of the need for an ecosystem approach to governance of the Arctic Marine Environment, and explained that Arctic States' active defense of their sovereignty impedes implementation of that approach. Young Kil Park of the Korea Maritime Institute provided a northeast Asian perspective on Arctic governance, focusing on the roles of China and Korea.[30] Dr. Hyunkyo Seo of the Korea Polar Research Institute closed the panel presentations with commentary on the role of two key Korean institutions: the Korea Polar Research Institute and the Korean Arctic Research Consortium.

Following the panel, the discussion highlighted the comparison between the multifaceted regime complex in the Antarctic and the singular dominance of the Arctic Council over the Arctic. It centered on the reality that the Arctic Council is heavily influenced by the Arctic States' tendency to protect as much sovereign power as possible. The Antarctic regime complex has successfully engaged a variety of governmental and non-governmental actors and international institutions. The downside of its non-hierarchical, overlapping governance system, however, is that the elements of that system sometimes operate with differing goals and divergent principles.

3 Managing Fish as a Common Resource

Much of the twentieth century was dominated by a laissez-faire attitude regarding freedom to fish in the oceans.[31] This approach led to a classic tragedy of the commons as many States rushed to exploit fisheries for their own gain, to the detriment of global fish stocks. Modern technology, which has made it possible to find and catch enormous quantities of fish at long distances from any shore, abetted this global fish grab. By 2018, the United Nations Food and Agriculture Organization (FAO) reported that over 70 percent of fisheries are maximally- or over-fished.[32] The impact of overfishing falls especially hard on those nations most dependent on ocean fish for food security.

---

30 This volume, Chapter 4.

31 Ronan Long, *Regulating and Managing Fisheries Resources: Five Decades of Triumph and Failure in the European Union*, in OCEAN LAW DEBATES 287 (Harry N. Scheiber, Nilufer Oral, and Moon Sang Kwon eds., 2018).

32 UN Food and Agricultural Organization, *The State of World Fisheries and Aquaculture: Meeting the Sustainable Development Goals*, (2018), http://www.fao.org/3/i9540en/I9540EN.pdf.

Over time, there has been a shift toward more active regulation of fisheries, with an increased focus on sustainability. The UN's Sustainable Development Goals, which entered into force in 2016, offer one example.[33] This change in resource management approach, while an improvement, is not without its difficulties. Some of the complications of management arise from the fact that fish are not distributed evenly throughout sovereign waters and the high seas; rather, 90 percent of the world's fish catch comes from only 3 percent of the ocean space. Furthermore, regulations mean little without enforcement, which, given the vast scope of the seas, poses both resource and logistical challenges.[34]

We asked a panel of experts to discuss the extent to which ocean fish are currently managed as a common resource, and the effectiveness of those management efforts. Michael Gerrard of Columbia University Law School chaired the panel. David VanderZwaag of the Marine & Environmental Law Institute at Dalhousie University described the nature and work of the North Atlantic Salmon Conservation Organization, a longstanding multilateral approach to managing an important transboundary fish stock.[35] Lorna Inniss of UN Environment discussed UN Oceans, a program comprised of over 20 different UN bodies and other organizations whose goal is global integrated ocean governance. Katrina Wyman of New York University School of Law suggested greater unilateral action by the United States barring import to the United States of fish caught on the high seas could significantly reduce high seas fishing more rapidly than an international agreement.

Following the presentations, discussion focused on the challenges of transboundary fishery management, including asymmetric access to information and uneven commitment to, and capacity for, enforcement. Conversation then turned to climate change. The prevailing single-stock assessment approach used by most RFMOs may not be able to effectively account for the multifaceted impacts of a changing climate. A more holistic ecosystem approach may be necessary. Scientific uncertainty and modeling challenges also increase the need to apply the precautionary principle. Separately, it can be difficult to measure the success of private fisheries management initiatives.

33 Ronan Long, *Regulating and Managing Fisheries Resources*, 287–288.

34 FAO, *The State of World Fisheries and Aquaculture*, 82.

35 This volume, Chapter 6.

4 Institutional Approaches to Managing the Ocean Commons

Governance of the ocean commons has historically been based on the freedom of the seas concept that dominated for centuries. Under this principle, no sovereign has ownership or control over the commons, and all are welcome to use it. The commons nature of the high seas contrasts sharply with the principle of sovereignty that informs the governance of territorial waters.[36] States have absolute control over the management of their territorial waters. Against this backdrop a sectoral and zonal management scheme has emerged.

Concerns about ocean health and resilience suggest that the current governance scheme requires augmentation to effectively manage the ocean commons and its resources. Sectoral management addresses specific ocean sectors from fishing to shipping.[37] Zonal management is spatially determined.[38] Both approaches often lead to fragmented and disjointed ocean governance,[39] particularly in light of differing stakeholder interests.[40] There is no uniform procedure for resolving conflicts between sectors or across boundaries,[41] and the cumulative effects of various marine activities are difficult to assess.[42] Furthermore, spatially-based management schemes can be at odds with the boundary-less and transient nature of marine ecosystems and species.[43] In light of these problems, interest in an integrated approach to ocean governance has grown since the second half of the 20th century.[44]

We asked a panel of experts to discuss the challenges of current institutional approaches to ocean governance. Each presented a case study, of a sector, a large-scale governance institution, and an innovative geographically focused institution. Seline Trevisanaut of Utrecht University School of Law spoke about the institutional framework governing the offshore energy sector, noting gaps, overlaps, and a lack of integration. She suggested a stronger role for global oversight. Gabriele Goettsche-Wanli of the UN Office of Legal Affairs,

---

36 Yoshifumi Tanaka, *A Dual Approach to Ocean Governance: The Cases of Zonal and Integrated Management* (London and New York: Routledge 2016).

37 L.B. Crowder et al., "Resolving Mismatches in U.S. Ocean Governance," *Science* 313 (2006): 617.

38 Tanaka, *A Dual Approach to Ocean Governance*, 6.

39 Crowder et al., *Resolving Mismatches in U.S. Ocean Governance*, 617.

40 Ibid.

41 Ibid.

42 Tanaka, *A Dual Approach to Ocean Governance*, 7.

43 Ibid.

44 Lawrence Juda, "Changing National Approaches to Ocean Governance: The United States, Canada, and Australia," *Ocean Development & International Law*, 34 (2003): 161.

Division of Ocean Affairs and the Law of the Sea, noted the tension between the sectoral regulatory framework encouraged by UNCLOS and the UN General Assembly's commitment to holistic consideration of ocean issues. She noted the General Assembly's primary role in guiding BBNJ negotiations as an example of its ability to facilitate cooperation and coordination among global and regional sectoral entities. David Freestone of George Washington University Law School and the Sargasso Sea Commission discussed the past, present, and future of the Sargasso Sea Commission.[45] William Eichbaum of the World Wildlife Fund chaired the panel and moderated the ensuing discussion.

Common themes that emerged from the presentations include the importance of identifying the proper geographic level of governance—regional versus global—and the need to avoid undermining existing governing institutions when developing new initiatives. The following discussion covered a variety of topics, including the ongoing BBNJ process, which has already played a positive role in governance development simply by bringing many new players to the table. Another topic was strengthening UN Oceans, which is a good institutional candidate for overcoming current fragmentation. Factors that might help UN Oceans grow its role could be the creation of a searchable database of sectoral activities, highlighting governance gaps, and increased funding for effective interagency coordination.

5 Marine Scientific Research Supporting Commons Governance

Marine scientific research (MSR) involves disciplines as diverse as geology, chemistry, biology, biotechnology, physics, geophysics, hydrography, oceanography, and ocean drilling and coring.[46] Researchers may focus on large or small geographic areas, confined to one State's jurisdiction or crossing multiple jurisdictional lines. Crucially, MSR highlights the effects of human activities on ocean systems and populations. For example, MSR is used to advance responsible fishing practices and prevent overfishing.[47] It is used to map the seabed

45 This volume, Chapter 7.

46 Marko Pavliha & Norman A. Martinez Guiterrez, "Marine Scientific Research and the 1982 United Nations Convention on the Law of the Sea," *Ocean & Coastal Law Journal* 16 (2010): 115.

47 Michael Lodge & Vladimir Ryabini, "Deep Sea Marine Science is Key to Unlocking the Potential of Our Oceans, International Institute for Sustainable Development" (May 16, 2019), http://sdg.iisd.org/commentary/guest-articles/deep-sea-marine-science-is-key-to-unlocking-the-potential-of-our-oceans/.

and tectonic movements of the ocean floor, to clarify the relationship of the ocean and the atmosphere, and to study waves and currents; and it advances States' national security interests by helping ships and submarines navigate the seas.[48]

UNCLOS directly governs MSR, but leaves many uncertainties.[49] Most notably, it does not define what constitutes marine scientific research, because State parties to the negotiations were unable to agree on one.[50] They did agree that MSR must be conducted "exclusively for peaceful purposes," and MSR carried out in the Area must also be "for the benefit of mankind as a whole."[51] This leaves considerable room for debate over what obligations States and researchers have when conducting MSR. The ongoing BBNJ discussions also directly implicate MSR on the high seas.

We asked a panel of experts to discuss the ways in which MSR supports governance of the ocean commons. Sherry Broder of the Jon Van Dyke Institute at the University of Hawai'i Richardson School of Law chaired the panel and facilitated the discussion. Dr. Nilufer Oral of the International Law Commission and Istanbul Bilgi University highlighted the need to balance the freedom to conduct MSR on the high seas with the obligation to promote community interests rather than those of individual States. Neil Davies of the University of California Gump South Pacific Research Station offered a case study, from the Station's work in Moorea, of how local studies can be effectively generalized to larger systems. Seung Shin of the University of Rhode Island College of Business delved into ocean data as a common resource that could be shared and integrated worldwide.

The discussion following the panel presentations focused in large part on the sociological challenges of MSR data management. There appear to be many barriers to sharing information. First and foremost, data are valuable assets, particularly to the academic scientists who gather them, fundamental to success in competitive careers. Not surprisingly, they resist sharing those assets absent an incentive to do so, whether that be compensation or acknowledgment. In contrast, there have been some data sharing networks that have been more successful in the private sector. Perhaps data

48 Pavliha & Guitierrez, "Marine Scientific Research and the 1982 United Nations Convention on the Law of the Sea," 116.

49 UNCLOS Part XIII, Marine Scientific Research (arts. 238–265).

50 U.N. Office of Legal Affairs, Division for Ocean Affairs and the Law of the Sea, *Marine Scientific Research: A Revised Guide to the Implementation of the Relevant Provisions of the United Nations Convention on the Law of the Sea Paras. 6–14* (2010).

51 UNCLOS arts. 143, 240.

sharing networks which provide mutual benefits to all MSR participants can help surmount the incentive hurdle. Other barriers to sharing may still remain, however, such as regulatory hurdles that restrict data sharing. A scientist's national origin, for example, can prevent access to another country to collect or share data. Complying with multiple inconsistent national regulations can be a burden.

Widespread conservation and management efforts require robust information collection and sharing. To maximize usability, such systems would benefit from incentives for standardization, which is not currently a focus of the scientific community. Protocols for language, digital file type, and database structure are crucial to creating a useful and effective system for data collection and use. Data management solutions should also be distributed, so that no one entity bears the burden of storing and managing data, and all relevant communities can access and use data as needed. Legal experts must play a role, ensuring that rights to use data, with appropriate acknowledgment, are clear and sufficiently broad.

6 Managing Biodiversity as a Common Resource

Marine biodiversity has the potential to spur innovation in sectors such as medicine and engineering, but it is also critical to the health and productivity of marine ecosystems.[52] Without a diversity of species and the functions they perform, ecosystems risk collapse. The marine areas beyond national jurisdiction (ABNJ) make up two-thirds of the global ocean. Biodiversity in these areas is under immense stress, due to the persistent problem of underregulation and overuse of the global commons. Policymakers are increasingly focused on conservation in these areas, however, as biodiversity has become seen as fundamental to reducing poverty and achieving sustainable development.[53]

The first session of the flagship Convention on Biological Diversity, the primary global treaty on biodiversity conservation and benefit sharing, took place in 1993.[54] While an important accomplishment, the Convention applies only within areas subject to national jurisdiction, leaving out the high seas. Biodiversity beyond national jurisdiction (BBNJ) was not explicitly mentioned

52 "Marine Biodiversity—a Vital Resource," in *World Ocean Review* (2010), http://worldoceanreview.com/en/wor-1/marine-ecosystem/biodiversity/.

53 Convention on Biological Diversity, "Convention on Biological Diversity and the World Summit on Sustainable Development," https://www.cbd.int/archives/review/wssd/.

54 Convention on Biological Diversity, "Introduction," https://www.cbd.int/intro/.

until the World Summit on Sustainable Development in 2002.[55] The Summit focused on sharing genetic resources and the benefits that come from these genetic resources, as well as technology transfer and biosafety.[56]

UNCLOS Article 192, which directs States to "protect and preserve the marine environment," provides a foundation for BBNJ conservation. Efforts have advanced on two fronts. First, regional agreements such as the Convention for the Protection of the Marine Environment of the North-East Atlantic (OSPAR Convention) have sought to protect specific ecosystems, representing an incremental approach to protecting biodiversity.[57] Second, there is an ongoing international effort to create a global and legally binding instrument to protect BBNJ. In 2004, the United Nations' General Assembly established the Ad Hoc Open-Ended Informal Working Group which issued a decision to create a legally binding instrument on biodiversity protection under UNCLOS.[58] Since then, the BBNJ Preparatory Committee has met myriad times to explore what should be included in the instrument.

We invited a panel of experts to discuss ways in which marine biodiversity can be managed as a common resource. Kristina Gjerde of the International Union for Conservation of Nature served as Chair. Harriet Harden-Davies of the University of Wollongong took up the issue of marine genetic resources and benefit sharing, a key challenge in BBNJ negotiations. She emphasized that the benefits to be shared should include scientific research capacity. Cymie Payne of Rutgers University suggested the public trust doctrine as a mechanism to ensure protection of BBNJ. Elizabeth Mendenhall of the University of Rhode Island noted that the BBNJ negotiations are plagued by tension between the two goals of biodiversity protection and biodiversity utilization.

Much of the discussion focused on implementation of the public trust doctrine in the global ocean commons. The public trust doctrine could provide a guiding principle, although some mechanism to ensure accountability and enforcement would be necessary. The inevitability of conflicting interests in ocean governance, including in the BBNJ negotiations, was noted. While there

---

55 Ronan Long, *Regulating and Managing Fisheries Resources*, 287.

56 Convention on Biological Diversity, "Convention on Biological Diversity and the World Summit on Sustainable Development," https://www.cbd.int/archives/review/wssd/.

57 David Freestone et al., "Can Existing Institutions Protect Biodiversity in Areas Beyond National Jurisdiction? Experiences from Two Ongoing Processes," *Marine Policy* 49 (2014): 167.

58 "Summary of the First Session of the Preparatory Committee on Marine Biodiversity of Areas Beyond National Jurisdiction," 25 *Earth Negotiations Bulletin* 25 (2016): 106, http://enb.iisd.org/vol25/enb25106e.html.

is always tension between economic exploitation and conservation, perhaps conflict between sectors or among States can be used to promote sustainability.

7 Conclusion

A few themes emerged repeatedly in presentations and discussion that characterize the dilemmas of managing the global ocean commons.

The first theme is the need for delineation. As we learned from Clive Schofield and Leonardo Bernard,[59] it is technically difficult to draw the line between the global marine commons and sovereign waters and submerged lands. But there is more to the delineation problem than that. Any resource from which it is difficult to exclude requires management with attention to the potential for the problem of overuse. But not all such resources deserve affirmative recognition as the common heritage of mankind. Going forward, we need principles for identifying those resources that rightly belong to the public commons, and must be managed for the benefit of the global community.

The second is the challenge of commons management. In his *Tragedy of the Commons*, Hardin advocated two solutions: privatization and regulation.[60] The international community has tried both for ocean resources. But the primary solution to date has been expansion of national sovereignty in the seas. Grotius conceived the ocean commons as inevitable: the seas were simply too vast and inaccessible to be managed or controlled. Today, however, coastal States enjoy sovereignty over vast exclusive economic zones and continental shelves. Yet even these vast areas do not exhaust human reach. Technology has made the oceans ever more accessible, allowing us to reach resources far distant from shore and far below the surface. We now recognize that all ocean resources are exhaustible. They therefore must be managed. But in areas beyond national jurisdiction we have few effective management institutions, and few effective strategies for creating new ones. That leaves us with an enduring dilemma of how to create and nourish international institutions with the capacity and incentives to manage global resources in the global interest.

59 This volume, Chapter 1.

60 In this volume, Chapter 5, Harry Scheiber elucidates how the tension at the center of Hardin's formulation of the tragedy of the commons was central to ocean law and policy debates for many years before his seminal work was published.

Third, we have yet to answer a fundamental question: for what and for whom are we managing our common resources? Should principles of allocation, to achieve equity or economic efficiency take precedence? Should the ultimate goal of commons management be biological or social sustainability? Or are there still other goals we should seek to achieve? It will be difficult to effectively manage the oceans' common resources without the guidance of shared underlying principles.

The world's oceans face daunting challenges from climate change, population growth, escalating pollution, and rapidly evolving technologies that speed the reach and pace of resource extraction. Individual nations and the global community, private actors and public, have both self-interested reasons and ethical obligations to restore and maintain ocean health. These shared interests in protecting ocean resources should motivate collaborative management efforts. But accelerating those efforts and making them effective will require that scientists, lawyers, politicians, and others work together to update and improve ocean governance institutions. We hope this Conference and this Volume provide some preliminary guidance for that work.

PART 1

The Area

CHAPTER 1

The Uncertain Limits of the Commons

Clive Schofield and Leonardo Bernard

1 Introduction

The regime of the high seas applies to those parts of the world ocean seawards of exclusive economic zone (EEZ) limits. Beyond these limits—and beyond the outer limits of the continental shelf—lies the international seabed area, generally termed the Area. These areas beyond national jurisdiction (ABNJ), encompassing an estimated sixty-four percent of the surface of the oceans and nearly ninety-five percent of its volume,[1] constitute the ocean Commons.

The precise spatial limits of the Commons are presently uncertain. This is because the outer limits of most national zones of maritime jurisdiction have yet to be clearly defined and, indeed, may change over time. While most coastal States have made claims to EEZs to 200 nautical miles (M) measured from baselines along the coast, the outer limits of these zones are generally not precisely delineated. The baselines from which such claims are measured may also change over time, creating uncertainty as to the scope of coastal States' claims to maritime jurisdiction. Consequently, the scope of both national maritime claims and that of the Commons are potentially continually in flux. This is of particular concern against the backdrop of rising sea levels.

The maritime claims of certain coastal States are also arguably excessive in character. For example, a number of States have made problematic baseline claims or have asserted EEZ and continental shelf rights from insular features whose capacity to support such claims is questionable. Further, where States have rights over continental shelf beyond 200 M, these can only be finalised following recommendations from the Commission on the Limits of the Continental Shelf (CLCS),[2] which has a significant backlog of submissions to evaluate. Moreover, Commons rights persist to some extent in these areas of

1 Rachael Scrimgeour et al., *A Review of Area-based Planning Tools. What Is the Potential for Cross-sectoral Planning in Areas Beyond National Jurisdiction?* (Cambridge, UK: UN Environment World Conservation Monitoring Centre, 2018), 4.

2 For information on the United Nations Commission on the Limits of the Continental Shelf (CLCS) *see*, "The Commission, It's Purpose and Functions," Commission on the Limits of the Continental Shelf (Aug. 15, 2019), http://www.un.org/Depts/los/clcs_new/clcs_home.htm.

 | DOI:10.1163/9789004514218_003

'extended' or 'outer' continental shelf seawards of 200 M EEZ limits, although how these rights will be realised in practice remains unclear.[3]

This Chapter will discuss the expansion of claims to maritime jurisdiction offshore and examine the challenges in establishing the outer limits of the EEZ and continental shelf which mark the beginning of the Commons. The Chapter will also explore the roles of States and institutions established under the 1982 Convention on the Law of the Sea (LOSC)[4]—notably the CLCS and the International Seabed Authority (ISA)—not only in determining these limits but in the operation of what can may be regarded as residual Commons rights relating in areas of continental shelf seawards of 200 M.

2 Creeping Jurisdiction of Coastal States

An enduring theme in the development of the international law regime relating to the oceans has been the gradual expansion of national claims to maritime jurisdiction offshore, a phenomenon often dubbed "creeping coastal State jurisdiction."[5] The tension between freedom of the seas for all States, especially freedom of navigation, and advancing coastal States' maritime claims offshore is symbolised by classic works in the law of the sea. In particular, *Mare Liberum* (Freedom of the Seas)[6] by Hugo Grotius, published in 1609,[7] championed the former view while John Selden's *Mare Clausum* (Closed Seas), published in 1635, took the latter.[8] For a considerable period, the demand for freedom of the seas in the interests of ensuring global trade meant that the Grotian view appeared to carry the day. Consequently, the maritime claims of coastal States

3 Either of the terms 'outer' or 'extended' continental shelf are generally accepted. In this chapter the former term will be used.

4 United Nations Convention on the Law of the Sea, *opened for signature* Dec. 10, 1982, 1833 U.N.T.S. 397 (entered into force Nov. 16,1994).

5 The term "creeping jurisdiction" was coined by Dr John Craven of the US Navy in the 1960s, who predicted that sovereign rights claims over the seabed by coastal States would soon be followed by similar claims to the water column above it. John Craven, "Sea Power and the Sea Bed," *US Naval Institute Proceedings* 92 (1966), 49.

6 Hugo Grotius, *The Freedom of the Seas Or The Right Which Belongs to the Dutch to Take Part in the East Indian Trade*, James Brown Scott, ed., R. Van Deman Magoffin, trans. (New York: Oxford University Press, 1916).

7 "Hugo Grotius" is the commonly used anglicised version of the Dutch "Huig de Groot." With apologies to de Groot, the anglicised version is used here.

8 John Selden, *Of the Dominion, or, Ownership of the Sea*, Marchamont Nedham, trans. (London: William du Guard by appointment of the Council of State, 1652; Clark, NJ: Lawbook Exchange, 2004).

were largely restricted to a narrow coastal belt of territorial waters. While no consensus was reached on the maximum breadth of territorial waters, they were generally thought not to extend more than 3 M offshore in accordance with what became generally known as the "cannon shot rule."[9]

While efforts were made towards the codification of the international law of the sea, for example at the Hague Conference on the Codification of International Law of 1930, little progress had been achieved by the mid-Twentieth Century. However, technological advances, particularly in relation to the exploration for and exploitation of oil offshore, proved to be a major driver for the advance in coastal State maritime claims seawards. Notable early developments in this regard include the division of the seabed of the Gulf of Paria between the United Kingdom (on behalf of Trinidad and Tobago) and Venezuela in 1942,[10] and Argentina's continental shelf Decree of 1944.[11] A 1945 United States Presidential Proclamation, Policy of the United States With Respect to the Natural Resources of the Subsoil and Sea Bed of the Continental Shelf, often termed the 'Truman Proclamation',[12] is generally regarded as a key catalyst for the expansion of coastal State claims to maritime jurisdiction further offshore. The Truman Proclamation was especially influential given that it was the United States making this assertion. The Proclamation relating to the continental shelf, stated that:

> ... the Government of the United States regards the natural resources of the subsoil and sea bed of the continental shelf beneath the high seas but contiguous to the coasts of the United States as appertaining to the United States, subject to its jurisdiction and control.[13]

9 The cannon shot rule purportedly equated to the distance a cannon could throw a ball, as proposed by the Dutch in negotiations with the English as early as 1610. *See* C. Sanger, *Ordering the Oceans: The Making of the Law of the Sea* (Toronto: University of Toronto Press, 1986), 12.

10 *See* Jonathan I. Charney and Lewis M. Alexander, eds., *International Maritime Boundaries* (Dordrecht and Boston: Martinus Nijhoff, 1993), 639–654. It is, however, worth noting in the present context that Article 5 of treaty provides that the agreement refers "solely to the submarine areas of the Gulf of Paria, and nothing herein shall be held to affect in any way the status of the islands, islets or rocks above the surface of the sea together with the territorial waters thereof." Ibid, 653.

11 This was the first explicit claim to coastal State jurisdiction over the continental shelf, termed the "epicontinental sea" of Argentina. *See* "Decree No.1, 385 Concerning Mineral Reserves, January 24, 1944, Boletin Oficial de la Republica Argentina, Vol.52, no.14, 853 (17 March 1944)," in United Nations, *Laws and Regulations on the Regime of the High Seas*, U.N. Doc. St/LEG/SER.B/1 (1951).

12 *See* Proclamation No. 2667, C.F.R. 67 (1943–48).

13 Ibid.

As this language indicates, the Truman Proclamation was explicitly resource-oriented.[14] Of particular note for future developments was that the exercise of jurisdiction over continental shelf resources by the "contiguous nation" was presented as "reasonable and just."[15] The Proclamation argued that this was because efforts to utilise or conserve seabed and subsoil resources would rely upon "cooperation and protection from shore" and because "the continental shelf may be regarded as the extension of the land mass of the coastal nation and thus naturally appurtenant to it."[16] This latter statement appears to represent an alternative way of saying "natural prolongation," with the resources in question frequently forming "a seaward extension of a pool or deposit lying within its territory."[17] While asserting control over the seabed and subsoil, the Truman Proclamation did, however, include a clear statement that "[t]he character as high seas of the waters above the continental shelf and the right to their free and unimpeded navigation are in no way thus affected."[18] The United States similarly claimed the right to designate fishery conservation zones in the high seas beyond the U.S.-claimed territorial sea.[19]

These developments sparked a profusion of extended claims to maritime jurisdiction. Such assertions included claims to sovereignty over both seabed and water column up to 200 M offshore, which in turn led to diplomatic protests from the United States, United Kingdom, and others.[20] This situation led to renewed efforts to codify the international law of the sea in the

14 The Truman Proclamation stressed the "long range world-wide need for new sources of petroleum and other minerals" and their probable presence beneath "many parts" of the continental shelf off the coasts of the United States, together with the technological developments to make their recovery practicable, either at the time or in the near future. Ibid. Further, jurisdiction over the continental shelf was claimed in order to ensure the "conservation and prudent utilization" of such resources, as development took place, and on security grounds, with "self-preservation" compelling the coastal nation to "keep close watch over activities off its shores." Ibid.

15 Ibid.

16 Ibid.

17 Ibid.

18 Ibid.

19 It is notable, however, that the fisheries proclamation refers to the regulation and control of fishing and offers to enter into agreements with other States. By contrast, the continental shelf proclamation claims "jurisdiction and control." Proclamation 2668, 3 C.F.R. 68 (1945).

20 For example, in a joint declaration dating from 1952, Chile, Ecuador, and Peru asserted their "sole sovereignty and jurisdiction over the area of sea adjacent to the coast ... and extending not less than 200 nautical miles from the said coast." Reproduced as Annex I in: U. S. Department of State, *Maritime Boundary: Chile-Peru*, Limits in the Seas No. 86 (Washington, D.C.: Office of the Geographer, Bureau of Intelligence and Research, July 2, 1979).

post-World War II period. In 1949, the International Law Commission (ILC) decided to study and codify the topic of the high seas, including to take "a careful study of the new doctrine of the control of natural submarine resources, known as the 'doctrine of the continental shelf.'"[21] The works and recommendations of the ILC served as the negotiating text for the First United Nations Conference on the Law of the Sea (UNCLOS I), which took place in Geneva in 1958. The Conference yielded four Conventions:[22] the Convention on the Territorial Sea and Contiguous Zone,[23] the Convention on the Continental Shelf,[24] the Convention on the High Seas,[25] and the Convention on Fishing and Conservation of the Living Resources of the High Sea.[26]

Despite the significant progress that the 1958 Conventions represented, uncertainty still prevailed concerning the limits of maritime claims. For example, consensus on the breadth of the territorial sea was lacking at UNCLOS I. Moreover, the breadth of the continental shelf under the 1958 Convention on the Continental Shelf was less than specific. Article 1 of the Convention provided for continental shelf limits coinciding with either a depth of 200 metres or, beyond that limit, to a depth where exploitation of resources was possible.[27] This linking of the outer limits of the continental shelf to an exploitability criterion, and thus to continuing technological developments, was widely viewed as problematic. This criterion was seen as open-ended,[28] lacking certainty,[29] and without any link to the natural physical continental shelf.[30]

Agreement on the contentious issues of territorial sea and continental shelf limits proved to be just out of reach at the conclusion of the Second United

---

21 *Summary Records and Documents of the First Session Including the Report of the Commission to the General Assembly*, (1949) 1 Y. B. Int'l L. Comm'n 3, U.N. Doc. A/CN.4/SER.A/1949, 237.

22 Collectively these Conventions are often termed the "Geneva Conventions" or the "1958 Conventions."

23 Convention on the Territorial Sea and Contiguous Zone, Apr. 29 1958, 516 U.N.T.S. 205.

24 Convention on the Continental Shelf, Apr. 29 1958, 499 U.N.T.S. 311.

25 Convention on the High Seas, Apr. 29 1958, 450 U.N.T.S. 11.

26 Convention on Fishing and Conservation of the Living Resources of the High Sea, Apr. 29 1958, 559 U.N.T.S. 285.

27 Convention on the Continental Shelf, art. 1, 311.

28 Kenneth O Emery, "Geological Aspect of Sea-floor Sovereignty," in Lewis M Alexander, ed., *The Law of the Sea: Offshore Boundaries and Zones* (Columbus, Ohio: The Ohio State University Press, 1967), 155.

29 Gilbert Gidel, "The Continental Shelf," *University of Western Australia Law Review* 3 (1954): 89–90.

30 Piers R Gardiner, "Reasons and Methods for Fixing the Outer Limit of the Legal Continental Shelf Beyond 200 Nautical Miles," *Iranian Review of International Relations* 11–12 (1978): 149.

Nations Conference on the Law of the Sea (UNCLOS II) in 1960.[31] These shortcomings were largely addressed during the Third United Nations Conference on the Law of the Sea (UNCLOS III), leading to the drafting of the LOSC in 1982. A key achievement of LOSC was the definition of clear spatial limits for national claims to maritime jurisdiction, something that had, as noted above, eluded earlier codification efforts.

Under LOSC, an agreement was reached on 12 M as the maximum breadth of the territorial sea.[32] The LOSC also provides for a contiguous zone out to 24 M from relevant baselines.[33] Additionally, and significantly, the concept of EEZ gained general international acceptance at UNCLOS III, with agreement reached on the breadth of the EEZ at 200 M from the baselines.[34] Concerning the continental shelf, complex criteria were laid down in Article 76 of LOSC whereby the outer limits of the continental shelf may be determined in partnership with a scientific and technical body established through the Convention—the CLCS. The LOSC has gained widespread international recognition and, at the time of writing, there were 168 parties to it.[35] For its parties, LOSC provides the binding legal framework governing maritime jurisdictional claims (see Figure 1.1). Indeed, those parts of the Convention dealing with maritime claims and maritime boundary delimitation can be considered declaratory of customary international law and, as such, legally binding on all States regardless of whether they are party to the Convention.[36]

---

31 For example, agreement on a formula of a 6 M territorial sea with a 6 M fishing zone seaward failing to secure the necessary two-thirds majority for adoption by a single vote (54 votes to 28 with 5 abstentions). *See* Second United Nations Conference on the Law of the Sea, *Official Record*, U.N. Doc. A/CONF.19/C.1/L.1 (Mar. 17-Apr. 26, 1960), 30.

32 Article 3 provides that every State has the right to establish the breadth of the territorial sea "up to a limit not exceeding 12 nautical miles," measured from baselines determined in accordance with the Convention. Article 4 further states that "the outer limit of the territorial sea is the line every point of which is at a distance from the nearest point of the baseline equal to the breadth of the territorial sea."

33 Ibid, art 33.

34 Ibid, art. 57.

35 Comprising 167 States plus the European Community. *See* United Nations, *Status of the United Nations Convention on the Law of the Sea, of the Agreement Relating to the Implementation of Part XI of the Convention and of the Agreement for the Implementation of the Convention Relating to the Conservation and Management of Straddling Fish Stocks and Highly Migratory Fish Stocks* (Mar. 31, 2018), available at: http://www.un.org/Depts/los/reference_files/status2018.pdf.

36 *See* Continental Shelf (Tunisia v. Libyan Arab Jamahiriya), Judgment, 1982 I.C.J. Reports 18, paras. 47, 100 (Feb. 24). A notable non-party to LOSC is the United States. The United States does, however, make its maritime claims and conduct its ocean policy in keeping with LOSC on the basis that it is largely reflective of customary international law. *See*

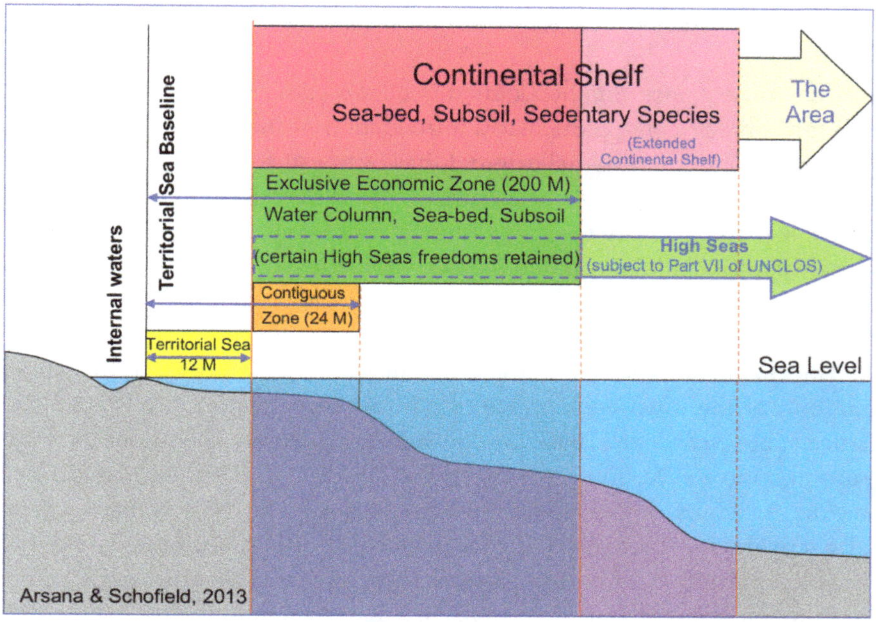

FIGURE 1.1 Baselines and claims to maritime jurisdiction
SOURCE: SCHOFIELD AND ARSANA, IHO (INTERNATIONAL HYDROGRAPHIC ORGANIZATION), *A MANUAL ON TECHNICAL ASPECTS OF THE UNITED NATIONS CONVENTION ON THE LAW OF THE SEA—1982 (TALOS)*. SPECIAL PUBLICATION NO. 51, (5TH EDITION, MONACO: INTERNATIONAL HYDROGRAPHIC BUREAU, 2014), CHAPTER 5, 3.

3 Defining the Commons under the UN Convention on the Law of the Sea

The vast majority of coastal States have proved to be enthusiastic claimants in terms of maritime jurisdictional zones.[37] These claims are predominantly in conformity with the distance-based outer limits to maritime zones prescribed by the LOSC. Indeed, a number of earlier claims that exceeded the

J. Ashley Roach and Robert Smith, *United States Responses to Excessive Maritime Claims*, 2nd ed. (Leiden and Boston: Martinus Nijhoff Publishers, 2012), 5.

37 *See* Division for Ocean Affairs and the Law of the Sea, Office of Legal Affairs, United Nations, *Table of Claims to Maritime Jurisdiction* (2011), available at: http://www.un.org/Depts/los/LEGISLATIONANDTREATIES/PDFFILES/table_summary_of_claims.pdf.

limits prescribed by LOSC were "rolled back" after the Convention entered into force.[38]

The consequence for the Commons of the extension in the breadth of the territorial sea and, particularly, introduction of the EEZ has been a radical reduction in their spatial extent. It has been estimated that, should every coastal State make territorial sea claims out to 12 M and EEZ claims out to 200 M (as is predominantly the case), these claims would encompass 43 million square nautical miles (147 million square kilometres) of maritime space.[39] This amounts to approximately 41% of the area of the oceans, meaning that the remaining 59% of the ocean comprises the high seas.[40]

The EEZ regime gives coastal States exclusive jurisdiction over the resources not only of the water column, but also of the seabed and subsoil,[41] to a distance of 200 M from the coast. Coastal States' entitlement over the seabed and subsoil up to 200 M from their coast, however, is not only based on the EEZ regime. Article 76, paragraph 1 of the LOSC, dealing with the continental shelf, also provides that coastal States have jurisdiction over the continental shelf to a distance of 200 M from their coasts.[42] Thus, within 200 M, the coastal State's jurisdiction over the seabed and subsoil is based on both the EEZ and continental shelf regimes. Beyond 200 M, coastal States may have jurisdiction over the seabed and subsoil if their continental margins extend beyond that limit.[43]

As the area beyond national jurisdictions constitute the ocean Commons, the outer limits of the EEZ and continental shelf beyond 200 M serve as the "boundary" for the Commons, which consists of the water column beyond the EEZ and the seabed beyond the continental shelf. It should be noted that coastal States could claim the outer limits of their EEZ for less than 200 M from their baselines. However, since the rights of coastal States over the continental shelf do not depend on any proclamation,[44] the continental shelf regime would still extend to 200 M or beyond that distance to the edge of the continental margin, even if States claimed less than the maximal EEZ.

38 *See* Roach and Smith, *Excessive Maritime Claims*, 138–143. Whilst most excessive territorial sea claims have been rolled back to the international norm of 12 M, a number of coastal States retain claims to 200 M territorial seas (e.g., Benin and Peru). Ibid.

39 Philip Symonds, Senior Advisor on Science and the Law of the Sea, Geoscience Australia (personal communication, July 2011).

40 Ibid. *See* also, J.R. Victor Prescott and Clive Schofield, *The Maritime Political Boundaries of the World* (Leiden: Brill Nijhoff Publishers, 2005), 9.

41 LOSC, art. 56(1)(b).

42 Ibid, art. 76(1).

43 Ibid.

44 Ibid, art 77(3).

In order to have clear limits between areas subject to national jurisdiction and the Commons, coastal States are required to publicise the outer limits of their EEZ either on charts or lists of geographical coordinates, and to deposit such charts or lists with the Secretary General of the United Nations.[45] To establish the outer limits of a continental shelf beyond 200 M, coastal States must receive recommendation from the CLCS,[46] a scientific body established under the LOSC. The CLCS considers all information submitted by coastal States in proposing the outer limits of their continental shelf beyond 200 M.[47] If the coastal State disagrees with the recommendations of the CLCS, the coastal State can make a new or revised submission within a reasonable time.[48] The CLCS, however, lacks the mandate to assess competing assertions by coastal States to the same areas of outer continental shelf. Consequently, the Commission will not consider any submission in which a land or maritime dispute exists,[49] unless prior consent is given by all States that are parties to such a dispute.[50] Since such submissions cannot be considered by the CLCS, coastal States raising objections to a submission can therefore indefinitely block definitive delineation of the outer limits of the continental shelf beyond 200 M. This is just one source of uncertainty for the limits of the Commons.

4 The Uncertainty of the Commons' Limits

While the legal definition of the Commons is clear—the area of the ocean beyond national jurisdiction—the actual spatial limits of the Commons are uncertain. One notable obstacle to clarifying the spatial dimensions of the Commons is that many maritime claims remain ill-defined. Only rarely do coastal States provide specific unilateral definitions as to the precise extent of their maritime jurisdictional claims. Instead, many States simply advance maritime claims according to the maximum breadth of the particular maritime claims, for instance asserting blanket EEZs out to 200 M from baselines

45 Ibid, art 75(2).

46 Ibid, art 76(8).

47 Ibid, Annex II, art 3.

48 Ibid, Annex II, art 8.

49 Commission on the Limits of the Continental Shelf, *Rules of Procedure of the Commission on the Limits of the Continental Shelf*, U.N. Doc. CLCS/40/Rev.1 (Apr. 17, 2008), Annex I, art 5(a).

50 Ibid.

along the coast, regardless of the proximity of neighbouring States. This general lack of precision regarding the exact dimensions of maritime claims leaves the extent of the Commons in question. The spatial scope of coastal State maritime claims is likewise rendered uncertain as a consequence of arguably excessive baselines claims, the potential for baselines and the outer limits of maritime claims to move accordingly and as a result of excessive maritime claims associated with islands.

5 Excessive Baselines

The LOSC provides a clear spatial framework for coastal State maritime claims, which are to be measured from baselines along the coast. In addition to normal baselines, the LOSC allows for a number of other types of artificial straight-line type baselines to be constructed along the coast. These include straight baselines (LOSC, Article 7), river closing lines (Article 9), bay closing lines (Article 10), and in respect of archipelagic States (Article 47). Among these, the provisions related to straight baselines have proved to be the most open to flexible interpretation and thus suffer the most abuse.

As early as 1935, Norway established a series of straight baselines joining the outer points of islands and rocks fringing part of its northern coastline, from which it measured its 4 M-breadth exclusive fisheries zone. These claims led to a case before the International Court of Justice (ICJ) between the United Kingdom and Norway seeking a ruling on the legitimacy of Norway's straight baselines.[51] In finding in favour of Norway, and confirming the validity of the Norwegian straight baseline system, the Court stipulated that: "Where a coast is deeply indented and cut into" the use of straight baselines, "within reasonable limits, may depart from the physical line of the coast"[52] but that "the drawing of baselines must not depart in any appreciable extent from the general direction of the coast."[53]

The ruling of the ICJ in the Anglo-Norwegian Fisheries case inspired the provisions on straight baselines contained in Article 4 of the 1958 Convention on the Territorial Sea and Contiguous Zone.[54] The provisions of Article 4 were largely retained as Article 7 of the LOSC. However, Article 7 goes beyond the

51 Anglo-Norwegian Fisheries Case, Judgment, 1951 I.C.J. Reports 116, 6 (Dec. 18).

52 Ibid, 128–30.

53 Ibid, 129.

54 *Report of the International Law Commission Covering the Work of its Fifth Session, 1 June—14 August 1953, Official Records of the General Assembly, Eighth Session, Supplement No. 9 (A/2456)*, (1953) Y. B. Int'l L. Comm'n 2, U.N. Doc. A/CN.4/76, 262.

1958 Convention by providing guidance in relation to baselines on highly unstable coastlines and allows for the possibility of using low-tide elevations without lighthouses as basepoints in a straight baseline system so long as such lines have acquired general international recognition.[55]

These additional provisions of Article 7 are intended to deal with particularly complex coastal geography, where the configuration of the coastline is such that using "highly irregular"[56] normal baselines would result in similarly irregular maritime limits such as, for example, a complex mosaic of enclaves or pockets of non-territorial sea areas within a State's territorial sea.[57] However, in practice, these provisions allow States to depart from the application of the normal baseline and measure maritime jurisdictional zones from straight baselines drawn along selected parts of their coastlines.[58]

The key requirements for the definition of straight baselines are contained in Article 7(1) of the LOSC, which states that straight baselines may be applied in localities "where the coastline is deeply indented and cut into, or if there is a fringe of islands along the coast in its immediate vicinity." Subsequent paragraphs of the article can be viewed as being dependent on this first paragraph, providing guidance on how straight baselines are to be defined but not in themselves offering justifications for their construction. It is, however, unclear how many and how deep the indentations need to be to constitute a "deeply indented and cut into" coastline; how many and how close the islands need to be to one another in order to form a "fringe" of islands; and how far offshore such a fringe of islands may lie and still fulfil the requirement that they be in the coastline's "immediate vicinity." Article 7 similarly fails to provide any specific rule for determining whether the sea area enclosed by a particular straight baseline system is "sufficiently closely linked to the land to be considered subject to the regime of internal waters."[59]

---

55 It can be observed that the provision concerning the use of low-tide elevations lacking lighthouses on them as potential basepoints in a system of straight baselines was likely included in Article 7 of the LOSC because Norway's system of straight baselines includes basepoints on such features and the ICJ had concluded that these straight baselines were "not contrary to international law." See, Anglo-Norwegian Fisheries Case, Judgment, 31.

56 International Hydrographic Organization and International Association of Geodesy, *Manual on Technical Aspects of the Law of the Sea*, Special Publication No. 51 (Monaco: International Hydrographic Bureau, 2014), chap. 4, 6.

57 United Nations, *Baselines: An Examination of the Relevant Provisions*.

58 *See, e.g.*, Prescott and Schofield, *The Maritime Political Boundaries of the World*, 137–164.

59 While the United States has published its own guidelines on the proper application of Article 7, these guidelines do not have international standing. *See* United States Department of State, *Developing Standard Guidelines for Evaluating Straight Baselines*, Limits in the Seas No. 106 (Washington, D.C.: Bureau of Oceans and International

As a result of the uncertainties inherent in Article 7, its terms have been interpreted—to put it politely—very flexibly by many coastal States, leading to a proliferation of excessive application of straight baselines,[60] which capture or enclose overly large marine spaces as internal waters and simultaneously advance the coastal State's starting point for measuring its maritime claims. These liberal applications of straight baselines have included the use of allegedly fringing islands that are far offshore and/or widely dispersed, such that the straight baselines in question are not in the "immediate vicinity" of the coast, and the waters so enclosed cannot genuinely be considered as suitable for the regime of internal waters.[61] The United States routinely protests against any practice that it deems to be excessive or contrary to the provisions of Article 7 of the LOSC.[62]

Overall, as Prescott observed, "the imprecise language [of Article 7] would allow any coastal country, anywhere in the world, to draw straight baselines along its coast."[63] Nonetheless, it is worth noting that the ICJ, in its decision in the *Qatar/Bahrain Case*, stated unequivocally that the method of straight baselines in accordance with Article 7 of LOSC, as "an exception to the normal rules" for the definition of baselines, "must be applied restrictively."[64] Excessive claims to straight

---

Environmental and Scientific Affairs, Aug. 31, 1987). In this context it is worth noting that the objective of the U.S. study was to suggest standard *guidelines* in order to allow a "reasoned evaluation" of straight baseline systems claimed around the world, making it possible to identify "with a certain degree of confidence" those straight baseline systems conforming to international law and those which do not. But it is noted that the guidelines are not, "benchmarks against which all such systems should be measured," and are not offered as "unequivocal yardsticks of the legality of straight baseline systems." *See* ibid, 2; *see also* J. Ashley Roach and Robert W. Smith, "Straight Baselines: The Need for a Universally Applied Norm," *International Journal of Marine and Coastal Law* 31 (2000): 47–80.

60 *See* Prescott and Schofield, *The Maritime Political Boundaries of the World*, 139–166; *see also* Roach and Smith, *Excessive Maritime Claims*, 72–130.

61 J. Ashley Roach, *Excessive Maritime Claims*, 4th ed. (Leiden and Boston: Martinus Nijhoff Publishers, 2021), 28.

62 For an excellent overview of such "excessive" claims from a US perspective, *see*, Roach and Smith, *Excessive Maritime Claims*, 57–161.

63 J.R. Victor Prescott, *The Maritime Political Boundaries of the World* (London: Methuen, 1985), 64; *see also* Prescott and Schofield, *The Maritime Political Boundaries of the World*, 162–164.

64 Case Concerning Maritime Delimitation and Territorial Questions between Qatar and Bahrain (Qatar v. Bahrain), Judgment, 2001 I.C.J. Rep 40 (Mar. 16), para. 212 (hereinafter, the *Qatar/Bahrain Case*). In the context of that case, the Court declined to employ straight or archipelagic baselines to the Bahraini coast, citing Bahrain's failure to declare archipelagic status and thereafter define a system of archipelagic straight baselines. *See* ibid, paras. 212–15.

baselines potentially advance coastal State claims offshore and—where overlapping claims with neighbouring States do not occur—these claims have the potential to reduce the scope of the high seas and thus the extent of the Commons.[65]

6 Retreating Baselines and Shifting Limits

It has long been recognised that parts of many coasts are dynamic and can change location and configuration in relatively short periods. Coastlines often change in a cyclical manner over time, alternately shifting seawards through deposition or accretion of material and then landwards because of erosion.[66]

The predominant type of baselines provided for under the LOSC are "normal" baselines that are coincident with "the low-water line along the coast as marked on large-scale charts officially recognized by the coastal State."[67] As normal baselines coincide with the low-water line, they move or "ambulate" over time, so the maritime jurisdictional limits measured from them will also shift and change.[68] Thus, where the baseline advances, the outer limits of the maritime claims measured from that baseline will expand seawards. Conversely, where the normal baseline recedes, the coastal State may lose maritime areas as the outer limits of their maritime zones are pulled back.

The shifting of the low-water line would also affect the location of other types of straight-line baselines, as these baselines are still dependent on the location of normal baselines. Specifically, in order for straight-line baselines to be valid they need to be connected back to the low-water line,[69] such that each system of baselines is "closed."[70]

---

65 Some caution is advisable in this context, however. The islands which often provide the turning points for such straight baselines may themselves be capable of generating EEZ and continental shelf rights thus limiting or moderating the impact of apparently excessive straight baselines claims.

66 *See, e.g.*, William Hirst and David Robertson, "Geographic Information Systems, Charts and UNCLOS: Can They Live Together?," *Maritime Studies* 136 (2014): 1–6.

67 LOSC, art. 5. Normal baselines are effectively a coastal State's default baselines as they do not need to be expressly claimed unlike other types of baselines provided for under LOSC, merely "marked on large scale charts officially recognized by the coastal state." Ibid.

68 Michael W. Reed, *Shore and Sea Boundaries Volume 3: The Development of International Maritime Boundary Principles through United States Practice* (Washington, D.C.: United States Government Printing Office, 2000), 185.

69 *See* LOSC, art. 7, 9, 10, 47; *see also* Anglo-Norwegian Fisheries Case (United Kingdom v. Norway), Order, 1951 I.C.J. 117, 128–29 (Jan. 18).

70 The UN Group of Technical Experts on Baselines indicated that, for straight baselines for example, this meant that "whether the baselines are drawn along the coast of an island

Global sea level rise also threatens to significantly alter baselines and, thus, the limits of the Commons. There exists broad consensus in the scientific community that global mean sea level is rising. For example, the Intergovernmental Panel on Climate Change (IPCC) in its Fifth Assessment Report (AR5), projected sea level rise of 52–98 cm by the end of the century if greenhouse gas emissions are not meaningfully curtailed.[71] Further, the IPCC's 2019 IPCC Special Report on the *Ocean and the Cryosphere* suggests the figure of 1.1 metres of global mean sea level rise by 2100.[72] More recently, in 2021 the IPCC released the first element of its Sixth Assessment Report (AR6), dealing with the physical science basis including the finding that the average rate of sea level rise has accelerated substantially from 1.3mm yr-1 in the period 1901-1971 to 3.7mm yr-1 in 2006-2018 with human influence considered to be very likely to be the main driver for these changes.[73] Here it can be observed that IPCC estimates are generally regarded as conservative, particularly due to uncertainties over the potential contribution to sea level rise from thermal expansion of the oceans as well as the melting of land-based or grounded ice.[74]

or of the mainland, the system must start and finish on or above the low water line" and that where straight baselines were drawn connecting a fringe of islands "all the intermediate basepoints must be located on or above the low water line." *See* United Nations, *Baselines: An Examination of the Relevant Provisions of the United Nations Convention on the Law of the Sea* (New York: UN Office for Ocean Affairs and the Law of the Sea, 1989), 23.

71 The IPCC 2013 AR5 medium confidence level projection is for global mean sea level rise of 0.52–0.98 m under its representative concentration pathways (RCP) 8.5 scenario, which envisages continued very high greenhouse gas emissions and a resulting increase in global mean temperature likely to exceed 2°C. *See* Intergovernmental Panel on Climate Change (IPCC) Working Group I, "Climate Change 2013: The Physical Science Basis," in IPCC, *Fifth Assessment Report of the Intergovernmental Panel on Climate Change* (Cambridge and New York: Cambridge University Press, 2013), 1139–40, available at: http://www.climatechange2013.org/images/report/WG1AR5_ALL_FINAL.pdf.

72 Under Representative Concentration Pathway (RCP) 8.5, corresponding to a high pathway for which radiative forcing reaches greater than 8.5 W m^{-2} by 2100 and continues to rise for some amount of time. See, Intergovernmental Panel on Climate Change (IPCC), *Special Report on the Ocean and Cryosphere in a Changing Climate* (IPCC Special Report), approved at its 51st Session held from 20–23 September 2019, available online: <https://www.ipcc.ch/srocc/home/>, Summary for Policymakers, 23.

73 IPCC, *Climate Change 2021 The Physical Science Basis*, Working Group I contribution to the Sixth Assessment Report of the Intergovernmental Panel on Climate Change, Summary for Policymakers (SPM), 7 August 2021, SPM-6, available at https://www.ipcc.ch/report/ar6/wg1/.

74 *See, e.g.*, Clive Schofield, "Climate Change and Changing Coasts: Geophysical and Jurisdictional Implications of Sea Level Rise," *Korean Journal of International and Comparative Law* 5 (2017): 38–43.

Rising seas could potentially lead to substantial reductions in the scope of claims to maritime jurisdiction.[75] It is, however, important to take into consideration the complex interactions between sea level and the shape and elevation of the land, that is, *relative* sea level rise. This suggests that sea level rise does not automatically translate into recessions in the location of low-water lines. Further, it can be noted that only the outermost points of a coastal State's baseline are critical for the definition of the outer limits of maritime claims, which are commonly constructed through the "envelope of arcs" method (see Figure 1.2).[76] Nonetheless, particularly for States with low elevation coasts, significant sea level rise has the potential to pose a distinct threat to critical base points from which maritime zones are measured and thus the extent of national maritime jurisdictional claims. This has led to threatened States to declare their baselines and the outer limits of their maritime zones with a view to preserving their existing maritime entitlements.[77]

7 Overly Expansive Claims from Islands

Another type of excessive maritime claim relates to islands and, in particular, to the claiming of EEZ and continental shelf rights from insular features that arguably should not support such claims. As provided by Article 121 of the LOSC, an island consists of "a naturally formed area of land, surrounded by water, which is above water at high tide."[78] In principle, such features are to be treated just as any other land territory and therefore generate the full suite of maritime claims.[79] However, paragraph 3 of Article 121 states that "[r]ocks which cannot sustain human habitation or an economic life of their own shall have no exclusive economic zone or continental shelf."

This distinction between islands capable of generating extended claims to maritime jurisdiction and a disadvantaged sub-category of island, the "rock," has enormous implications in terms of potential maritime claims. If an island has no maritime neighbours within 400 M, it could generate 125,664 M^2 (431,014km^2) of territorial sea, EEZ and continental shelf rights. In stark

75 *See* David Freestone and Clive Schofield, "Securing Ocean Spaces for the Future? The Initiative of the Pacific SIDS to Develop Regional Practice Concerning Baselines and Maritime Zone Limits," *Ocean Yearbook* 33 (2019).

76 Christopher M. Carleton and Clive Schofield, *Developments in the Technical Determination of Maritime Space: Charts, Datums, Baselines, Maritime Zones and Limits*, International Boundaries Research Unit Maritime Briefing 3 (Durham, U.K: University of Durham, 2001), 62.

77 *See* Freestone and Schofield, *supra* note 75.

78 LOSC, art. 121(1).

79 LOSC, art. 121(2).

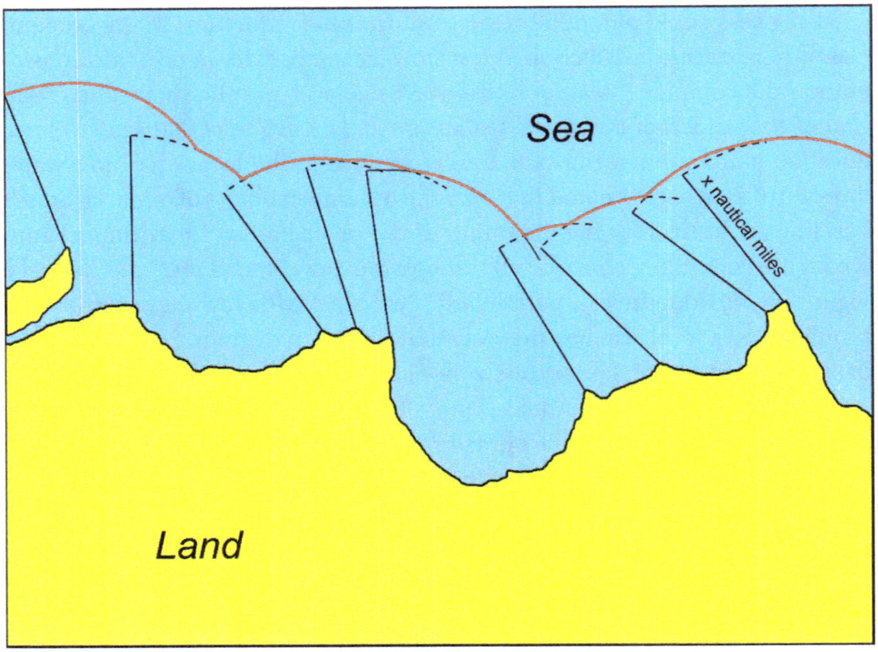

FIGURE 1.2 Delineating the outer limits of maritime zones through an envelope of arcs
SOURCE: SCHOFIELD AND ARSANA, IHO (INTERNATIONAL HYDROGRAPHIC ORGANIZATION), *A MANUAL ON TECHNICAL ASPECTS OF THE UNITED NATIONS CONVENTION ON THE LAW OF THE SEA—1982 (TALOS)*. SPECIAL PUBLICATION NO. 51, (5TH EDITION, MONACO: INTERNATIONAL HYDROGRAPHIC BUREAU, 2014), CHAPTER 5, 3.

contrast, if the same feature were deemed a mere "rock" incapable of generating EEZ and continental shelf rights, only a territorial sea of 452 M^2 (1,550km^2) could be claimed.[80]

Distinguishing between islands capable of generating extended maritime claims and mere rocks which cannot has proved to be a longstanding conundrum in the law of the sea. However, on 12 July 2016, the Arbitral Tribunal in the case between the Philippines and China published its Award on the Merits, which includes crucial—and controversial—findings concerning the status of certain insular features in the South China Sea.[81] The Tribunal's detailed

80 For the sake of this theoretical calculation the features in question are assumed to have no land area.

81 In the Matter of the South China Sea Arbitration Before an Arbitral Tribunal Constituted Under Annex VII to the 1982 United Nations Convention on the Law of the Sea Between

analysis of Article 121 represents the first judicial interpretation of these important, yet challenging to interpret, provisions of the Convention.

In particular, the Tribunal concluded that the assessment of a particular feature was not to be based on geological or geomorphological criteria.[82] That is, that the term "rocks" is not meant to apply only to features "composed of solid rock."[83] Rather, the Tribunal ruled that assessment should be on the basis of the feature's "natural capacity" to sustain human habitation or an economic life of its own, "without external additions or modifications intended to increase its capacity" to do so,[84] and indicated in explicit terms that "a rock cannot be transformed into a fully entitled island through land reclamation."[85]

The Tribunal went on to determine that only features with a capacity to sustain either "a stable community of people"[86] or economic activity that is "oriented around the feature itself and not focused solely on the waters or seabed of the surrounding territorial sea" and not dependent on outside resources or purely extractive in nature are capable of generating extended maritime claims.[87] It also made clear that the text of Article 121(3) is disjunctive, meaning that either the capacity to sustain human habitation or an economic life of its own is required in order for a feature to escape being classified as a "rock,"[88] and that the assessment of insular features concerns their capacity to sustain human habitation or an economic life of their own, rather than whether they presently do or have historically done so.[89]

Regarding the phrase "human habitation," the Tribunal was of the view that "(t)he mere presence of a small number of persons on a feature does not constitute permanent or habitual residence there and does not equate to habitation." It ruled that the critical factor was that the habitation be "non-transient in character" such that the population involved "can fairly be said to constitute

the Republic of the Philippines and the People's Republic of China, PCA Case No. 2013-19, Certified Award (Permanent Court Arbitration, 2006), available at: https://pca-cpa.org, at https://pcacases.com/web/view/7 (hereinafter South China Sea Award). It is noted that the first author of this Chapter served as an independent expert witness in this case.

82 Ibid, para. 540.

83 Ibid. In reaching this conclusion the Tribunal pointed out that the dictionary definition of the term rock also included "aggregates," "organic matter," and "soft materials such as clays" rather than exclusively hard rock. Ibid, para. 480.

84 Ibid, para. 541.

85 Ibid, para. 508.

86 Ibid, para. 542.

87 Ibid, para. 543.

88 Ibid, para. 544.

89 Ibid, para. 545.

the natural population of the feature."[90] Importantly, the Tribunal found that the capacity of an insular feature to generate EEZ rights depended on the presence of a population to benefit from the resources within that zone,[91] reasoning that the meaning of the text of Article 121(3) is shaped by "the inherent connection between this provision and the concept of the exclusive economic zone."[92]

In reaching this conclusion, the Tribunal referred to the history of the Convention, finding that Article 121(3) was included as a "counterpoint" to the introduction of the EEZ, serving to prevent the expansion in maritime rights provided by the EEZ "from going too far" by disabling tiny features from:

> … unfairly and inequitably generating enormous entitlements to maritime space that would serve not to benefit the local population, but to award a windfall to the (potentially distant) State to have maintained a claim to such a feature.[93]

Tellingly, on the basis of the *travaux préparatoires*, the Tribunal determined that Article 121(3) is a "provision of limitation" with "the object and purpose of preventing encroachment on the international seabed reserved for the common heritage of mankind and of avoiding the inequitable distribution of maritime spaces under national jurisdiction."[94]

On the basis of this interpretation of Article 121 of the LOSC, the Tribunal found that none of the above high-tide features in the Spratly Islands "are capable of sustaining human habitation or an economic life of their own" and that, therefore, they are legally rocks without EEZ or continental shelf entitlements.[95] This ruling clearly sets a high bar for islands to generate EEZ and continental shelf rights. It also suggests that expansive maritime claims from small, remote and especially uninhabited features are excessive in character.

The Tribunal's ruling runs counter to the maximalist trend in the maritime claims advanced by coastal States from numerous obscure and uninhabited insular features. Were the Tribunal's standard for islands to generate EEZ and continental shelf rights to be applied on a global basis, many expansive maritime claims from small features would need to be rolled back and the

90 Ibid, para. 542.
91 Ibid.
92 Ibid, para. 512.
93 Ibid, para. 516.
94 Ibid, para. 535.
95 Ibid, para. 646.

Commons substantially enhanced in terms of its area. To date there is scant sign of this occurring in practice. Here it can be observed that the Award of the Tribunal in the South China Sea case is binding solely on the parties to that case, the Philippines and China with the latter resoundingly rejecting its findings.[96] Nonetheless, as the sole detailed, and unanimous, international judicial interpretation of the Regime of Islands, it has the potential to inform future negotiations between coastal States, for instance in maritime delimitation scenarios involving islands as well as future international jurisprudence.

8 Un-delineated ECS Limits

The legal limits for the continental shelf regime under international law is closely linked to the development of the legal definition of the shelf itself. During the negotiations of UNCLOS III, the "margineers," or broad-shelf States group,[97] considered the notion of including the entire continental margin in the legal definition of continental shelf, as supported by geological considerations.[98] However, this view received strong resistance from the land-locked and geographically disadvantaged States,[99] who took the view that the goals of establishing the Commons "would not be attained if the continental shelf regime were retained beyond [200 M]."[100] As a compromise, the CLCS was created with a role to establish the outer limits of coastal States' continental shelf beyond 200 M, as well as to limit the seaward extension of coastal States' jurisdiction.[101]

96 See, for e.g., "Statement of the Ministry of Foreign Affairs of the People's Republic of China on the Award of 12 July 2016 of the Arbitral Tribunal in the South China Sea Arbitration Established at the Request of the Republic of the Philippines", <https://www.fmprc.gov.cn/mfa_eng/wjdt_665385/2649_665393/t1379492.shtml>.

97 The group consisted of 13 States: Argentina, Australia, Brazil, Canada, Iceland, India, Ireland, Madagascar, New Zealand, Norway, Sri Lanka, the United Kingdom and Venezuela. Myron H. Nordquist, ed., *United Nations Convention on the Law of the Sea, 1982: A Commentary*, vol. I (Dordrecht: Martinus Nijhoff Publishers, 1982–2003), 76.

98 Makhdoom Ali Khan, "The Juridical Concept of the Continental Shelf," *Pakistan Horizon (Karachi)* 38 (1985), 19, 32.

99 Third United Nations Conference on the Law of the Sea, *Summary Records of 18th Meeting of the Second Committee*, U.N. Doc. A/CONF/.62/C.2/SR.18 (July, 29 1974), 151.

100 Third United Nations Conference on the Law of the Sea, *Summary Records of 19th Meeting of the Second Committee*, A/CONF.62/C.2/SR.19 (July 30, 1974), 157.

101 Rüdiger Wolfrum, "The Role of International Dispute Settlement Institutions in the Delimitation of the Outer Continental Shelf," in Rainer Lagoni and Daniel Vignes, eds., *Maritime Delimitation* (Dordrecht: Martinus Nijhoff, 2006), 19, 21.

Overall, as many as 87 coastal States have made or may ultimately be in a position to make submissions for outer continental shelf rights to the CLCS.[102] The CLCS, however, is not well-equipped to deal with such a large number of submissions; out of the 92 submissions, less than one third have received the Commission's recommendation.[103] Furthermore, as mentioned above, if a submission from a coastal State involves a disputed area, the CLCS cannot consider it[104] unless prior consent were given by all States parties to the dispute.[105] Consequently, in such disputed areas, there are no clear limits between coastal States' jurisdiction and the Commons. At least until the relevant States resolve or decide to set aside their dispute, allowing the Commission to proceed with its evaluation of submissions and, in due course, to provide recommendations on the basis of which coastal States can delineate outer continental shelf limits.

9 Residual Commons Rights in the ECS?: The Article 82 Conundrum

A further aspect of the package deal negotiated at UNCLOS III relates to what have been characterised as residual Commons rights persisting in areas of outer or extended continental shelf.[106] These Commons rights are enshrined in Article 82 of the LOSC and their inclusion was necessary in order to secure the consent of the land-locked and geographically disadvantaged States to the broad continental margin States securing rights over continental shelf areas seawards of the 200 M EEZ limits.[107] This Section outlines the content

102 Robert Van de Poll, personal communication (Dec. 6, 2018).

103 For a list of all submissions and recommendations, see the CLCS website at: Commission on the Limit of the Continental Shelf (May 31, 2022), http://www.un.org/Depts/los/clcs_new/clcs_home.htm.

104 *Supra* note 49.

105 Ibid.

106 *See*, e.g., International Law Association (ILA), Committee on the Outer Continental Shelf, 'Report on Article 82 and the 1982 UN Convention on the Law of the Sea,' 2008, para. 1.3. An alternative view is that the common heritage of mankind principle does not apply to continental shelf areas seawards of 200 M limits and that instead the provisions of Article 82 are better viewed as a negotiated outcome and form of compensation for developing and land-locked States as a result of outer continental shelf areas falling under coastal State jurisdiction rather than being governed as part of the Ocean Commons. *See*, Joanna Mossop, *The Continental Shelf Beyond 200 Nautical Miles: Rights and Responsibilities* (Oxford: Oxford University Press, 2016) 129–130. *See* also, Stephen C. Vasciannie, *Land-locked and Geographically Disadvantaged States in the International Law of the Sea* (Oxford: Clarendon Press, 1990) 127.

107 SP Jagota, *Maritime Boundaries* (Martinus Nijhoff Publishers, 1985), 41.

of Article 82 of the LOSC and highlights the ambiguities and uncertainties in implementing Article 82—an issue that is becoming more urgent in character as an increasing number of coastal States are looking to exploit the resources of their continental shelf beyond 200 M.

Historically, Article 82 has been regarded as a dormant provision of the Convention.[108] However, as of the time of writing, 21 coastal States have issued exploration blocks for oil and gas exploration seawards of their 200 M EEZ limits, thus providing a compelling indication of exploration interest in these areas.[109] Further, a discovery has been made in one such block located on Canada's extended continental shelf.[110] If developed, this would be the first hydrocarbons exploitation project to occur on the extended continental shelf.

A number of issues arise in the interpretation and application of Article 82 of LOSC; it appears that these will need to be addressed in the relatively near future.[111] It is clear from the text of Article 82 that payments and contributions are to be made in relation to the exploitation of, rather than exploration for, non-living resources from continental shelf areas seawards of 200 M limits. The level of these payments and contributions is also explicit: 1% from year

---

108 Aldo Chircop, "Implementation of Article 82 of the United Nations Convention on the Law of the Sea: the Challenge for Canada," in Catherine Banet, ed., *The Law of the Seabed* (Leiden: Brill-Nijhoff, 2020), 372.

109 *See* Robert Van de Poll and Clive Schofield, "Pushing Beyond the 200 Nautical Mile Limit: Progress and Challenges in Exploration Efforts on the Extended Continental Shelf," in *Proceedings of the Advisory Board on the Law of the Sea (ABLOS) Conference on UNCLOS: Advances in Managing the Blue World* (International Hydrographic Bureau, Monaco, Oct. 9–11, 2017).

110 See Chircop. *supra* note 117, 374–5.

111 Article 82 reads as follows:

Payments and contributions with respect to the exploitation of the continental shelf beyond 200 nautical miles,

1. The coastal State shall make payments or contributions in kind in respect of the exploitation of the non-living resources of the continental shelf beyond 200 nautical miles from the baselines from which the breadth of the territorial sea is measured.
2. The payments and contributions shall be made annually with respect to all production at a site after the first five years of production at that site. For the sixth year, the rate of payment or contribution shall be 1 per cent of the value or volume of production at the site. The rate shall increase by 1 per cent for each subsequent year until the twelfth year and shall remain at 7 per cent thereafter. Production does not include resources used in connection with exploitation.
3. A developing State which is a net importer of a mineral resource produced from its continental shelf is exempt from making such payments or contributions in respect of that mineral resource.
4. The payments or contributions shall be made through the Authority, which shall distribute them to States Parties to this Convention, on the basis of equitable sharing

6 of production with an increase of 1% per annum through years 7–12 and a maximum of 7% from year 12 to termination of production.

What is less clear is how Article 82 will be implemented by the coastal State. For instance, it is uncertain who exactly is to make these payments, the coastal State or the contractor involved in the production. Since Article 82 is part of the LOSC, it would necessarily seem to apply to all States parties. That said, it appears to be up to the coastal State to interpret this provision as it sees fit. Undoubtedly, it is up to the coastal State to define the terms of its contractual terms with the companies, likely international oil and gas companies, involved in production from outer continental shelf areas. Coastal States therefore may impose obligations through contractual terms on the companies involved. While it would seem to be to the advantage of the coastal State to transfer the burden of payments and contributions to the contractor in this manner, this would likely dampen and perhaps forestall interest among international oil and gas companies in what are already likely to be risky ventures, as they are necessarily remote from shore, often deep or ultra-deep 'frontier' provinces for exploration activities.

Further sources of uncertainty involve how payments are to be made. Notably, the "contributions in kind" envisaged under Article 82(1) are to be "made through the (International Seabed) Authority" consistent with Article 82(4). Moreover, how active or passive the ISA's role is remains open to debate. For example, it is unsettled whether the ISA might have powers related to monitoring compliance in implementation of Article 82 obligations or is merely a passive receiver of payments and contributions. A number of terms contained within Article 82 are also open to interpretation and thus, potentially, to disagreement. These include: "resource," "all production," "value," "volume," "site," "payments," "contributions in kind," and "annually." As Article 82 has yet to be implemented, State practice that could shed light on these questions is not so much scant as entirely absent.

The ISA has, to its credit, recognised this deficit and has initiated a series of workshops to address the conundrum of Article 82. In 2009, the ISA convened a seminar related to the challenges posed by Article 82 at the Royal Institute of International Affairs (RIIA), Chatham House, London, United Kingdom, leading to the publication of two Technical Studies.[112] A follow-up seminar took place in Beijing, China in 2012, leading to the publication of a series of

criteria, taking into account the interests and needs of developing States, particularly the least developed and the land-locked among them.

112 International Seabed Authority, *Non-living Resources of the Continental Shelf Beyond 200 Nautical Miles: Speculations on the Implementation of Article 82 of the United*

additional Technical Studies.[113] Responding to a recommendation made at the latter meeting, the ISA undertook research regarding the interpretation of the terms contained in Article 82 and issued a further Technical Report.[114] This study provides an analysis of how key terms contained in Article 82 of the LOSC are interpreted, primarily with respect to hydrocarbons, across nine jurisdictions.[115] It demonstrates that whilst some commonalities in interpretation of terms is evident between jurisdictions, considerable variations in interpretation also exist.[116]

10 A Canadian Precedent?

As noted above, it appears that Canada is likely to be the first State faced with the practical implementation of Article 82. Canada made its submission relating to continental shelf seawards of its 200 M limits in the Atlantic Ocean on December 6, 2013.[117] However, in light of the backlog in submissions to the CLCS, Canada may need to wait on the order of 10–15 years to receive recommendations on its submission. Despite this, Canada has issued oil and gas exploration blocks which include areas of continental shelf seawards of its 200 M limits.[118] These outer continental shelf areas are highly likely to be

Nations Convention on the Law of the Sea, ISA Technical Study No. 5 (Kingston, Jamaica: International Seabed Authority, 2010); International Seabed Authority, *Issues Associated with the Implementation of Article 82 of the United Nations Convention on the Law of the Sea*, ISA Technical Study No. 4 (Kingston, Jamaica: International Seabed Authority, 2009).

113 *See, e.g.*, International Seabed Authority, *Implementation of Article 82 of the United Nations Convention on the Law of the Sea. Report of the International Workshop Convened by the International Seabed Authority in Collaboration with the China Institute for Marine Affairs in Beijing, the People's Republic of China, 26–20 November, 2012*, ISA Technical Study No. 12 (Kingston, Jamaica: International Seabed Authority, 2013).

114 *See* Wylie Spicer and Elizabeth McIsaac, *A Study of Key Terms in Article 82 of the United Nations Convention on the Law of the Sea*, ISA Technical Study No. 15 (Kingston, Jamaica: International Seabed Authority, 2016).

115 The nine jurisdictions covered by the Technical Report are the United States, Brazil, Alberta (Canada), Newfoundland and Labrador (Canada), Australia, Nigeria, the Russian Federation, the United Kingdom, and Norway. Ibid, 11.

116 Ibid, 13–14.

117 *See* Government of Canada, *Partial Submission of Canada to the Commission on the Limits of the Continental Shelf: Executive Summary* (Dec. 6, 2013), available at: https://www.un.org/depts/los/clcs_new/submissions_files/can70_13/es_can_en.pdf.

118 *See* Chircop. *supra* note 117, 374–5.

included well within any final delineation of Canada's outer continental shelf limit. Exploration in the area known as the Flemish Pass east of Newfoundland suggests the presence of substantial quantities of oil which potentially warrant commercial development. For example, the Bay du Nord and Baccalieu oil fields discovered in this area are estimated to hold mean recoverable reserves of 300–600 million barrels of oil,[119] the development of which represents a C$6.8 billion (c.US$5.1 billion) project.[120] However, these discoveries have been made in an area located approximately 500 km (270 M) east of St. John's, Newfoundland. These areas of extended continental shelf are therefore necessarily remote, as well as being in relatively deep water (c.1,200m deep) that is prone to harsh weather conditions including the presence of hazards such as icebergs.[121]

Of particular note, the bid information for these Canadian Blocks includes a notice that the Canada-Newfoundland and Labrador Offshore Petroleum Board:

> … informs prospective bidders for these parcels, which are entirely or partially beyond Canada's 200 nautical mile zone, that it has been advised by the Government of Canada that, in order to meet obligations arising pursuant to Article 82 of the United Nations Convention on the Law of the Sea, additional terms and conditions may be applied through legislation, regulations, amendments to licences or otherwise.[122]

This would seem to suggest that Canada is contemplating shifting the burden of making payments or contributions from the State to the contractor. The Canadian government has been rather coy on this issue, however, so it remains uncertain that this will become Canadian policy. An added complication in the Canadian context is that there is ongoing disagreement domestically as to whether the Canadian Federal Government is responsible for the obligations under Article 82 of the LOSC or whether this responsibility falls to the

---

119 *See* "Bay du Nord Project," Offshore Technology (2020), https://www.offshore-technology.com/projects/bay-du-nord-project/.

120 "N.L., Equinor Announce $6.8B Offshore Deepwater Oil Project," Canadian Broadcasting Corporation (July 26, 2018), https://www.cbc.ca/news/canada/newfoundland-labrador/oil-gas-announcement-premier-dwight-ball-1.4762299.

121 *See* Jamie Fitzpatrick, "Does the Flemish Pass Hold the Future of Offshore Oil?," Canadian Broadcasting Corporation (May 25, 2017), https://www.cbc.ca/news/canada/newfoundland-labrador/flemish-pass-basin-oil-1.4127739.

122 *See, e.g.*, "C-NLOPB Announces 2013 Call for Bids," Canada-Newfoundland and Labrador Offshore Petroleum Board (May 16, 2013), https://www.cnlopb.ca/news/nr20130516/.

government of the Province of Newfoundland, to which the revenues from any development will flow.[123] It remains to be seen how Canada will implement Article 82 in practice, but doing so is clearly on the policy-making horizon.

11 Conclusions

The seabed beyond national jurisdiction is under the responsibility of the ISA, and currently negotiation is on-going to establish a framework to use and conserve the biodiversity found in the waters beyond national jurisdiction. The framework resulting from these negotiations would likely provide the geographical scope of the Commons, or areas beyond national jurisdiction, on which the framework would be applicable. However, the exact geographical limits of the Commons remains radically unclear.

One reason for continuing confusion is excessive claims by coastal States. The LOSC establishes various maritime zones that fall under the jurisdiction of coastal States. However, it left coastal States with considerable discretion in establishing the limits of their maritime jurisdiction. Not surprisingly, coastal States in general have tended to expand their jurisdiction as far seaward as possible, through excessive maritime claims. Many coastal States have made liberal use of straight baselines, applying them in areas where normal baselines could and should be used. This practice not only converts a large area of what should be territorial sea or even EEZ into internal waters, but also potentially pushes the limits of national jurisdiction seaward to the detriment of the Commons. Some coastal States also claim EEZ and continental shelf from small features, which might properly be designated rocks that cannot sustain human habitation or economic life of their own, and thus not entitled to an EEZ and continental shelf.

In addition to excessive claims, most coastal States also do not provide clear statements of the limits of their national jurisdiction. Of the 152 coastal States

---

123 *See, e.g.*, Rowland J. Harrison, "Article 82 of UNCLOS: The Day of Reckoning Approaches," *Journal of World Energy Law and Business* 10 (2017): 488–504. *See* also, Rowland J. Harrison, "Offshore Oil Development in Uncharted Legal Waters: Will the Proposed Bay du Nord Project Precipitate Another Federal-Provincial Conflict," *Energy Regulation Quarterly* 6(4), December 2018; and, Aldo Chircop, "Implementation of Article 82 of the United Nations Convention on the Law of the Sea: the Challenge for Canada," in C. Banet (ed.) *The Law of the Seabed,* (Leiden: Brill-Nijhoff, 2020): 371–394.

in the world,[124] less than a third have published and deposited the outer limits of their EEZ with the Secretary General of the United Nations[125] as required by Article 75 of the LOSC.[126] The statistic is slightly better on the limits of continental shelf beyond 200 M. Of the 152 coastal States, as many as 87 coastal States have made or may ultimately be in a position to make submissions for outer continental shelf rights to the CLCS.[127] Among these coastal States, 83 had, at the time of writing, made either full submissions or submissions of preliminary information as a prelude to making full submissions to the CLCS regarding outer continental shelf rights.[128] In total, 100 distinct outer continental shelf submissions or submissions of preliminary information being deposited with the CLCS, comprising 81 full submissions and 19 preliminary submissions.[129] However, because the CLCS cannot consider any submission that is disputed by other States, such submissions have been put on hold until the States involved resolved the dispute or give their consent to have the CLCS consider the submission. Accordingly, in multiple areas, the outer limits of continental shelf beyond 200 M, and thus the limits of the Area, remain un-delineated.

Finally, the LOSC is itself unclear about the existence of what have been termed residual Commons rights on the continental shelf beyond 200 M. Article 82 of the LOSC on the revenue sharing regime for the exploitation of continental shelf resources beyond 200 M contains important ambiguities. For example, it is not clear whether the coastal State or the companies exploiting

124 This figure excludes three States, Azerbaijan, Kazakhstan and Turkmenistan, whose only coastlines are those on the Caspian Sea, which is not connected to the global ocean save via rivers and canals and is therefore not included.

125 Deposited charts are available at the website of the UN Division of Ocean Affairs and Law of the Sea. "Deposit of Charts," UN Division of Ocean Affairs and Law of the Sea (Dec. 31, 2019), http://www.un.org/Depts/los/LEGISLATIONANDTREATIES/depositpublicity.htm.

126 LOSC, art. 75.

127 Robert Van de Poll, personal communication (Dec. 6, 2018).

128 CLCS, *Submissions, through the Secretary-General of the United Nations, to the Commission on the Limits of the Continental Shelf, pursuant to article 76, paragraph 8, of the United Nations Convention on the Law of the Sea of 10 December 1982*, http://www.un.org/depts/los/clcs_new/commission_submissions.htm.

129 Note that a number of these submissions are joint or partial and these figures are inclusive of multiple partial submissions for different areas by some States. Additionally, preliminary submissions are gradually being replaced by full submissions. Thus, while the CLCS lists 47 submissions of preliminary information, most of these have been supplanted by full submissions such that only submissions of preliminary information remain to be, as it were, 'upgraded' to full submissions. *See*, "The Commission, It's Purpose and Functions," Commission on the Limits of the Continental Shelf (Aug. 15, 2019), http://www.un.org/Depts/los/clcs_new/clcs_home.htm.

the resources have to make revenue contributions. This is an issue that appears to be an increasingly pressing one, as an increasing number of coastal States are looking to exploit the resources of their continental shelf beyond 200 M.

Taken together, these factors suggest that the precise spatial limits of the Commons, as well as the limits of residual Commons rights in areas of extended or outer continental shelf, are a long way from being realised with certainty.

Acknowledgements

The authors are indebted to Dr I Made Andi Arsana of the Department of Geodetic and Geomatic Engineering at Universitas Gadjah Mada, Indonesia for his kind assistance in preparing the figures included in this Chapter. These figures were produced by Dr Arsana and the first author for inclusion in the International Hydrographic Organization (IHO) and International Association of Geodesy (IAG) *Manual on Technical Aspects of the United Nations Convention on the Law of the Sea—1982* (TALOS Manual). These figures are reproduced with the kind permission of the IHO and IAG subject to the following notice:

Material from IHO-IAG publication C-51, *A Manual on Technical Aspects of the United Nations Convention on the Law of the Sea—1982* (TALOS), Edition 5.0.0 dated June 2014 is reproduced with the permission of Professor Clive Schofield and Dr I Made Andi Arsana, authors of the animated graphics, and of the Secretariat of the International Hydrographic Organization (IHO) and the Executive Council of the International Association of Geodesy (IAG) (Permission N° 8/2020) acting for the International Hydrographic Organization (IHO) and the International Association of Geodesy (IAG), which do not accept responsibility for the correctness of the material as reproduced: in case of doubt, the IHO-IAG's authentic text shall prevail. The incorporation of material sourced from IHO-IAG shall not be construed as constituting an endorsement by IHO or IAG of this product.

The first author would also like to acknowledge the generous funding of the World Maritime University (WMU)-Sasakawa Global Ocean Institute by The Nippon Foundation.

CHAPTER 2

Korea's Deep Seabed Activities and Domestic Legislation on the Exploration for and Exploitation of Resources in the Deep Seabed Area

An Abortive Attempt and Moving Forward

Seokwoo Lee

1 Introduction

As mineral extraction activities in the area beyond national jurisdiction (the Area) move from the exploration stage towards exploitation, the need for domestic regulation of these activities grows increasingly urgent. In 2012, the Republic of Korea began the process of enacting the Korean Law on Exploration for and Exploitation of Resources in the Deep Seabed Area (hereinafter referred to as the Korean Law on Deep Seabed Area).[1] The enactment of the Korean domestic law, in addition to accommodating for the domestic measures required by the United Nations Convention on the Law of the Sea (UNCLOS or Convention), is understood as a measure of Korean nationals to actively comply with the international and domestic standard of activities in the Area and to ensure sincere implementation of such activities. Naturally, since the Korean Law on Deep Seabed Area itself is an integration of UNCLOS and the International Seabed Authority (ISA or the Authority) rules into Korean law, with an aim to administer Korean nationals' activities in the Area and to strengthen the international performance of it, this Korean Law on Deep Seabed Area will not be prominent except for the procedural contents related to notification, authorization, and issuance of warranty. Unfortunately, however, the proposed legislation was dropped in 2018 when the National Assembly did not adopt it due to a disagreement among the parties.

However, it is worth noting that the Authority's management capacity during the later exploitation phase, as was the case with exploration phase,

1 2018 Draft of the Korean Law on Exploration for and Exploitation of Resources in the Deep Seabed Area (on file with author). Though this proposed legislation was dropped in 2018, it is likely that there will be another opportunity when this bill will be re-introduced given the relative importance of this matter.

 | DOI:10.1163/9789004514218_004

needs to be improved. Efficient management of activities in the Area has significant limits in its function and effectiveness, notwithstanding fulfillment of the sponsoring States' and contractors' duties. As such, it is meaningful that the Korean Law on Deep Seabed Area re-angled its focus from exploitation to management of activities in the Area. This Chapter provides background on the legal regime that applies to resources of the Area, focusing on the international legal mandate for domestic legislation. It then turns to the example of Korea, discussing the need for such regulation before detailing the proposed Korean Law on the Deep Seabed Area. Finally, the Chapter considers the more contentious and less-examined issue of mineral exploitation activities on the extended continental shelf within national jurisdiction. It concludes with the suggestion that the developing regulatory regime for activities in the Area could provide guidance to the international community as it tackles the challenge of regulating activity on the extended continental shelf.

2 United Nations Convention on the Law of the Sea and the International Seabed Authority in General

According to Article 157(1) of UNCLOS, the ISA is an "autonomous international organization through which state parties to the Convention organize and control activities in the Area, particularly with a view to administering the related mineral resources." Article 145 articulates that the fundamental competences of the Authority are to "regulate exploration and mining in the deep seabed and to ensure that the marine environment is protected from any harmful effects, which may arise during exploration and mining activities." The limits of the Authority are expressed in Articles 87, 112, and 147.

One of the crucial roles of the Authority is its organizational function. It is through the ISA that state parties to the Convention are to "organize and control the activities in the Area, particularly with a view to administering the resources of the Area."[2] Therefore, analogous to other issues pertaining to the Area, large industrialized states and smaller developing states are largely divided as regards to how much power is vested in the Authority. The Authority comes into play because the mineral resources located in the Area are part of the "common heritage of mankind,"[3] meaning no one party (state or individual investor) has exclusive rights of exploitation to the same. In fact, it is for

2 United Nations Convention on the Law of the Sea, opened for signature Dec. 10, 1982, 1833 U.N.T.S 3 (entered into force Nov. 16 November, 1994) [hereinafter LOSC], art. 157(1).

3 Ibid, art. 136–37.

this very reason that the Authority is necessary—to safeguard investors that intend to carry out long-term development of the resources in the Area, by giving them exclusive rights to the resources of those areas for the duration of their contracts or licenses with the Authority.

However, conflicts between states regarding the Authority as detailed in Part XI of the Convention were not resolved until the Agreement relating to the implementation of Part XI of the UNCLOS of 10 December 1982 was enacted in 1994. The 1994 Agreement in essence altered the decision-making process so that an individual state's interest overrides that of mankind's. This was primarily due to the protest of large-margin states that, as in the words of the United States, the common heritage regime "unfairly and unnecessarily granted a disproportionate voice to developing countries that have little or no investment in seabed mining operations."[4] Further, the implementing agreement changed the relationship of the internal organs of the Authority, namely the Assembly, Council and Secretariat. Finally, it guaranteed that the state with the largest GDP to always have a seat on the Council, thereby allowing policies of developed states to dominate "mankind." As can be observed from the overview of issues regarding the provisions of the Convention, this chapter will provide a modest proposal to come to amicable solutions on the responsibilities of states versus international bodies in regulating activities within common areas of the ocean, coupled with growing environmental concerns that, at times, sit in tension with state interests.

3 Korea's Legislative Direction for Exploitation of Resources in the Deep Seabed and Ocean Floor

In anticipation of proceeding to the phase of exploitation of resources of the deep seabed and ocean floor (the Area), various issues including procurement of the sponsoring States' profit structure, threat to environment caused by resource exploitation, and the like conflict structure was raised broadly for the purposes of international alignment of interest between the international community and sponsoring States. As such, the international community is taking measures to minimize damage to the marine environment caused by activities in the Area, for instance, by instructing that the best environment practices apply.

4 Steven J. Molitor, "The Provisional Understanding Regarding Deep Seabed Matters: An Ill-Conceived Regime for U.S. Deep Seabed Mining," 20(1) *Cornell International Law Journal* (1987), p.226.

The Authority's demand for individual states to legislate or implement administrative measures related to the Area became official in 2011, when the International Tribunal for the Law of the Sea (ITLOS) Seabed Disputes Chamber issued an advisory opinion on the responsibilities and obligation of states with respect to activities in the Area.[5] While the 2011 ITLOS advisory opinion is not legally binding, there is a fair chance that it will be raised during the Authority's site consideration process as a measure to procure implementation, an important factor for the sponsoring State. As such, a state's domestic measures could operate as a means to encourage active participation for common heritage of mankind, because it requires its nationals' activities in the Area to comply with international duties and sponsors implementation in the areas of environment, technology, finances and so forth.

Negative perceptions towards exploitation of resources of the Area and the insistence on revenue return at the exploitation phase both stems from the difference in how the common heritage of mankind is used. Korea, as a pioneer investor, has already enhanced its understanding of the Area by conducting exploration in the Area over twenty years and thereby applied the best environment practice while attempting to minimize hazardous elements associated at the exploitation phase.

The enactment of the Korean domestic law, in addition to accommodating for the domestic measures required by UNCLOS, is understood as a measure of Korean nationals to actively comply with the international and domestic standard of activities in the Area and to ensure sincere implementation of such activities. Naturally, since the Korean Law on Deep Seabed Area itself is an integration of UNCLOS and the ISA rules into the Korean law with an aim to administer Korean nationals' activities in the Area and to strengthen the international performance of it, the law will not be prominent except for

5 International Tribunal for the Law of the Sea, Seabed Disputes Chamber, *Responsibilities and obligations of States with respect to activities in the Area*, Advisory Opinion, 1 Feb. 2011, ITLOS Reports 2011, 10. The Advisory Opinion addressed a question which had been referred to ITLOS by the ISA, on the responsibilities and obligation of states with respect to activities in the Area. In answering the question, the Tribunal opined, among other things, that principles of international environmental law, including due diligence and the precautionary approach, apply to activities in the Area and that states sponsoring activities in the Area have a duty to ensure those principles are upheld. ITLOS further noted that developing states should be given preference with respect to activities in the Area, in keeping with the objective of UNCLOS to create an equitable ocean governance regime. The opinion then stated that each state-party to UNCLOS is required to enact domestic measures reflecting these principles, and provided specific guidance on what domestic legislation should entail under various circumstances.

the procedural contents related to notification, authorization, and issuance of warranty. Nevertheless, particularly given the limitations of the Authority, it is meaningful that the Korean Law on Deep Seabed Area re-angled its focus from exploitation to management of activities in the Area.

The international community's approach on resources of the "Area" used to be that its resources were considered purely under the purview of International Seabed Authority (the "Authority"/ISA). The other approach in the area outside the limits of national jurisdiction, however, is anticipated to focus on the 200 nautical miles of the area newly incorporated into the continental shelf of the coastal state in accordance with Articles 76–82 of UNCLOS. Accordingly, Korea's legal or political response must also mirror this dichotomy in its approach and analysis. It goes without saying that under Article 76 of the Convention, exploitation of the resources in the areas expanded as extended continental shelf of the coastal state and exploitation of resources in the Area differ in their legal character in that they are separately governed by Article 82 of the Convention (continental shelf) and Part XI of the Convention and 1994 Implementing Agreement (the Area). However, both share the commonality that the distribution of interests occurs in accordance with the Authority's discussion and that both are deep sea areas with distinct features of the development of resources on land and in the water, and as such, we may approach or respond to both in much the same way.

However, it is worth noting that the Authority's management capacity during the later exploitation phase, as was the case with exploration phase, needs to be improved. Efficient management of activities in the Area has significant limits in its function and effectiveness notwithstanding fulfillment of the sponsoring States' and contractors' duties.

Korea is in urgent need of implementing a legislative structure which incorporates institutional support for the advancement of Koreans and resources of the Area beyond the national jurisdiction. Precedents of early legislation on the resources of the Area include Unites States' Deep Seabed Hard Mineral Resources Act, and Germany's Act of Interim Regulation of Deep Seabed Mining[6] in 1980, the United Kingdom's Deep Sea Mining Temporary Provisional Act and France's Law on the Exploration and Exploitation of Mineral Resources of the Deep Seabed in 1981, Japan's Law on Interim Measures for Deep Seabed

6 After becoming a signatory of the Convention in 1994, Germany has enacted legislation with an overall character on the marine environment in 1995, organized one section of which is dedicated to regulation of the exploitation of the Area. Korea Ocean Research & Development Institute, *Report on Development of Deep Sea Mineral Resources* (CRPM32100-1782-5) (Ansan, South Korea: Ministry of Land, Transport and Maritime Affairs, 2006), at 60.

Mining and Russia's Edict on Provisional Measures to Regulate the Activity of Soviet Enterprises Relating to the Exploration and Exploitation of Mineral Resources of Seabed Areas Beyond the Limits of the Continental Shelf in 1982, and Italy's Law on the Exploration and Exploitation of the Mineral Resources of the Deep Seabed in 1985. But such legislation was applied merely as a transitional measure before the Convention took effect and does not include environmental changes related to exploitation of the Area.

The Authority's demand for each state's legislation or implementation of administrative measures related to the Area became official through the 2011 Seabed Disputes Chamber's advisory opinion. Considering that the Seabed Disputes Chamber made recommendations as to the specific details of what should be incorporated into the domestic law depending on different circumstances, more meaningful material on practical legislation on the Area would be the enactment of the legislation after 2011. For instance, according to the Seabed Disputes Chamber, the sponsoring State's obligation under the treaty and related documents is divided into obligation to secure compliance and direct obligation. In particular, the Seabed Disputes Chamber suggests States have: (1) obligations to assist the Authority by taking all measures necessary to ensure compliance under Article 153(4) of the Convention; (2) obligations to apply a preventative approach; (3) obligations to best environmental management measures; (4) obligations to take measures to ensure the provision of compliance in the event where the Authority issues an emergency order for protection of the marine environment; (5) obligations to specify means of achieving compliance; and (6) obligations to conduct assessment of the impact on the marine environment and the like. Additionally, the Seabed Disputes Chamber stated that the sponsoring State's legislation should include provisions to be included in addition to the Convention and the Authority's Exploitation Regulation on mineral resources of the Area (in draft form as of the writing of this Chapter), such as the contracting party's financial and technological capabilities, conditions for the issuance of certificate, and sanctions for the contracting party's failure to fulfill its obligations. With respect to the domestic measures, while recognizing discrepancies among different legal systems, it is advised that the contracting party be closely supervised and also that an implementing agency for adjustment of activities with the Authority be established.

According to the progress of legislation reported to the Authority, Korea is one of approximately 30 different states that have reported on the status of enactment of the related legislation. Of these, only certain states have actually enacted such legislation, including: Cook Island's Seabed Minerals Act 2019; Czech Republic's Prospecting Exploration for and Exploitation of Mineral

Resources from the Seabed beyond Limits of National Jurisdiction (Act No. 158/2000 of 18 May 2000); Germany's Seabed Mining Act of 6 June 1995, amended by article 74 of the Act of 8 December 2010 (Federal Law Gazette I, p. 1864); the United Kingdom's Deep Sea Mining (Temporary Provisions) Act 1981 and enactment of its legislation (Deep Sea Mining Act 2014); Singapore's Deep Seabed Mining Act 2015 (No. 6 of 2015); Law of the People's Republic of China on Exploration for and Exploitation of Resources in the Deep Seabed Area 2016; Tonga's Seabed Minerals Act 2014; Fiji's International Seabed Mineral Management Decree 2013; Federated States of Micronesia's Seabed Resources Act of 2014; Tuvalu's Tuvalu Seabed Minerals Act 2014, and so forth.[7]

Each legislation is differently composed, depending on each respective state's legislative structure and some legislation qualifies only as a legislation for simple exploitation of marine mineral resources instead of broader legislation on the Area advised by the Authority. Some legislations target the marine mineral resources both within and outside the national jurisdiction and several share a highly similar set of provisions and contents. For instance, Fiji and Nauru's official legislations on the Area beyond the national jurisdiction contain 57 and 56 provisions respectively and both establish a Seabed Minerals Authority to domestically administer the related activities.[8] The similarity of both state's legislation is attributable to the EU's model law of Pacific-African Caribbean Pacific (P-ACP) region,[9] which served as their basis. On the other hand, both Tuvalu's legislation and Tonga's differ from this model law in that they encompass marine mineral resources both within and outside the national jurisdiction, and consist of 129 and 121 provisions respectively. These two states, in particular, include diverse financial burdens such as application fee, sponsorship payments, taxes, loyalty and so forth.[10]

States with relatively simpler legislative systems include China, Singapore, and Korea, which is currently in the progress of initiating enactment of the legislation. These states' laws on the Area are composed of 29 provisions (China), 25 provisions (Singapore), and 28 provisions (Korea). In addition, the

7 ISA, National Legislation Database, https://isa.org.jm/national-legislation-database.

8 Fiji International Seabed Mineral Management Decree (Act. No. 21/2013), art. 6; Nauru International Seabed Minerals Act (Act. No. 26/2015), art. 7.

9 The P-ACP group includes the Cook Islands, Federated States of Micronesia, Fiji, Kiribati, Marshall Islands, Nauru, Niue, Palau, Papua New Guinea, Samoa, Solomon Islands, Timor Leste, Tonga, Tuvalu and Vanuatu. https://ec.europa.eu/trade/policy/countries-and-regions/regions/pacific/.

10 Tonga Seabed Minerals Act (Act No. 10/2014), art. 93–94; Tuvalu Seabed Minerals Act (Act No. 14/2014), art. 100.

Korean and the Chinese legislation incorporate step-by-step rules on securing the mines from the Authority. Distinctive features of the Korean legislation include rules on "prospecting, exploration or exploitation," procedures for notification in the case of prospecting, and procedures for obtaining permits in the case of exploration or exploitation. By contrast, the laws of Singapore and China only include the exploration or exploitation of the resources within their permit systems.[11] A noteworthy feature of the Chinese legislation is that it facilitates the overall management of information by the nation through the support of construction and operation of public infrastructure related to the Area; exchange and cooperation of science and technology related to the Area, and sharing of achievements'[12] dissemination of deep sea science;[13] and submission of copies of all materials and samples.[14] Likewise, the Korean Law on Deep Seabed Area encourages development of science and technology for support of the activities in the Area and provision of information and dissemination of international cooperation achievements. But the legislation does not directly require submission of information related to the activities in the Area. However, both the Korean and Singaporean legislation include regulations to impose conditions,[15] and thereby could potentially foster holistic management policies by, for instance, requiring submission of related information as a prerequisite of the permit.

Another distinctive feature of the Korean Law on Deep Seabed Area is that, unlike other legislations which mandate the imposition of measures of marine environment protection as an obligation of the contracting party, it simultaneously regulates the obligations of the state and the obligations of private entities engaged in activities in the Area.[17] In particular, the Korean Law requires, as part of the obligations of the state, the duty to take measures to protect the marine environment and to implement emergency action plans to be triggered in case of serious infringement on the marine environment. In this way, the law requires the state to take measures which may be necessitated by the activities in the Area over and above simple supervision and inspection.

---

11 Law of the People's Republic of China on Exploration for and Exploitation of Resources in the Deep Seabed Area (promulgated by Standing Committee of the National People's Congress, Feb. 26, 2016, effective May 1, 2016), art. 8 [hereinafter, China DSM Law]; Singapore Deep Seabed Mining Act (Act No. 6/2015), art. 6.

12 China DSM Law, art. 16.

13 Ibid, art. 17.

14 Ibid, art. 18.

15 Korean Law on Deep Seabed Area, art. 10; Singapore Deep Seabed Mining Act, art. 10.

17 Korean Law on Deep Seabed Area, art. 19.

4 The Korea Law on Exploration for and Exploitation of Resources in the Deep Seabed Area

4.1 *The Need for Legislation*

There is an absence of domestic regulation for implementation of international treaty related to activities in the deep seabed and ocean floor (hereinafter the "Area"). 'Resources of the Area' are collectively managed by the international community in accordance with the UNCLOS and international law related to the Area strongly requires the enactment of pertinent regulations. 'Resources of the Area' refers to all mineral resources *in situ* in the Area and subsoil thereof, beyond the limits of national jurisdiction and as of 2017, approximately 30 States have officially enacted their respective legislations. As the international community moves towards commercialization of resources of the Area for the first time, there is a defect in the domestic legislation as to the regulation of Korea's secured mining lot in the Area. Korea is in urgent need of enacting a domestic law pertinent to the Authority and ITLOS' implementation of the duty to manage and fulfillment of state liability exemption prerequisites.

There is the need to procure ground rules on implementation of domestic measures for immunity of States that sponsor activities in the Area (hereinafter sponsoring States). UNCLOS Article 139, Article 153(4), and Annex III Article 4(4), and ISA's Decision of the Council (ISBA/17/C/20, para.3) and Decision of the Council (ISBA/18/C/8, Add.1), demand a provision in the domestic law that secures activities in the Area. Further, in its 2011 Advisory Opinion, ITLOS recommended that the sponsoring States put forward domestic legislation in order to be exempt from related state liability. The advisory opinion also spoke to the sponsoring States' indirect and direct obligations, and emphasized that specific measures be legislated into the sponsoring State's domestic law.

The Korean Law on Deep Seabed Area establishes ground rules for stable exploitation of resources of the Area as follows:

The first rule is stable exploitation of resources of the Area in accordance with nationals' support of activities in the Area and enactment of a law on exemption from state liability in accordance with duty to comply with international law. This rule represents a paradigm change from the international community's active management of the Area's resources which follows the 'first-come, first-served basis,' and reinforcement of the state party's management obligation.

The second rule is that Korea needs to cater to the demand to internationally conform by, among other things, renewing its manganese nodule exploration contract (expired in 2016) for five additional years, and preparing to proceed into the commercial (exploitation) phase within the next five years.

Reflecting these developments, there has been progress in Korea in introducing the law on exploitation of mineral resources of the Area. Domestically, the exploitation of resources of the Area has been under the purview of the Ministry of Trade, Industry and Energy. However, there are currently no legislations with a focus on exploitation of mineral resources of the Area, the commercial development period of which has been uncertain. The Korean Ministry of Ocean and Fisheries' approach in regards to the exploitation of resources of the Area rests in the pre-commercial stage, with the focus on "investigation—securing the mining area—selection of priority mining area," and there is insufficient recognition of the need for legislation on exploitation.[18]

Recently, however, the Authority has been giving more weight to the establishment of domestic law as a precondition for the granting of a mining block. In the absence of enacted Korean legislation, the Authority's position could operate as an obstacle to the further securing of lots in the mining area and entrance into the exploitation phase. When Brazil applied for the exploitation of manganese nodules, states such as the Netherlands raised an issue about the absence of domestic legislation related to the Area.

Within the next five years, Korea, as a contracting State of the Area, is in urgent need of a legal basis to support the policy, for the promotion of marine enterprise, and for leading technological development for transition into the commercial phase. Enactment of legislation related to the Area ensures exploitation of the resources of the Area as the leading features of the Korean Ministry of Ocean and Fisheries. It could contribute towards stabilization of Korea's strategic mineral supply, which as of now heavily relies on foreign sources. Mining of the Area—which necessitates cutting-edge marine development technology and tremendous investment costs—requires institutional and financial support measures. It also needs the basis for promotion of the industry in the Area provided by stimulating participation of private enterprises.

In 2012, the Ministry of Ocean and Fisheries, then known as the Ministry of Land, Transport, and Maritime Affairs, initiated the domestic legislation in accordance with the Authority's trend of expanding activities in the Area. In 2013, it devised its first draft, known as the Marine Mineral Resources Development Act.[19]

18 This is the reason why the proposed legislation was abandoned in 2018 when the National Assembly did not adopt it.

19 Marine Mineral Resources Development Act, Law No. 14679, Sep. 22, 2017.

4.2 *Legislative Direction and Organizational Structure*

4.2.1 Legislative Direction

The new legislation, which governs the authorization process for conducting exploration and exploitation of resources of the Area, accepts international law related to activities in the Area and administers the activity of Korean nationals in the Area. It also clarifies the international obligation for the guarantee of implementation of obligations.

The proposed legislation is comprised of basic plans of work for exploitation of resources of the Area and the authorization process for the people engaged in the Enterprise. It also includes provisions ensuring compliance with international norms and protection of the marine environment, including basic plans of work for activities in the Area (Section 2), authorization of activities in the Area (Section 3), and supplementary rules (Section 5).The legislation also ensures international competitiveness of activities in the Area by regulating support of activities in the Area, establishment of the Enterprise (Section 4), encouragement of joint ventures (Section 3), and promotion of activities in the Area.

4.2.2 Structure of the Law

The Korean Law on the Deep Seabed is composed of 6 Sections and 28 provisions. Section 1 (General Provisions) points out the purpose, definitions, and relationship with international conventions, as well as responsibility and liability. Section 2 (Basic Plans of Work for Activities in the Area) concerns formulation of basic plans of work for exploration and exploitation activities in the Area, establishment of a review committee for activities in the Area, and so forth. Section 3 (Authorization of Activities in the Area) touches upon issues such as notification of prospecting, issuance of the Enterprise permit, encouragement of joint ventures, issuance of certificates, revocation of the Enterprise permit, termination of support, rights and obligations of the persons engaged in the Enterprise, and transfer of rights of persons engaged in the Enterprise. Section 4 (Promotion of Activities in the Area) covers topics such as assistance with activities in the Area, establishment of the Enterprise, and delegation of rights. Section 5 (Supplementary Rules) has provisions on protection and preservation of marine environment, protection and preservation of rare or fragile ecosystems, emergency measures, inspection and supervision, corrective orders, and charges. Finally, Section 6 (Penalties) mentions penalties, joint penal provisions, and administrative fines.

4.2.3 Main Contents of the Law

The main contents of the Korean Law on Deep Seabed Area are as follows. First, the application and scope of administration specify inclusion of activities in the Area beyond the national jurisdiction.[20] In particular, the legislation provides for regulation of implementation of international obligations and domestic procedure for Korean nationals engaged in activities in the Area administered by the Authority (prospecting, exploration, exploitation). These provisions define "Resources of the Area" as all mineral resources *in situ* in the Area and subsoil thereof, beyond the limits of national jurisdiction, which are defined by UNCLOS as the 'common heritage of mankind,' meaning all rights in the resources of the Area are vested in mankind as a whole, on whose behalf the Authority shall act.

Second, the law provides formulation of basic plans of work for exploration and exploitation of the Area, and establishes a review committee for activities in the Area.[21] It formulates basic plans of work for systematic and effective management of the exploitation of resources of the Area and refers matters related to the development and alteration of basic plans to the review committee for activities in the Area.

The legislation provides for submission of contents such as the basic purpose of activities in the Area, direction and strategies of activities in the Area, promotion and support of the Enterprise, scientific and technological development for activities in the Area, international cooperation related to activities in the Area, securing resource supply stability in cases of emergency, and collection and distribution of information needed for activities in the Area. The legislation also provides for establishment of the review committee comprised of related departments to review matters related to authorization, modification, revocation, and termination of the Enterprise. The Chairperson of the committee shall act as a deputy minister of the Ministry of Oceans and Fisheries, and the committee shall consist of no more than 20 members.

Third, the legislation provides that Korean nationals who seek to undertake prospecting are categorized into notification (prospecting) and permitting (exploration, exploitation) depending on the level of activities.[22] Nationals must also submit related plans and applications to the review committee depending on their activities. The legislation's approach in prospecting, exploration, and exploitation is the same as that of the Authority's draft Exploitation

20 Korean Law on Deep Seabed Area, art. 1–4.

21 Ibid., art. 6–7.

22 Ibid., art. 8–9, 11–13.

Regulation approach of notification and authorization.[23] Specifically, the legislation requires persons seeking to undertake prospecting to report to the Minister of the Ministry of Oceans and Fisheries and to first undergo the notification process. The legislation then requires persons who seek to conduct an Enterprise to obtain a use permit from the Minister of the Ministry of Oceans and Fisheries (valid for 10 years), and to separately apply for the exploration permit and exploitation permit. To obtain these permits, applicants must submit: proof of financial, investment, and technical capabilities for the Enterprise; assessment of the impact of exploration or exploitation on the marine environment; and an emergency action plan to be triggered in case of serious infringement on the marine environment.

The legislation strengthens implementation of international law and measures to administer compliance by Korean nationals by stipulating that the persons engaged in the Enterprise shall not proceed with the exploration or exploitation until having become a contracting person through an exploration or exploitation contract with the Authority.

The legislation provides that the applications for the Enterprise be reviewed in the order of submission. Where deemed necessary, joint ventures of two or more persons to the Enterprise are recommended with a view to strengthen international competitiveness. The Authority's Exploitation Regulation also reviews applications in the order they were submitted, and while this principle has been domestically adopted, the possibility of strengthening national coordination has been introduced.

The legislation also provides that in the case of issuing a permit for the Enterprise, the Minister of the Ministry of Oceans and Fisheries must issue a certificate which is necessary for persons engaged in the Enterprise to enter into a contract with the Authority. Thus, the permit for the Enterprise is a domestic procedure for issuance of a certificate necessary for persons engaged in the Enterprise to enter into a contract with the Authority and, as such, the government assesses the ability of the applicant to implement international obligations during the procedure of issuing a permit.

In addition to revocation of the permit, the legislation provides for termination of support in certain cases, such as obtaining the permit through deceit or other illegal means. In such a case, the Minister of the Ministry

23 The Authority's Exploitation Regulation requires persons seeking to undertake prospecting to notify the Secretary General of the Authority, and to refrain from carrying out the prospecting until confirmation that such notification has been filed. International Seabed Authority, *Draft Regulations on Exploitation of Mineral Resources in the Area*, ISA Doc. SBA/25/C/WP.1 (Mar. 25, 2019).

of Oceans and Fisheries shall submit a written submission to the Authority and the termination will take effect 6 months after the Secretary General of the Authority's receipt of the submission in order to protect the rights of the sponsor.

The Fourth aspect of the legislation concerns rights and obligations, including transfer of rights that vest in persons engaged in the Enterprise.[24] The legislation provides that the persons engaged in the Enterprise hold exclusive exploration or exploitation rights only to certain resources within the territory of the contract signed with the Authority and urges the fulfillment of contractual obligations. The legislation clarifies the rights of persons engaged in the Enterprise and urges implementation of contractual duties with the Authority and provides for compliance of domestic regulations related to safety. The legislation also provides for the assignment or assumption of rights and obligations to be made only to the people of the Republic of Korea. In addition, the law lays out procedures for modification of the permit. The Enterprise hinges on a state's international responsibility and, as such, deems assignment of its rights as a critical modification in the permit.

Fifth, the law encourages joint ventures of more than two persons for the purpose of strengthening international competitiveness and promoting efficiency, as the Enterprise is accompanied by large-scale budget and technology development.[25] In particular, the legislation provides for adjustments to resolve an overlap where there is more than one person who intends to undertake the Enterprise in the same area for the same resources of the Area prescribed by the Authority.

Sixth, and finally, the legislation ensures support for the promotion of activities in the Area such as provision of relevant information, training of professional personnel, development of science and technology equipment, and international cooperation.[26] It also includes support for industries related to activities in the Area by providing training of professional personnel and support of research institutes related to activities in the Area. The legislation further provides for establishment of the professional Enterprise group for implementation and support of the activities in the Area and provides that the group may carry out the government's mandate related to such activities.

24 Korean Law on Deep Seabed Area, art. 14–15.

25 Ibid, art. 10.

26 Ibid, art. 16–18.

5 Response to Development of Extended Continental Shelf beyond 200 Nautical Miles of the Coastal States under Article 76 of the Convention

Given the status of technological developments related to exploitation of the Area, distribution of coastal states' interests pursuant to Article 82 of the Convention does not appear likely to be executed in the very foreseeable future.[27] However, considering the adoption of relevant rules for exploration of manganese nodules in the past and discussions around hydrothermal exploration regulations, at this point the international community needs to initiate specific discussions related to Article 82. This is because the conflict of intergovernmental interests will be stronger in the case of Article 82 of the Convention, because it discusses the distribution of profits from the development of continental shelf that was incorporated into the sovereign jurisdiction of one country; whereas the discussion of the Area is one that involves the common heritage of mankind, which is necessarily outside the jurisdiction or control of any one state.

With the gradual stabilization of the spatial parameters of the Area, creation of an order for the purposes of legal interpretation and implementation of development of non-living resources in the continental shelf beyond 200 nautical miles of the coastal states became the new task for the international law of the sea. The Convention is working on a device to return the resources of the Area, which is a common heritage of mankind susceptible to interference by expansion of the coastal states' continental shelf, to the international community. Article 82 of the Convention is part of such an effort. Accordingly, Article 82 is assessed to be one of the most controversially compromised and one of the most innovative products of the Convention. However, before a realistic power of execution can be achieved, the exploitation of resources and the associated profit-sharing in the continental shelf beyond 200 nautical miles of the coastal states, which the state has sovereign rights to, remains as a problem to be solved. Ultimately, with respect to international law, while the method of reaching an appropriate compromise between competing states at the time of signing UNCLOS would be followed, an important controversy remains in that process as to what extent the views of coastal states with the expanded continental shelf will be accepted.

27 Permanent Mission of the PRC to International Seabed Authority (Feb. 24, 2009), http://china-isa.jm.chineseembassy.org/chn/xwdt/t539030.htm.

One issue likely to breed contention is determining when coastal States are obligated to begin making payments. To begin, "all products produced in the mining area in the period beginning five years after the start of production" or "evaluation on and value of products" and relationship with obligations, runs the risk of freezing exploitation of the resources in a state's continental shelf beyond 200 nautical miles.[28] These issues may create new conflicts in the process of making regular in-kind donations and cash payments. For instance, the issue of how to realistically achieve realization of the investment loss in the case where development is delayed due to a *force majeure* event at the development stage of coastal states, or in the case of resuming a previously delayed work for a certain reason, is likely to lead to a long debate between the international community and coastal states.

With respect to the *force majeure* factor at the phase of exploration or exploitation, the Regulation on Exploitation of Manganese Nodules in the Area instructs that:

> [T]he Contractor shall not be liable for an unavoidable delay or failure to perform [any of its obligations/the Exploitation Activities] under this Contract due to *force majeure*, provided the Contractor has taken all reasonable steps to overcome the delay or obstacle to performance … has failed to complete the preparations necessary to proceed in to the exploitation phase or is under the economic circumstances where the Contractor cannot proceed into the development phase, the Contract may apply for an extension of the exploration plan for no more than five years, under the recommendations of the committee and with the permission of the board of directors.

Such a *force majeure* clause related to the Area may operate as a flexible negotiating factor inducing a compromise between parties in the case of the expanded continental shelf of the coastal state that falls within the parameters of Article 82 of the Convention. However, notwithstanding the need to adequately reflect environmental conditions for promoting development of the coastal states, it is imperative that there be measures for the distribution of development benefits to the international community and for the acceleration of commercial development.

---

28 Hee-Cheol Yang, "Korea's Deep Seabed Activities on the Exploration for and Exploitation of Resources," in *The United Nations Convention on the Law of the Sea: Contemporary Issues and Challenges* (in Korean), Korean Society of the Law of the Sea (2012), p.258.

With respect to establishing a fair method of distribution, it is clear that the discussions on the distribution method and standard of development of non-living resources in the extended continental shelf will proceed with much controversy and complexity compared to discussions regarding the Area. While it is necessary to recognize the difference in stance on distribution by targeting the continental shelf within the national jurisdiction, it is anticipated that a certain standard for equitable distribution can be provided by the regulation on exploitation of mineral resources of the Area.

From February 11 to February 13, 2009, the Authority and Chatham House of the United Kingdom jointly conducted a seminar in London on the issue of financial or in-kind payment associated with the development of non-living resources in the continental shelf beyond 200 nautical miles of the coastal states, which is regulated by Article 82 of the Convention. During the seminar it was predicted that, given the recent application progress for the continental shelf of coastal states and the related exploitation of resources, the receipt of payment would be conducted under Article 82 of the Convention in 2015, at the earliest.[29] Admittedly, the build-up of issues were also highlighted with respect to the jurisdiction and procedural problems between coastal states and the Authority when it comes to the issue of profit-sharing under Article 82 of the Convention. Besides the national implementation of Article 82, it is clear that the legal relationship surrounding mutual distribution of benefit and rights will be complicated if domestic interests are involved. Moreover, for the obligations imposed on states by international law, the relevant state must establish domestic legal regulations as to whether the state will shoulder the payment of relevant costs or whether such burden will be shifted to the producers.

Indeed, Article 82 of the Convention is not directly connected to Korea's understanding with respect to jurisdiction. However, expansion of a coastal state's continental shelf by the Commission on the Limits of the Continental Shelf means that resources of the Area (minerals, energy, and other) that were previously under the control of the Authority will be reduced and, as such,

29 During the meeting, there were discussions of payment of costs or payment in kind associated with the exploitation of mineral resources, the amount and time of such payments, and the direct powers and dispute settlement mechanisms of the Authority in the relevant area for the purposes of enforcing the specific problems of the aforementioned clauses. The results of the seminar were to be referred by the Conference of the Parties or the Authority. *See* "International Seabed Authority Holds Seminar on Issues Related to the Implementation of Article 82 of the United Nations Convention on the Law of the Sea," Permanent Mission of PRC to International Seabed Authority (Feb. 24, 2009), http://china-isa.jm.chineseembassy.org/chn/xwdt/t539030.htm.

ultimately signifies a serious narrowing down of room for economic advancement. That is, regardless of whether or not the direct profit sharing target under Article 82 is realized, there must be a formulation of theoretical and policy directions related to Article 82 of the Convention, which is bound to arise as the new agenda for Korea's profits of the Area and the international maritime order. At the heart of such discussions lies Korea's interest in participation, in the sense that these discussions will involve the issue of exploitation of resources of the Area connected to the coastal state's continental shelf, the issue of profit-sharing, and the major mineral resources and all other nonliving resources as currently discussed by the Authority.

6 Conclusion

The Area and its resources are defined by UNCLOS as the common heritage of mankind. Related norms of the Convention and the Authority require all state parties to take domestic legal and administrative measures necessary for support and implementation of the activities in the Area. According to Article 1(3) of UNCLOS, "activities in the Area" means all activities of exploration for, and exploitation of, the resources of the Area.

In response to the limits in the current law and the need for new domestic legislation related to the Area, as a State Party to the Convention and the Authority, Korea has drafted legislation that would require Korean nationals' activities in the Area to be conducted in accordance with international law. Further, as a sponsoring State, the legislation seeks to enforce Korea's legal responsibilities and obligations as prescribed by international law and international judicial bodies and other law enforcement as agencies as part of the domestic law.[30] It designs to provide necessary procedures such as support of Korean nationals' activities in the Area and provides for cooperation and compliance with international legal norms, thereby promoting enterprises in the Area that secure a stable supply of resources.

Key factors in the legislation include sponsorship obligations of Korean nationals who engage in the enterprise beyond the limits of national

30 *See* UNCLOS, art. 139; Responsibilities and Obligations of States Sponsoring Persons and Entities with Respect to Activities in the Area, Case No. 17, Advisory Opinion of Feb. 1, 2011, ITLOS Rep. 10; International Seabed Authority, *Laws, Regulations and Administrative Measures Adopted by Sponsoring States and Other Members of the International Seabed Authority with Respect to the Activities in the Area*, ISA Doc. ISBA/18/C/8/Add.1 (Jun. 26, 2012).

jurisdiction, measures to prevent environmental pollution, the support of related industries, domestic accommodation of international norms, long-term promotion of enterprise in the Area, ensuring implementation of international norms by the persons engaged in the enterprise, sharing of information about the Area, and cooperation.

Despite this desirable direction to move forward, it is a pity that there has been no progress in terms of adoption at the National Assembly in Korea, and it is hope that this proposed legislation will be re-introduced in due course.

PART 2

The Polar Regions

CHAPTER 3

Governing the Ocean Commons

Lessons from the Antarctic

Karen N. Scott

1 Introduction*

This chapter will draw lessons from one of the oldest and, in some ways, most successful 'commons' regimes—the Antarctic—and seek to apply those lessons more generally. The commons is in fact a contested concept in the Antarctic, but nevertheless, a Southern Ocean 'regional seas' regime for commons governance has been established within the framework of the Antarctic Treaty System (ATS). The ATS provides examples of good governance in areas under increasing pressure as political dynamics change within the region and resource constraints impact day-to-day management.

The regime governing the Antarctic is arguably one of the most successful commons management regimes ever implemented. The regime was initiated at the height of the Cold War with the entry into force of the 1959 Antarctic Treaty in 1961, and has continued to successfully navigate significant changes in global geopolitics through to the present day. The Antarctic Treaty built on the significant level of scientific cooperation between states which took place during the 1957–58 International Geophysical Year, and developed a set of principles that prioritised science and peace. Its most important provision, Article IV, allowed for successful mediation of the different positions between claimant and non-claimant states, and facilitated cooperation in respect of scientific research, environmental protection, management of resources and tourism. The Antarctic Treaty provided a foundation for the development of the Antarctic Treaty System, which today comprises three instruments focused on resource management and environmental protection. This chapter will critically assess the three key instruments of the ATS—the 1959 Antarctic Treaty, 1991 Environmental Protocol and the 1980 Convention for the Conservation of Antarctic Marine Living Resources (CAMLR Convention)—as well as

* The text of this chapter was completed in April 2019.

 | DOI:10.1163/9789004514218_005

the broader regime complex that governs activities taking place within the Southern Ocean.

The success of the Antarctic regime may provide valuable lessons for global commons management more generally; lessons that are particularly important in light of ongoing negotiations in respect of a legally binding global instrument for the conservation of biodiversity beyond areas of national jurisdiction. This chapter, after introducing the Antarctic Treaty System, will identify four such 'lessons.' These lessons will comprise examples of good governance in the Antarctic, but examples that are also under contemporary pressure as political dynamics change within the region and resource constraints impact day-to-day management. The lessons identified comprise: transparency and open inspection; freedom of scientific research and dissemination of that research; ecosystem and integrated environmental management; and cooperation navigating the Southern Ocean regime complex. These lessons from the Antarctic demonstrate what can be achieved in a commons context whilst simultaneously illustrating the challenges of oceans commons governance.

2 Contested Commons and Antarctica

The commons (defined as an area beyond the jurisdiction of states) in the Antarctic is a contested and potentially complicated concept. The presence of seven disputed and largely unrecognised claims to the continent of Antarctica has created significant uncertainty as to the jurisdictional status of the water column and the seabed immediately adjacent to Antarctica. Moreover, the regime created by the Antarctic Treaty System can be characterised as going beyond even an atypical regional seas regime and, rather, operating as something approaching a proxy for coastal state jurisdiction. The ambiguous status of much of the Southern Ocean has, in some ways, created opportunities for more extensive collaboration than is typically seen in commons areas, while limiting cooperation in other ways—particularly in respect of enforcement. This section will detail the ambiguous jurisdictional regime in the Antarctic and explore its implications for ocean commons management.

2.1 *Maritime Zones Subject to the Jurisdiction of Coastal States in the Sub-Antarctic*

Some areas of the Southern Ocean are claimed as sovereign territory while others are considered part of the high seas. The parts of the Southern Ocean that lie under the jurisdiction of states consist of maritime zones associated with largely uncontested claims to Antarctic and sub-Antarctic islands. For example: Prince Edward Islands (South Africa); Crozet Islands and Kerguelen Island (France); Heard and McDonald Islands, Macquarie Island (Australia); Auckland Island, Campbell Island (New Zealand); South Shetlands, South Orkneys (UK); South Sandwich Islands, South Georgia (UK, contested by Argentina); Bouvet Island (Norway). Within these maritime zones, states exercise rights and duties over resources, navigation and scientific research as set out under Parts II, V and VI of the 1982 United Nations Convention on the Law of the Sea (UNCLOS).[1] These areas are also subject to the jurisdiction of the 1980 Convention on the Conservation of Antarctic Marine Living Resources (CAMLR Convention)[2] in respect of Southern Ocean fisheries management, although coastal states may choose not to apply measures adopted under the Convention to their maritime zones.[3] Moreover, to the extent that the continental shelf associated with these islands extends south of 60° South Latitude into the Antarctic Treaty Area, activities on the shelf are likely to be subject to the 1959 Antarctic Treaty[4] and the 1991 Environmental Protocol to the 1959 Antarctic Treaty,[5] in particular, the ban on minerals exploitation under Article 7 of the Protocol.

It is also notable that all of the features noted above are claimed as "islands" pursuant to Article 121(1) of UNCLOS with the full panoply of maritime zones. As early as 1988, at least one commentator questioned whether the sub-Antarctic islands were indeed "islands" rather than "rocks" on account of their size, absence of permanent population and distance from the metropolitan claimant state.[6] If these features are, in fact, rocks rather than islands, they do not generate maritime zones over which states may assert jurisdiction. In 2016, in The South China Sea Arbitration (The Republic of Philippines v. The People's Republic of China), the UNCLOS Annex VII Tribunal adopted a narrow view of the requirement that islands must be able to "sustain human

1 1982 United Nations Convention on the Law of the Sea, Dec. 10, 1982, 1833 U.N.T.S. 397, 21 I.L.M. 1261, entered into force Nov. 16, 1994 [hereinafter 1982 UNCLOS].

2 1980 Convention for the Conservation of Marine Living Resources, May 20, 1980, 1329 U.N.T.S. 47, entered into force Apr. 7, 1982 [hereinafter CAMLR Convention].

3 See the Chairman's Statement appended to the 1980 CAMLR Convention. Although the statement refers specifically to Crozet Islands and Kerguelen Island (under the jurisdiction of France) it has been interpreted as being of application to the maritime zones of sub-Antarctic islands more generally.

4 1959 Antarctic Treaty, Dec. 1, 1959, 402 U.N.T.S. 71, 12 U.S.T. 794, entered into force Jun. 23, 1969.

5 1991 Protocol on Environmental Protection to the Antarctic Treaty, Apr. 10, 1991, 30 I.L.M. 1461, entered into force Jan. 14, 1998 [hereinafter Environmental Protocol].

6 Christopher C. Joyner, "The Exclusive Economic Zone and Antarctica: The Dilemmas of Non-Sovereign Jurisdiction," *Ocean Development and International Law* 19 (1988): 469, 477.

habitation or economic life of their own,"[7] demanding that a feature must have "conditions sufficiently conducive to human life and livelihood for people to inhabit, rather than merely survive on, the feature."[8] Moreover, the Tribunal asserted that "purely extractive economic activities, which accrue no benefit for the feature or its population, would not amount to an economic life of the feature as 'of its own.'"[9] This interpretation is supported by the negotiating history of UNCLOS, whereby Article 121(3) was intended to operate as a constraint on the declaration of exclusive economic zones (EEZs) by serving to "disable tiny features from unfairly and inequitably generating enormous entitlements to maritime spaces that would serve not to benefit the local population, but to award a windfall to the (potentially distant) State to have maintained a claim to such a feature."[10]

Applying this interpretation of Article 121(3) to sub-Antarctic features could potentially preclude their classification as "islands" for the purposes of UNCLOS. Whilst most would be capable of "sustaining" life in the sense of providing water, sustenance and basic shelter, it is questionable whether a population could "inhabit" rather than merely "survive." Indeed, past attempts at inhabitation have failed.[11] Moreover, to the extent that these islands support an economic life through fishing (and perhaps tourism) it is unarguable that this economic life benefits the distant metropolitan state rather than any local population. On the other hand, claims to the sub-Antarctic are long-standing and uncontested, suggesting that other states have, at the very least, acquiesced to the designation of these features as "islands" (and thus capable of generating maritime zones) and it is notable that the Tribunal in the South China Sea Arbitration was remarkably, perhaps even negligently, dismissive of state practice in this area.[12]

---

7 1982 UNCLOS, art. 121(3).

8 The South China Sea Arbitration (The Republic of Philippines v. People's Republic of China), PCA Case No. 2013-19, Order of Jul. 12, 2016, [489], available at: https://pcacases.com/web/sendAttach/2086.

9 Ibid, [500].

10 Ibid, [517].

11 For example, the settlement of Enderby Island in the Auckland Islands (New Zealand) between 1849 to 1852. *See* Conon Fraser, *Beyond the Roaring Forties. New Zealand's Subantarctic Islands* (Wellington: Government Printing Publishing, 1986), chap. 9.

12 The Tribunal briefly stated that "there is no evidence for an agreement based upon State practice on the interpretation of Article 121(3) which differs from the interpretation of the Tribunal as outlined in the previous sections." *South China Sea Arbitration*, [553].

2.2 *Maritime Zones off the Coast of the Continent of Antarctica*

The seas surrounding the continent of Antarctica itself are the subject of unambiguous disputes as to their jurisdictional status. Six of the seven claimant states (Argentina, Australia, Chile, France, New Zealand and the UK) claim a territorial sea off their respective coastlines and Norway reserves a right to do so.[13] A contiguous zone (up to 24 nautical miles) is claimed by Australia, Argentina, Chile, France and New Zealand.[14] And Australia, Argentina, Chile and France also claim a 200 nautical mile EEZ.[15] Further, although states do not need to proclaim a continental shelf under Article 77(3) of UNCLOS as coastal state sovereign rights over the continental shelf flow automatically from their control over territory, Australia, Argentina and Chile have formally claimed continental shelves off their Antarctic territories.[16] These claims (maritime and terrestrial) are not generally recognised by the 185 non-claimant states and, indeed, are not fully recognised among the claimant states themselves.[17]

In 1959 the narrow and uncertain width of the territorial sea and the absence of significant activity associated with the continental shelf off Antarctica meant that the issue of Antarctic maritime zones could be largely ignored by all states operating within the region.[18] Article IV of the 1959 Antarctic Treaty operates to preserve existing claims or bases of claims but provides that no new claims or enlargement of existing claims may take place whilst the Treaty is in force. Article IV also stipulates that activities taking place under the Treaty do not serve to support or undermine existing claims (or the bases of claims) or the recognition (or otherwise) of those claims. This clever compromise has operated as the foundation for cooperation in the region to this day, and has allowed states to avoid a direct confrontation over maritime claims even though the adoption of the 1982 UNCLOS substantially shifted the balance (at least in theory) in favour of the putative claimant states through increasing waters subject to the

13 Tim Stephens, "An Icy Reception or a Warm Embrace? The Antarctic Treaty System and the International Law of the Sea" in Klaus Dodds, Alan D. Hemmings and Peder Roberts, eds., *Handbook on the Politics of Antarctica* (Cheltenham: Edward Elgar Publishing, 2017), chap. 28, 442.

14 Ibid.

15 Ibid. New Zealand has not claimed an EEZ but reserves a right to do so under section 9(3) of the Territorial Sea, Contiguous Zone, Exclusive Economic Zone Act 1977.

16 Ibid.

17 Australia, France, New Zealand, Norway and the UK mutually recognise one-another's claims and Chile and Argentina also recognise one-another's claims although they have not agreed on a boundary between the claims.

18 M. J. Peterson, "Antarctic Implications of the New Law of the Sea," *Ocean Development and International Law* 16 (1986): 137, 141.

control of coastal states at the expense of the high seas. Moreover, the parties to the 1959 Antarctic Treaty were successful in "forestalling formal discussion of Southern Ocean issues at UNCLOS III,"[19] and the application of Part XI of UNCLOS—which establishes a common heritage of mankind regime in respect of the seabed beyond the jurisdiction of states and its mineral resources—to the Antarctic Treaty area was, and remains, ambiguous.

The relationship between the Antarctic Treaty and the modern law of the sea has been the subject of robust discussion over the years,[20] but compromise and clever diplomacy has allowed states to walk the tightrope between rights claimed by claimant states, Antarctic Treaty party states and other states when developing a regime for fisheries management,[21] negotiating a convention facilitating the exploitation of Antarctic minerals,[22] and engaging in the UNCLOS process for confirming the limits of the continental shelf beyond 200 nautical miles.[23] Claimant states have generally been cautious in actively asserting their claims, and do not take enforcement action on the basis of domestic legislation against foreign vessels or in respect of states, relying instead on international rules and standards.[24] Whilst non-claimant states take steps to preserve their position of non-recognition[25] they have nevertheless not prevented claimant

19 Ibid.

20 *See, e.g.*, Stephens, "An Icy Reception"; Peterson, "Antarctic Implications"; Joyner, "The Exclusive Economic Zone," 469; Bernard H. Ozman, "Antarctica and the New Law of the Sea," *Cornell International Law Journal* 19 (1986): 211; Shirley V. Scott, "The Evolving Antarctic Treaty System: Implications of Accommodating Developments in the Law of the Sea" in Erik J. Molenaar, Alex G. Oude Elferink and Donald R. Rothwell, eds., *The Law of the Sea and the Polar Regions. Interactions between Global and Regional Regimes* (Leiden: Martinus Nijhoff Publishers, 2013), chap. 2.

21 1980 CAMLR Convention.

22 1988 Convention on the Regulation of Antarctic Mineral Resource Activities, Nov. 25, 1988, 27 I.L.M. 868, not yet in force.

23 1982 UNCLOS, art. 76(8).

24 For example, even though an Australian NGO obtained an injunction in 2008 against Japanese whalers under the Australian Environment Protection and Biodiversity Conservation Act, for whaling inside the Australian Antarctic EEZ, this injunction was never enforced. *See Humane Society International v. Kyodo Senpaku Kaisha Ltd.*, [2004] FCA 15110; [2005] FCA 664; [2006] FCAFC 116; [2008] FCA 3. Instead, Australia argued—successfully—that Japan's whaling activities breached Article VIII of the 1946 International Convention on the Regulation of Whaling before the International Court of Justice. *See* Whaling in the Antarctic (Australia v. Japan; New Zealand Intervening), Judgment, 2014 I.C.J. Rep. 1062, [247].

25 For example, in response to Australia's submission to the Commission on the Limits of the Continental Shelf, the US, Russia, Japan, the Netherlands, Germany and India all lodged formal notes confirming that they do not recognise Australia's claim to Antarctica. *See* United Nations Division for Ocean Affairs & the Law of the Sea, *Commission on the*

states from taking action to maintain those claims, such as making submissions to the UNCLOS Continental Shelf Commission.[26]

2.3 *A 'Commons' Maritime Zone Managed by All Antarctic Treaty Consultative Parties?*

Christopher Joyner, in 1988, suggested that "when viewed in composite, the Antarctic Treaty System may present an acceptable surrogate in the Antarctic for jurisdiction tantamount to the coastal state-derived EEZ concept."[27] This is a limited version of the 'commons': a form of collective management perhaps approximating a form of condominium regime but not open to all states, at least not those states outside of the regime. In the absence of functional coastal states, the parties to the 1959 Antarctic Treaty and its associated instruments have developed rules and standards to govern activities such as scientific research, environmental protection, fisheries management, navigation and even the exploitation of mineral resources. Of course, this regime extends to the entire area south of 60° South Latitude, well beyond the limit of the various maritime zones claimed off Antarctica.[28] Whether this arrangement is regarded as a 'surrogate' for coastal state jurisdiction or merely an unusual regional seas regime is of little import on a day-to-day operational basis. It

---

Limits of the Continental Shelf (CLCS) Outer limits of the continental shelf beyond 200 nautical miles from the baselines: Submissions to the Commission: Submission by Australia (Nov. 5, 2012), available at: https://www.un.org/depts/los/clcs_new/submissions_files/submission_aus.htm.

26 Australia, Norway and Argentina have all provided information on the proposed outer limits of the continental shelf off their Antarctic claims to the Commission on the Limits of the Continental Shelf pursuant to Article 76(8) of UNCLOS. France, New Zealand and the UK have made partial submissions to the Commission and reserved a right to make a future submission in respect of their Antarctic territories. Chile has made a preliminary submission to the Commission and has noted that it may in the future submit information in respect of its Antarctic claim or it may make a reservation in respect of Antarctica. The Commission is unable to examine the Antarctic portion of any claim under its Rules of Procedure, which require the consent of all parties to a dispute prior to considering an area under dispute. *See* Commission on the Limits of the Continental Shelf, Rules of Procedure, CLCS/40/Rev.1 (Apr. 17, 2008), Annex 1, [5]. All submissions and relevant communications can be found on the webpage of the Commission. "Submissions, through the Secretary-General of the United Nations, to the Commission on the Limits of the Continental Shelf, pursuant to article 76, paragraph 8, of the United Nations Convention on the Law of the Sea of 10 December 1982," Commission on the Limits of the Continental Shelf, (Dec. 12, 2019), https://www.un.org/depts/los/clcs_new/commission_submissions.htm.

27 Joyner, "The Exclusive Economic Zone," 482.

28 1980 CAMLR Convention, art. 1(1).

does have implications, however, for potential access to resources—living and non-living—and the extent to which any regime of application to 'commons' resources is able to extend its reach into the Southern Ocean.

2.4 *The Southern Ocean as Res Communis*

For those states not party to the 1959 Antarctic Treaty (and for many who are) the Southern Ocean beyond the maritime zones of sub-Antarctic islands comprises the high seas: open to all states but subject to the sovereignty and control of no state.[29] The 1982 UNCLOS, whilst not specifically addressing the seas surrounding Antarctica, nevertheless intended to create a global legal order for the oceans[30] and thus cannot be interpreted to exclude the Southern Ocean from its remit. The 1959 Antarctic Treaty confirmed that "nothing in the present Treaty shall prejudice or in any way affect the rights, or the exercise of the rights, of any State under international law with regard to the high seas within that area."[31] Article 311(2) of the 1982 UNCLOS preserves the rights and obligations of states arising from other agreements (such as the 1959 Antarctic Treaty) provided those rights and duties "do not affect the enjoyment by other State Parties of their rights or the performance of their obligations under" UNCLOS.[32] The various principles and rules relating to peaceful purposes, scientific research and environmental protection are likely to be considered compatible with (if not supportive of) UNCLOS, at least to the extent that they are not imposed on states not party to the Antarctic Treaty. There is scope for dispute as to whether the ban on minerals exploitation under Article 7 of the Environmental Protocol is compatible with Part XI of UNCLOS, but the ban has yet to be challenged by any state not party to the 1959 Antarctic Treaty. Given that UNCLOS has been in force for over 20 years it might be argued that UNCLOS parties have acquiesced to or, alternatively, are estopped from challenging the ban.

3 The Southern Ocean 'Regional Seas Regime'

The Antarctic Treaty System (ATS) comprises an atypical 'regional seas regime' and provides the framework "for discrete but concomitant instruments" designed to manage maritime activities including coastal infrastructure,

29 1982 UNCLOS, art. 87(1), 89.
30 Ibid, pmbl.
31 1959 Antarctic Treaty, art. VI.
32 1982 UNCLOS, art. 311(2).

scientific research, tourism, fishing, navigation and minerals extraction.[33] It is unusual in that whilst the ATS undoubtedly applies to a geographic region, its membership comprises both states that are geographically proximate (relatively speaking) as well as states which are not but which have an interest in Antarctic or Southern Ocean resources. The 1959 Antarctic Treaty and the 1991 Environmental Protocol both apply to the area south of 60° South Latitude,[34] although the provisions of the Protocol also extend to "dependent and associated ecosystems."[35] The 1980 CAMLR Convention applies to the entire Antarctic ecosystem and includes the area between 60° South Latitude and the Antarctic Convergence.[36] Its focus on the Antarctic ecosystem is demonstrated through its expansive biological mandate, which includes "fin fish, crustaceans and all other species of living organisms, including birds" as well as their relationships with one another and with their physical environment.[37] Whilst the CAMLR Convention performs the functions of a regional fisheries management organization (RFMO) in the Southern Ocean, its strong conservation mandate means that it is more than an RFMO. One other convention also forms part of the ATS system: the 1972 Convention for the Conservation of Antarctic Seals (CCAS).[38] However, CCAS has yet to become operational owing to absence of commercial sealing activities in the Antarctic. Furthermore, an additional convention focused on resource management—the Convention on the Regulation of Antarctic Mineral Resources (CRAMRA)[39] adopted in 1988—is also not operational and is now unlikely to enter into force.

The Antarctic Treaty System is itself part of the broader regime complex for commons governance. The Southern Ocean regime complex, which might be defined as functionally overlapping, non-hierarchical institutions that impact one another's operations,[40] includes, in addition to the instruments described

33 Karen N. Scott and David L. VanderZwaag, "Polar Oceans and the Law of the Sea" in Donald R. Rothwell, Alex G. Oude Elferink, Karen N. Scott, and Tim Stephens, eds., *The Oxford Handbook of the Law of the Sea* (Oxford: Oxford University Press, 2015), 724, 741.

34 1959 Antarctic Treaty, art. VI; 1991 Environmental Protocol, art. 1(b).

35 1991 Environmental Protocol, art. 2.

36 1980 CAMLR Convention, art. 1(1).

37 Ibid, art. 1(2)-(3).

38 1972 Convention for the Conservation of Antarctic Seals, Jun. 1, 1972, 11 I.L.M. 251, entered into force Mar. 11, 1978 [hereinafter CCAS].

39 1988 Convention on the Regulation of Antarctic Marine Living Resources, Jun 2, 1988, 27 I.L.M. 868, not yet in force [hereinafter CRAMRA]. Following Australia and France's refusal to ratify CRAMRA, the Convention was effectively abandoned in favour of the 1991 Environmental Protocol, which was negotiated over 18 months and adopted in 1991.

40 *See* Kal Raustiala and David G. Victor, "The Regime Complex for Plant Genetic Resources," *International Organisation* 58 (2004): 277, 279; Thomas Gehring and Benjamin Faude,

above: the 1982 UNCLOS and 1995 Fish Stocks Agreement;[41] International Maritime Organization (IMO) Conventions regulating shipping and pollution;[42] the 1972 London Convention[43] and the 1996 Protocol;[44] the 1991 Agreement on the Conservation of Albatrosses and Petrels (ACAP);[45] the 1992 Biodiversity Convention;[46] the 1946 International Convention on the Regulation of Whaling;[47] the 1973 Convention on International Trade in Endangered Species (CITES);[48] the 1992 United Nations Framework Convention on Climate Change (UNFCCC);[49] and adjacent RFMOs including (but not limited to) the Southeast Atlantic Fisheries Organization (SEAFO),[50] the Commission for the Conservation of Southern Bluefin Tuna (CCSBT),[51] the Western Central Pacific Fisheries Commission (WCPFC)[52] and the South Pacific Regional Fisheries Management Organisation (SPRFMO).[53] These regimes and

---

"The Dynamics of Regime Complexes: Microfoundations and Systemic Effects," *Global Governance* 19 (2013): 119, 120; Karen J. Atler and Sophie Meunier, "The Politics of International Regime Complexity," *Perspectives on Politics* 7 (2009): 13, 13.

41 1995 Agreement for the Implementation of the Provisions of the United Nations Convention on the Law of the Sea of 10 December 1982 relating to the Conservation and Management of Straddling Fish Stocks and Highly Migratory Fish Stocks, Aug. 4, 1995, 2167 U.N.T.S. 88, entered into force Dec. 11, 2001 [hereinafter Fish Stocks Agreement].

42 *See, e.g.*, 1974 International Convention for the Safety of Life at Sea, Nov. 1, 1974, 1184 U.N.T.S. 278, entered into force May 25, 1980 [hereinafter SOLAS]; 1973 International Convention for the Prevention of Pollution from Ships as Modified by the Protocol of 1978 Relating Thereto, Nov. 2, 1973, 1340 U.N.T.S. 62, entered into force Oct. 2, 1983 [hereinafter MARPOL].

43 1972 Convention for the Prevention of Marine Pollution by Dumping of Wastes and Other Matter, Nov. 13, 1972, 1046 U.N.T.S. 120, entered into force Aug. 30, 1975 [hereinafter London Convention].

44 1996 Protocol to the London Convention on the Prevention of Marine Pollution by Dumping of Wastes and Other Matter, Nov. 7, 1996, 36 I.L.M. 1, entered into force Mar. 24, 2006.

45 2001 Agreement on the Conservation of Albatrosses and Petrels, Jun. 19, 2001, 2258 U.N.T.S. 257, entered into force Feb. 1, 2004 [hereinafter ACAP].

46 1992 Convention on Biological Diversity, Jun. 5, 1992, 1760 U.N.T.S. 79, entered into force Dec. 29, 1993 [hereinafter CBD].

47 1946 International Convention on the Regulation of Whaling, Dec. 2, 1946, 161 U.N.T.S. 72, entered into force Nov. 10, 1948 [hereinafter ICRW].

48 1973 Convention on International Trade in Endangered Species of Wild Fauna and Flora, Mar. 3, 1973, 993 U.N.T.S. 243, entered into force Jul. 1, 1975 [hereinafter CITES].

49 1992 United Nations Framework Convention on Climate Change, Jun. 4, 1992, 1771 U.N.T.S. 107, entered into force Mar. 21, 1994 [hereinafter UNFCCC].

50 South East Atlantic Fisheries Organisations (Apr. 14, 2015), http://www.seafo.org/.

51 Commission for the Conservation of Southern Bluefin Tuna, https://www.ccsbt.org/.

52 Western Central Pacific Fisheries Commission (Jan. 17, 2020), https://www.wcpfc.int/home.

53 South Pacific Regional Fisheries Management Organisation, https://www.sprfmo.int/.

institutions interact in the context of global principles and values, including precaution, sustainability and equity that provide the broader framework for Southern Ocean governance.[54] Against this backdrop, this Section will provide a brief overview of the three key components of the ATS.

3.1 *1959 Antarctic Treaty*

The 1959 Antarctic Treaty is founded on the principles of peace,[55] freedom of scientific research[56] and a prohibition on nuclear explosions and the disposal of nuclear waste within the Antarctic Treaty area.[57] These principles are consistent with and supportive of the modern law of the sea but pre-date and, in several cases, go beyond the principles applicable to the global commons more generally.[58] For example, Article I of the Antarctic Treaty prohibits the carrying out of military manoeuvres and the testing of any type of weapon within the Antarctic Treaty Area. Scientific research was designated a freedom of the seas in Article 87(1)(f) of the 1982 UNCLOS, more than twenty years after its guarantee under Articles II and III of the 1959 Antarctic Treaty in respect of the Southern Ocean South of 60° South Latitude. Although questions were raised early in the history of the Antarctic Treaty as to whether its provisions apply to the Southern Ocean, given that Article VI of the Treaty stipulates that "nothing in the present Treaty shall prejudice or in any way affect the rights, or the exercise of the rights, of any State under international law with regard to the high seas within that area," state practice confirms its application to the Southern Ocean south of 60° South Latitude. Under the 1959 Treaty, states must provide advance notice of all expeditions to and within Antarctica,[59] and must permit open inspection of their ships, stations and other facilities.[60] Through subsequent instruments adopted as part of the Antarctic Treaty System, in particular,

54 *See* Duncan French, "Regime Integrity *qua* Antarctic Security. Embedding Global Principles and Universal Values within the Antarctic Treaty System" in Alan D. Hemmings, Donald R. Rothwell and Karen N. Scott, eds., *Antarctic Security in the Twenty-First Century. Legal and Policy Perspectives* (London and New York: Routledge, 2012), chap. 4; Ruth Davis, "Global Legal Norms in the Antarctic" in Klaus Dodds, Alan D. Hemmings and Peder Roberts, eds., *Handbook on the Politics of Antarctica* (Cheltenham: Edward Elgar Publishing, 2017), chap. 35.

55 1959 Antarctic Treaty, art. I.

56 Ibid, art. II.

57 Ibid, art. V.

58 See for example Articles 301 and 141 of UNCLOS that relate to peaceful uses of the seas and the Area respectively and Articles 87(1)(f) and 238 that confirm that scientific research is a freedom of the high seas.

59 Ibid, art. VII(5)(a).

60 Ibid, art. VII(3).

the 1991 Environmental Protocol, Antarctic Treaty parties have developed wide-ranging controls over activities, including navigation, where those activities may have a negative impact on the fragile Antarctic environment.

3.2 *1991 Environmental Protocol to the 1959 Antarctic Treaty*

The 1991 Environmental Protocol to the 1959 Treaty commits the parties to the comprehensive protection of the Antarctic environment and dependent and associated ecosystems, and designates Antarctica as a natural reserve devoted to peace and science.[61] Article 3 of the Protocol sets out far-reaching environmental principles designed to guide activities taking place in the Antarctic Treaty area, requiring parties design and carry out activities avoiding adverse impacts on climate, water quality, biodiversity and sites of scientific, aesthetic or wilderness significance.

The principal tool for managing the impacts of activities under the Protocol is a process of environmental impact assessment. With the exception of fishing, all other activities, including tourism and scientific research, likely to have a minor or transitory impact on the marine environment south of 60° South Latitude are subject to an Initial Environmental Evaluation (IEE) under Article 8 and Annex I of the Protocol. Activities slated to have a more than minor or transitory impact must comply with a Comprehensive Environmental Evaluation (CEE), which is reviewed by the parties collectively at the annual Antarctic Treaty Consultative Meeting (ATCM).[62] In 2018, thirteen IEEs were carried out in respect of marine-based activities,[63] including tourist cruises,[64] scientific research[65] and bioprospecting.[66] It is notable that no CEE has been

61 1991 Environmental Protocol, art. 2.

62 Ibid, art. 8, Annex I, art. 3.

63 Details on IEEs and CEEs carried out to date can be found in the EIA database maintained by the Secretariat to the Antarctic Treaty. "Antarctic Treaty Database," Secretariat of the Antarctic Treaty (2020), https://www.ats.aq/devAS/ToolsAndResources/AntarcticTreatyDatabase?lang=e. The examples in footnotes 64 to 66 are all drawn from this database.

64 IEEs carried out by Canada, Poland and the US. Thus far in 2019, Germany has carried out IEEs in respect of 15 tourism voyages.

65 For example, Brazil has carried out IEEs in 2018 relating to the use of autonomous technologies and bottom water surveys, the pelagic food chain, and Cetacea visual surveys. Switzerland has carried out an IEE to survey microplastics in the Southern Oceans, as has the UK in respect of surveying the Larsen C Ice Shelf and attempt to locate the wreck of Shackelton's *Endurance*.

66 Brazil, IEE of the project entitled "Biodiversity, monitoring, survival strategies and bioprospection of extremofilous seaweeds along Maritime Antarctica."

carried out in respect of marine scientific research and IEE practice is inconsistent, particularly around tourism cruises.

The Protocol also provides for tight regulation around taking and interference with species not regulated by the 1982 CAMLR Convention, the 1972 CCAS and the 1946 ICRW. Annex II of the Protocol prohibits taking and interference with Antarctic species without a permit.[67] In addition, an area, including any marine area, can be designated an Antarctic Specially Protected Area (ASPA) or an Antarctic Specially Managed Area (ASMA) pursuant to Annex V of the Environmental Protocol and managed strictly in accordance with an appropriate management plan in order to protect environmental, scientific, historic, aesthetic or wilderness values.[68] Decisions to designate protected areas, like all decisions under the ATS are taken by consensus.

Minimising pollution is another strong focus of the Protocol.[69] Notably, the Protocol has addressed marine pollution from ships in Annex IV, complementing and, in the past, going beyond global shipping standards for certain discharges.[70] The parties to the Antarctic Treaty have developed significant regional initiatives in respect of the safety of polar ships,[71] the carriage of heavy fuel oil[72] and ballast water management,[73] and have strongly influenced the international agenda, particularly in respect of the adoption of the Polar Code by the IMO.[74] Antarctic Treaty parties have also been proactive in adopting measures relating to search and rescue in the region with a strong focus on information exchange and vessel position reporting.[75]

---

67 1991 Environmental Protocol, Annex II, art 3.

68 Ibid, Annex V, art. 2.

69 *See, e.g.*, Ibid, Annex III.

70 Today, global shipping standards in respect of discharges largely reflect or, in some cases, go beyond the 1991 Environmental Protocol.

71 ATCM Dec. 4, Guidelines for Ships Operating in Arctic and Antarctic Waters (2004).

72 ATCM Dec. 8, Use of Heavy Fuel (2005).

73 ATCM Res. 3, Ballast Water Exchange (2006).

74 IMO Res. M.S.C. 385(94), International Code of Safety for Ships Operating in Polar Waters (Nov. 21, 2014). Rules prohibiting the carried heavy fuel oil in the Antarctic have also been adopted by the IMO, see IMO Res. M.E.P.C. 189(60), Amendments to MARPOL Annex I to Add Chapter 9—Special Requirements for the Use or Carriage of Oils in the Antarctic Area (Mar. 26, 2010), as well as rules relating to ballast water exchange, see IMO Res. M.E.P.C. 163(56), Guidelines for Ballast Water Exchange in the Antarctic Treaty Area (Jul. 13, 2007).

75 ATCM Res. 6, Improving the Coordination of Maritime Search and Rescue in the Antarctic Treaty Area (2010); ATCM Res. 4, Improved Collaboration on Search and Rescue (SAR) in Antarctica (2013).

3.3 1980 *Convention for the Conservation of Marine Living Resources (CAMLR Convention)*

The 1980 CAMLR Convention seeks to conserve Antarctic marine living resources, although "conservation" for the purposes of the Convention also includes "rational use."[76] From the outset, therefore, the CAMLR Convention has been described as a conservation convention[77] rather than a regional fisheries management organisation (RFMO), although it carries out the functions of the latter within the Southern Ocean. Its strong conservation mandate is demonstrated through its early endorsement of an ecosystem approach[78] and its focus on associated and bycatch species[79] as well as broader threats to Southern Ocean ecology such as climate change.[80] The CAMLR Commission (CCAMLR) is required to adopt a precautionary approach to fisheries management[81] and may adopt, on a consensus basis,[82] measures relating to catch limits, gear specification, data reporting, research, bycatch minimisation, environmental protection, protected areas and compliance.[83] As an integral part of the Antarctic Treaty System, the CAMLR Convention reiterates Article IV of the Antarctic Treaty, asserting that activities under the Convention cannot be used as a basis to strengthen, undermine, recognise or deny any claim to Antarctica.[84]

4 Lessons from the Antarctic

The Antarctic regime is regarded as a relatively successful example of management within commons and disputed spaces and thus often regarded as a potential model for regions such as the Arctic[85] or the South China Sea.[86] The

---

76 1980 CAMLR Convention, art. II(1)-(2).

77 David M. Edwards and John A. Heap, "Convention on the Conservation of Antarctic Marine Living Resources: A Commentary," *Polar Record* 30 (1981): 353, 362.

78 1980 CAMLR Convention, art. II(3)(b).

79 *See infra* Conservation Measures listed in notes 150–52.

80 CCAMLR Res. 30/XXVIII, Climate Change (2009).

81 1980 CAMLR Convention, art. II(3)(c).

82 Ibid, art. XII(1).

83 Ibid, art. IX. A full list of CCAMLR Conservation Measures are available at: "Conservation Measures," CCAMLR (2020), https://www.ccamlr.org/en/conservation-and-management/conservation-and-managment.

84 1980 CAMLR Convention, art. IV.

85 *See, e.g.*, Donald Rothwell, "The Arctic in International Affairs: Time for a New Regime?," *Brown Journal of International Affairs* 15 (2008): 241.

86 *See, e.g.*, Shirley V. Scott, "What Lessons does the Antarctic Treaty System Offer for the Future of Peaceful Relations in the South China Sea?," *Marine Policy* 87 (2018): 295.

question for the purposes of this collection is: What lessons are applicable to the governance of global commons areas? This question is particularly apposite as negotiations for a new treaty for the conservation of biodiversity in areas beyond the jurisdiction of states are currently underway.[87] For the purposes of this chapter, four lessons from the Antarctic will be identified: transparency and open inspection; freedom of scientific research and dissemination of research; ecosystem and integrated environmental management; and cooperation navigating the Southern Ocean regime complex. The experience of the Antarctic Treaty System in these areas demonstrate both the potential of the Antarctic as a model for global commons governance as well as its limitations.

4.1 *Transparency and Open Inspection*

As a regime developed at the height of the Cold War, the 1959 Antarctic Treaty deliberately developed mechanisms to build trust between the various parties. A number of these mechanisms were designed to promote transparency in respect of facilities and activities in the Antarctic. Parties must, for example, provide information on their scientific programmes and scientific personnel on exchange in Antarctica,[88] as well as stations in Antarctica occupied by their nationals.[89] Parties must also inform all parties of expeditions to and within Antarctica by their ships, nationals and all expeditions to Antarctica organised in or leaving from their territory.[90] Whilst the Treaty permits military personnel and equipment to be used for scientific or other peaceful purposes,[91] personnel and equipment must be reported to the Antarctic Treaty parties on an annual basis.[92]

The current scope of the information to be provided is set out in Decision 7 (2019) on Information Exchange[93] and, since 2012, the information is loaded into the Electronic Information Exchange System (EIES).[94] Although the information in the EIES system is not publicly available, much of that information in summarised in the annual reports submitted by states and the reports

87 G.A. Res. 72/249, Intergovernmental Conference on an International Legally Binding Instrument Under the United Nations Convention on the Law of the Sea on the Conservation and Sustainable Use of Marine Biological Diversity of Areas Beyond National Jurisdiction (Dec. 24, 2017).

88 1959 Antarctic Treaty, art. III(1)-(2).

89 Ibid, art. VII(5)(b).

90 Ibid, art. VII(5)(a).

91 Ibid, art. I(2).

92 Ibid, art. VII(5)(c).

93 ATCM Dec, 7, Information Exchange (2019).

94 ATCM Dec. 4, Information Exchange, (2012).

containing permanent information available on the website of the Antarctic Treaty Secretariat.[95] In comparison to many other international regimes, these reporting requirements are relatively well complied with. For the year 2016/17, for example, 44 of 53 contracting parties submitted reports.[96] Of those which did not,[97] only Chile, South Korea, South Africa, the Ukraine and the US undertake significant activities in the Antarctic Treaty area. Reporting information on military personnel and equipment is, however, much more variable, with 18 states providing no formal indication as to whether they are using military assets in Antarctica, including China, Russia and the US.[98]

In support of requirements relating to information exchange, the 1959 Antarctic Treaty guarantees complete freedom of access at any time to all areas of Antarctica, including stations, installations, equipment, vessels and aircraft.[99] Aerial observation is also provided for.[100] Observers, who may be appointed by any Antarctic Treaty party, and remain nationals of and under the jurisdiction of that party, may carry out inspections pursuant to Article VII of the Treaty.[101] Typically these inspections are carried out on a collaborative basis involving multiple states. These provisions, which represent a remarkable agreement between opposing Cold War states, have provided the inspiration for (generally less comprehensive) observer and inspection regimes in major weapons treaties such as the 1968 Treaty on the Non-proliferation of Nuclear Weapons.

The 1991 Environmental Protocol builds on the Antarctic Treaty and provides for a similarly open system of inspection for the purposes of ensuring compliance with the rules under the Protocol.[102] Importantly, after the state which is the subject of the inspection has had an opportunity to respond to the report, the report must be made publicly available.[103] In practice, however,

95 Secretariat of the Antarctic Treaty (2020), https://www.ats.aq/index_e.html.

96 Information on annual country reports and permanent information (on infrastructure etc.) can be found on the Antarctic Treaty Secretariat website, ibid. All the information in footnotes 97 and 98, and 104 to 107 was obtained from this website.

97 Canada, Chile, Columbia, South Korea, Peru, South Africa, Ukraine and the United States.

98 Belarus, Belgium, Bulgaria, China, Czech Republic, Ecuador, Finland, Germany, Japan, Netherlands, Norway, Poland, Russia, Sweden, Turkey, United Kingdom, United States and Venezuela.

99 1959 Antarctic Treaty, art. VII(3); *see generally*, Julia Jabour, "The Utility of Antarctic Inspections: Symbolism Without Sanction?" in Daniela Liggett and Alan D. Hemmings, eds., *Exploring Antarctic Values* (Christchurch: Gateway Antarctica Special Publication, 2013), chap. 6.

100 1959 Antarctic Treaty, art. VII(4).

101 Ibid, art. VII(1).

102 1991 Environmental Protocol, art. 14.

103 Ibid, art. 14(3).

the number of actual inspections that take place on an annual basis are low and appear to have decreased over the last few years. For example, during the 2017/18 season Norway was the only state to carry out inspections.[104] Over the course of the 2016/17 season Australia inspected one station and one protected area[105] and Argentina and Chile carried out a joint inspection of two stations.[106] This represents a marked decrease from previous years where between 12 and 24 stations in addition to protected areas and vessels were inspected during a season.[107]

The 1980 CAMLR Convention was one of the earliest RFMOs to develop a comprehensive system of inspection and observation,[108] with the processes for appointing inspectors, who remain under the jurisdiction of their national states, and of inspection itself, being adopted in 1988.[109] Vessels carrying out harvesting and scientific research are subject to inspection in order to verify information provided to CCAMLR at the beginning of the season and compliance with CCAMLR conservation measures more generally. During the 2016/17 fishing season, inspections of seven vessels were carried out in statistical area 48.1 (the Antarctic Peninsula region) by Chile,[110] and New Zealand boarded and inspected 10 vessels in the Ross Sea region, with two potential compliance issues being reported to Ukraine and Spain as the relevant respective flag states.[111] The Scheme of International Scientific Observation (SISO) was

104 Norway inspected Halley (United Kingdom), Neumayer Station III (Germany), Princess Elisabeth (Belgium), SANAE IV (South Africa) and SANAP Summer Station (South Africa), in addition to two runways (both operated by Russia).

105 The Amundsen-Scott South Pole Station (US) and ASMA 5 (the Amundsen-Scott South Pole).

106 Johann Gregor Mendel (Czech Republic) and Rothera (UK).

107 For example, in 2015–16, China inspected 6 stations, Argentina and Chile inspected 6 stations and the US inspected 8 protected areas. In 2014–15, the Czech Republic and the UK inspected 13 stations, 1 refuge and 11 vessels. In 2012–13, Germany and South African inspected 4 stations, Russia and the US inspected 6 stations and the Netherlands, Spain and the UK inspected 14 stations, 1 refuge, 5 vessels, 3 protected areas and the Bahia Pariso wreck. Information on inspections can be found here: "Inspections Database," Secretariat of the Antarctic Treaty (2020), https://www.ats.aq/devAS/Ats/InspectionsDatabase?lang=e.

108 1980 CAMLR Convention, art. XXIV.

109 The text of the CCAMLR System of Inspection was adopted at CCAMLR VII (1988) and has been amended on a regular basis. *See generally* "Text of the CCAMLR System of Inspection," CCAMLR (Dec. 13, 2019), https://www.ccamlr.org/en/document/publications/text-ccamlr-system-inspection.

110 CCAMLR XXXVI, *Report of the Thirty-six Meeting of the Commission* (Hobart, Australia, Oct. 16–27, 2017), Annex 6, [58].

111 Ibid, [61].

adopted in 1992[112] and provides for an observer to remain on board a vessel for an extended period during the season. During the 2016/17 season, 58 scientific observers were appointed with 43 observing longline vessels, 3 on trawl vessels fishing for icefish and 12 on vessels fishing for krill.[113] All vessels fishing for toothfish must carry an observer, and CCAMLR aims to ensure that 50 percent of all krill vessels also carry an observer.[114] Of the 25 CCAMLR member states, 12 received a SISO appointed observer of their vessel and 7 members provided SISO observers with a different nationality to the vessel's flag state.[115] The SISO is as much about providing and facilitating the dissemination of scientific information as it is about enforcement. In particular, its primary function is to assess the impact of fishing on the wider Antarctic ecosystem and to support the development of measures designed to mitigate that impact.

The system of open inspection under the 1959 Antarctic Treaty has provided the basis for a relatively robust process to be developed by CCAMLR, which in turn has been emulated at the international level under the 1995 Fish Stocks Agreement and by other RFMOs. However, the system of open inspection under the 1959 Antarctic Treaty and the 1991 Environmental Protocol is less about compliance and more about building trust between nations and providing a mechanism of sharing best practice. It is this latter function that arguably provides a useful lesson for broader global commons governance.

4.2 *Freedom and Dissemination of Scientific Research*

The freedom to undertake scientific research is prioritised as an activity under Article II of the 1959 Antarctic Treaty and this is confirmed in Article 2 of the 1991 Environmental Protocol, which designates "Antarctica as a natural reserve, devoted to peace and science."[116] The pre-eminence of science within the Antarctic Treaty can be found in many places, not least in that which is "reflected in the attribution of powers to take decisions to further the principles and objectives of the Treaty."[117] As a consequence of this priority, science

112 The text of the CCAMLR SISO was adopted at CCAMLR XI (1992) and has been amended on a regular basis. The current text is available at: "CCAMLR Scheme of International Scientific Observation (SISO)," CCAMLR (2020), https://www.ccamlr.org/en/science/ccamlr-scheme-international-scientific-observation.

113 CCAMLR, *Report of the Thirty-sixth Meeting of the Commission*, Annex 5, [2].

114 "CCAMLR Scheme of International Scientific Observation (SISO)," CCAMLR (2020), https://www.ccamlr.org/en/science/ccamlr-scheme-international-scientific-observation.

115 CCAMLR, *Report of the Thirty-sixth Meeting of the Commission*, Annex 5, [2].

116 Emphasis added.

117 René Lefeber, "Marine Scientific Research in the Antarctic Treaty System" in Erik J. Molenaar, Alex G. Oude Elferink and Donald R. Rothwell, eds., *The Law of the Sea and the Polar Regions. Interactions between Global and Regional Regimes* (Leiden: Martinus

has been described as the "currency"[118] for cooperation within the Antarctic Treaty System and providing "symbolic capital,"[119] the return on which is participation in Antarctic governance, including resource issues. However, science is "not just the means through which Antarctic politics is mediated, but political in and of itself."[120] As Nayler et al. note, science did not replace political rivalry so much as emerge as a "subtle new form of geopolitics in Antarctica."[121] In contrast to the commons more generally, it can be said that Antarctica has been "constructed through science" as a geopolitical and legal space.[122]

The lesson for the commons however, is not so much the prioritisation of science as a privileged activity, but the Antarctic Treaty System's endorsement of free dissemination of scientific findings and cooperation and collaboration in research. Article III of the 1959 Antarctic Treaty requires parties to exchange information on plans for scientific programmes, on scientific personnel on exchange and "scientific observations and results" from research in Antarctica. Parties are also encouraged to cooperate with UN specialised agencies and with other international organisations having a scientific or technical interest in Antarctica.[123] Much scientific research in Antarctica has global implications, covering topics such as the ozone hole and climate change. The dissemination of such research is undoubtedly for the benefit of humankind. Although much

Nijhoff Publishers, 2013), chap. 14, 323. Article XI(2) stipulates that each original signatory to the Antarctic Treaty is designated a consultative party, able to fully participate in decision-making. In respect of subsequent states ratifying the Treaty, only those which demonstrate their "interest in Antarctica by conducting substantial scientific research activity there, such as the establishment of a scientific station or the despatch of a scientific expedition" are able to become a consultative party. To date, out of 53 state parties, 29 are consultative parties leaving 24 unable to participate in Antarctic decision-making.

118 R. Herr and R. Hall, "Science and Currency and the Currency of Science" in J. Handmer, ed., *Antarctica: Policies and Policy Development* (Canberra: Centre for Resource and Environmental Studies, 1989), 13.

119 A. Elzinga and I. Bohlin, "The Politics of Science in the Polar Regions" in A. Elzinga, ed., *Changing Trends in Antarctic Research* (Dordrecht: Kluwer, 1993), chap. 1, 22.

120 Karen N. Scott, "Scientific Rhetoric and Antarctic Security" in Alan D. Hemmings, Donald R. Rothwell and Karen N. Scott, eds., *Antarctic Security in the Twenty-First Century. Legal and Policy Perspectives* (London and New York: Routledge, 2012), chap. 15, 287.

121 S. Nayler, K. Dean and M. Siegert, "The IGY and the Ice Sheet: Surveying Antarctica," *Journal of Historical Geography* 34 (2008): 574, 591.

122 A. Elzinga, "Antarctica: The Construction of a Continent by and for Science" in E. Crawford, T. Shinn and S. Sörlin, eds., *Denationalizing Science: The Contexts of International Scientific Practice* (Dordrecht: Kluwer, 1992) chap 3, 77.

123 1959 Antarctic Treaty, art. III(2).

research is collaborative, the extent of that collaboration and the low number of jointly managed facilities has nevertheless been subject to criticism.[124]

Moreover, the principle of free dissemination of scientific research risks coming under pressure within the Antarctic Treaty System as the distinction between so-called 'pure' and 'applied' research becomes blurred. This question has arisen specifically in the context of bioprospecting and the increase in interest in Antarctic organisms for their genetic properties and their application for pharmaceutical and industrial processes.[125] The issue of regulating bioprospecting activities in Antarctica has been a regular agenda item for the ATCM since 1999,[126] but thus far the parties have failed to achieve consensus as to whether the activity requires separate rules beyond the requirements already applicable under the Antarctic Treaty and Environmental Protocol. In particular, the parties have failed to engage in the question of how the benefits from any discovery should be distributed. They have, however, confirmed that Article III of the 1959 Antarctic Treaty and, in particular, the principle that "scientific observations and results from Antarctica shall be exchanged and made freely available" applies to bioprospecting activities.[127] They have also confirmed that it is the Antarctic Treaty System that is the appropriate regulatory forum to manage bioprospecting activities taking place within the Antarctic Treaty area.[128] Nevertheless, there is no agreed definition of bioprospecting for the purposes of the Antarctic Treaty[129] nor is there agreement on the scope of the obligation to disseminate the results of research.

---

124 *See, e.g.*, Alan D. Hemmings, "Why Did We get an International Space Station Before an International Antarctic Station?," *The Polar Journal* 1 (2011): 5.

125 For background on this issue, see Dagmar Lohan and Sam Johston, *UNU-IAS Report: Bioprospecting in Antarctica* (2005), available at: http://www.ecosystemmarketplace.com/wp-content/uploads/archive/documents/Doc_415.pdf; Alan D. Hemmings and Michelle Rogan-Finnemore, eds., *Antarctic Bioprospecting*, Antarctica Special Publication Ser. No. 0501 (Christchurch: Gateway, 2005).

126 Christopher C. Joyner, "Bioprospecting as a Challenge to the Antarctic Treaty" in Alan D. Hemmings, Donald R. Rothwell and Karen N. Scott, eds., *Antarctic Security in the Twenty-First Century: Legal and Policy Perspectives* (London and New York: Routledge, 2012), chap. 11, 201.

127 ATCM Res. 7, Biological Prospecting (2005); ATCM Res. 9, Collection and Use of Antarctic Biological Material (2009).

128 ATCM Res. 9, Collection and Use of Antarctic Biological Material (2009); ATCM Res. 6, Biological Prospecting in Antarctica (2013).

129 This was noted as an issue in ATCM Resolution 6, Biological Prospecting in Antarctica. There have been multiple suggestions as to how the activity might be defined. The latest proposal was made by Brazil at the 2018 ATCM. Brazil suggested that bioprospecting for biotechnological applications be defined as "activities of cultivation, replication or modification processes of any Antarctic native organisms conducive to biotechnological

At the 2018 ATCM, most parties took the view that the ATCM should continue to address bioprospecting notwithstanding that negotiations for a global regime to manage marine genetic resources were initiated in 2017.[130] However, the US notably took the view that the Southern Ocean may be covered by any global regime, and suggested that the ATCM should wait until those negotiations conclude before signalling that marine genetic resources within the Antarctic Treaty area or CAMLR Convention Area should be excluded from any BBNJ regime.[131] The minority US position, however, did not prevail and the 2018 ATCM decided that an informal intersessional exchange of information would be established in order to obtain information on the collection and use of biological material in Antarctica and their implications for state obligations under Article III of the Antarctic Treaty. The Intersessional Exchange of Information was due to report to the 2019 ATCM.[132]

Scientific research in the context of CCAMLR may also involve issues of commercial sensitivity and therefore it is unsurprising that there are no explicit obligations under the CAMLR Convention relating to the dissemination of scientific research. There are, however, obligations associated with carrying out research, particularly in respect of new and exploratory fisheries and where research has implications for ecosystem health more generally.[133] However, the Second Performance Review of CCAMLR, reporting in 2017, highlighted the reliance of Commission on fishing vessels for scientific information and recommended that "CCAMLR implements practical mechanisms to coordinate and deliver research activities among Members to deliver the long-term

applications or industrial and commercial uses, including all organisms, their parts, as well as partial or whole genomes." *See* Brazil, Working Paper 27, *An Enhanced Definition on Bioprospection in Antarctica* (submitted to the XLI ATCM, Buenos Aires, Argentina, May 13–18, 2018). Some delegations, however, considered this definition to be too narrow. *See* ATCM, *Final Report of the Forty-first Antarctic Treaty Consultative Meeting* (Buenos Aires, Argentina, May 13–18, 2018), [55].

130 ATCM, *Final Report of the Forty-first Antarctic Treaty Consultative Meeting* (Buenos Aires, Argentina, May 13–18, 2018), [52].

131 Ibid, [51].

132 Ibid, [57]. This was also added to the ATCM Multi-Year Strategic Workplan (item i*bis*). *See* ATCM Dec. 3, Multi-Year Strategic Workplan for the Antarctic Treaty Consultative Meeting (2018).

133 *See, e.g.*, CCAMLR Conservation Measure 24-01, The Application of Conservation Measures for Scientific Research (2017); CCAMLR Conservation Measure 24-02, Longline Weighting for Seabird Conservation (2014); CCAMLR Conservation Measure 24-03, Establishing Time-limited Special Areas for Scientific Study in Newly Exposed Marine Areas Following Ice-shelf Retreat or Collapse in Statistical Areas 48.1 and 88.3 (2017); CCAMLR Conservation Measure 24-04, Fishing for Research Purposes Pursuant to Conservation Measure 24-01 (2018); CCAMLR Res. 30/XXVII; CCAMLR Res. 31/XXVIII, Best Available Science (2009).

research required by the Commission to achieve its objective, including better targeted fish stock research to ascertain productivity and yield of stocks across their ranges, and analyses of status and trends of those stocks and Antarctic marine living resources more generally."[134]

The freedom of scientific research and dissemination of scientific findings are already principles enshrined by UNCLOS. They provide an important component for any regime in the commons and, as demonstrated by the Antarctic Treaty, can operate as a basis for governance not predicated on territorial control or shared resource regimes such as common heritage of humankind.

4.3 *Ecosystem and Integrated Environmental Management*

The Antarctic Treaty System and, in particular, the CAMLR Convention are typically regarded as pioneer instruments with respect to ecosystem and integrated environmental management.[135] There is a significant level of coordination and cooperation between the Antarctic Treaty and CCAMLR with respect to marine ecosystem management. For example, the approval of CCAMLR is necessary prior to the designation of an ASPA or ASMA within the marine environment by the Committee for Environmental Protection (CEP) under Annex V of the 1991 Environmental Protocol.[136] CCAMLR and the CEP have been actively cooperating on the designation of marine protected areas (MPAs) since 2006[137] and the CEP has in effect delegated the task of developing a network of representative MPAs to the Commission.[138] Following the designation of the Ross Sea MPA by CCAMLR in 2016,[139] the ATCM adopted Resolution 5 (2017) in which it encouraged Antarctic Treaty parties not members of Commission to comply with the Ross Sea MPA management measures, and invited the CEP to consider any appropriate measures within the competence of the ATCM to support the objectives of the Ross Sea MPA, in particular, the designation of ASPAS

134 CCAMLR Performance Review Panel, *Second Performance Review of CCAMLR—Final Report of the Panel* (Aug. 23, 2017), Recommendation 8 [hereinafter "Second Performance Review of CCAMLR"].

135 *See e.g.*, Henrik Österblom and Olof Olsson, "CCAMLR: An Ecosystem Approach to the Southern Ocean in the Anthoprocene" in Klaus Dodds and Alan D. Hemmings, eds., *Handbook on the Politics of Antarctica* (Cheltenham: Edward Elgar, 2017) 408–421.

136 1991 Environmental Protocol, Annex V, art. 6(2).

137 ATCM Res. 1, CCAMLR in the Antarctic Treaty System (2006); *see also* Secretariat of the Antarctic Treaty, *Summary of the Work of the CEP on Marine Protected Areas* (Sept. 2018), available at: https://documents.ats.aq/ATCM41/ww/atcm41_ww007_e.pdf.

138 ATCM Res. 2, Guide to the Preparation of Management Plans for Antarctic Specially Protected Areas (2011).

139 CCAMLR Conservation Measure 91-05, Ross Sea Region Marine Protected Area (2016).

and ASMAs within the Ross Sea region.[140] This level of cooperation between a regional seas regime and a regional fisheries arrangement is unusual, with the only other comparable example being the more recent cooperation between the Commission for Protection of the Marine Environment of the North East Atlantic (OSPAR) and the North East Atlantic Fisheries Commission (NEAFC) over the designation of MPAs in the North East Atlantic.[141]

Nevertheless, within both the Antarctic Treaty and the CAMLR Convention there are indications that both the ecosystem and integrated approach to environmental management are under pressure. Although the 1991 Environmental Protocol has the overall objective of protecting the Antarctic environment including dependent and associated ecosystems,[142] the parties have not interpreted Article 2 of the Protocol as permitting the regulation of activities outside of the Antarctic Treaty area (south of 60° South Latitude). More significantly, although the CEP is required to identify areas which would benefit from a higher level of protection for the purposes of Annex 5 of the Protocol "within a systematic environmental-geographical framework,"[143] it has struggled to do this despite developing tools to identify Antarctic regions on a biogeographic basis.[144] Moreover, there is no functional system of strategic environmental assessment within the Antarctic Treaty System[145] and, occasionally, even a lack of coordination occurs between protected area proposals and CEEs in respect of activities within the proposed protected area.[146] Finally, until relatively recently, the ATCM has avoided directly engaging in action on climate change

140 ATCM Res. 5, Establishment of the Ross Sea Region Marine Protected Area (2017).

141 *See* K. Hoydal, D. Johnson and H.H. Hoel, "Regional Governance: The Case of NEAFC and OSPAR" in Serge M. Garcia, Jake Rice and Anthony Charles, eds., *Governance of Marine Fisheries and Biodiversity Conservation: Interaction and Coevolution* (Hoboken, N.J.: Wiley-Blackwell, 2014), 225; Ingrid Kvalvik, "Managing Institutional Overlap in the Protection of Marine Ecosystems on the High Seas: The Case of the North East Atlantic," *Ocean Development and International Law* 56 (2012): 35.

142 1991 Environmental Protocol, art. 2 (emphasis added).

143 Ibid, Annex V, art. 3.

144 *See* ATCM Res. 3, Revised Antarctic Conservation Biogeographic Regions (2017).

145 *See* Simon Marsden, "Introducing Strategic Environmental Assessment to the Madrid Protocol: Lessons from International Experience," *The Polar Journal* 1 (2011): 36; Ricardo M. Roura and Alan D. Hemmings, "Realising Strategic Environmental Assessment in Antarctica," *Journal of Environmental Assessment Policy and Management* 13 (2011): 483.

146 For example, the CEE in respect of the Indian research station at Larsemann Hills and ASMA 6, Larsemann Hills. Both proposals appeared to proceed independently initially although the CEP ultimately advised the ATCM that the Laresmann Hills station CEE was compatible with the proposals for an ASMA within the broader Larsemann Hills area. *See Final Report of the Thirtieth Antarctic Treaty Consultative Meeting* (New Delhi, India, Apr. 30-May 11, 2007), [86], Annex E, app. 3.

despite the centrality of this issue to the Antarctic and Southern Ocean.[147] This is, however, changing—to a limited extent—and climate change is now included in the ATCM Multi-Year Strategic Work Plan,[148] although action on climate change in the Antarctic is still largely research-focused or hortatory.

The 1980 CAMLR Convention was one of the earliest instruments to adopt an explicitly ecosystem approach to conservation and fisheries management in the Southern Ocean, including a definition of the Antarctic ecosystem.[149] It has implemented an ecosystem approach through a strong focus on managing bycatch,[150] incidental mortality of birds and marine mammals[151] as well as taking early and important measures to protect the marine environment more generally such as restrictions on bottom fishing,[152] driftnet fishing[153] and ballast water exchange.[154] This holistic approach to the Southern Ocean ecosystem has been described as a "model in international fisheries management."[155]

---

147 *See* Duncan French and Karen N. Scott, "International Legal Implications of Climate Change for the Polar Regions: Too Much, Too Little, Too Late?," *Melbourne Journal of International Law* 10 (2009): 631.

148 ATCM Dec. 3, Multi-Year Strategic Workplan for the Antarctic Treaty Consultative Meeting (2018).

149 The Convention defines the Antarctic marine ecosystem as "the complex of relationships of Antarctic marine living resources with each other and with their physical environment." CAMLR Convention, art. 1(3).

150 CCAMLR Conservation Measure 33-01, Limitation of the By-catch of *Gobionotothen gibberifrons*, *Chaenocephalus aceratus*, *Pseudochaenichthys georgianus*, *Notothenia rossii* and *Lepidonotothen squamifrons* in Statistical Subarea 48.3 (1995); CCAMLR Conservation Measure 33-02, Limitation of By-catch in Statistical Division 58.5.2 in the 2018/19 Season (2018); CCAMLR Conservation Measure 33-03, Limitation of By-catch in New and Exploratory Fisheries in the 2018/19 Season (2018).

151 CCAMLR Conservation Measure 25-02, Minimisation of the Incidental Mortality of Seabirds in the Course of Longline Fishing or Longline Fishing Research in the Convention Area (2018); CCAMLR Conservation Measure 35-03 (2018); ATCM Res. 22/XXV, International Actions to Reduce the Incidental Mortality of Seabirds Arising from Fishing Category 26: Environmental Protection (2006).

152 CCAMLR Conservation Measure 22-05, Restrictions on the Use of Bottom Trawling Gear in High-seas Areas of the Convention Area (2008); CCAMLR Conservation Measure 22-06, Bottom Fishing in the Convention Area (2017); CCAMLR Conservation Measure 22-07, Interim Measure for Bottom Fishing Activities Subject to Conservation Measure 22-06 Encountering Potential Vulnerable Marine Ecosystems in the Convention Area (2013); CCAMLR Conservation Measure 22-09, Protection of Registered Vulnerable Marine Ecosystems in Subareas, Divisions, Small-scale Research Units, or Management Areas Open to Bottom Fishing (2012).

153 ATCM Res. 7/IX, Driftnet Fishing in the Convention Area (1990).

154 ATCM Res. 28/XXVII, Ballast Water Exchange in the Convention Area (2008).

155 Österblom and Olsson, "CCAMLR: An Ecosystem Approach to the Southern Ocean in the Anthropocene," chap. 26, 413.

In 2011, CCAMLR adopted a general framework for the establishment of marine protected areas.[156] And in 2016, CCAMLR designated the largest MPA in an area beyond the jurisdiction of any states, the Ross Sea MPA.[157] The express objectives of the MPA include the conservation of all components of the Ross Sea region ecosystem, the provision of reference areas for monitoring natural variability and long-term change, the protection and promotion of research, the protection of coastal locations of importance and the protection of large-scale ecosystem processes responsible for the productivity and functional integrity of the ecosystem.[158] The Ross Sea MPA is the second large-scale designated MPA within the CCAMLR region, the South Orkney Islands Southern Shelf MPA being designated in 2009.[159] MPAs proposed for Eastern Antarctica and the Weddell Sea are currently under negotiation. Furthermore, in a rare direct response to the impact of climate change, CCAMLR adopted an innovative conservation measure in 2016, allowing the designation of time-limited Special Areas for scientific study in regions newly exposed by ice-shelf retreat or collapse.[160] This highly precautionary measure will allow restrictions on fishing activities in areas newly exposed by climate change, and, in response to the loss of a 5,800 km^2 section of floating ice from the Larsen C ice shelf in July 2017, the CCAMLR Commission endorsed a recommendation from the Scientific Committee that the initial Stage 1 Special Area for Scientific Study (limited to two years) be extended to a Stage 2 Special Area, for a period of 10 years.[161]

Despite being held as an example of an exemplary fisheries management arrangement, CCAMLR has struggled at times to implement holistic ecosystem management and these challenges would appear to be increasing, indicating a "limited capacity of CCAMLR to develop its international leadership further."[162]

---

156 CCAMLR Conservation Measure 91-04, General Framework for the Establishment of CCAMLR Marine Protected Areas (2011).

157 CCAMLR Conservation Measure 91-05. The Ross Sea MPA covers about 1.5 million km^2 with 1.12 million km^2 subject to full protection. *See* "Sea Region Marine Protected Areas," New Zealand Foreign Affairs & Trade, https://www.mfat.govt.nz/en/environment/antarctica/ross-sea-region-marine-protected-area/.

158 CCAMLR Conservation Measure 91-05, [3].

159 CCAMLR Conservation Measure 91-03, Protection of the South Orkney Islands Southern Shelf (2009).

160 CCAMLR Conservation Measure 24-04, Establishing Time-Limited Special Areas for Scientific Study in Newly Exposed Marine Areas Following Ice-shelf Retreat or Collapse in Statistical Subareas 48.1, 48.5 and 88.3 (2017).

161 CCAMLR, *Report of the Thirty-sixth Meeting of the Commission*, [5.84].

162 Österblom and Olsson, "CCAMLR: An Ecosystem Approach to the Southern Ocean in the Anthropocene," 414.

Although endorsing an explicit precautionary approach,[163] and being developed in order to manage the krill fishery before it had begun,[164] CCAMLR was arguably unprepared for the rapid expansion of the toothfish fishery, and the Olympic style of fishery management applied under CCAMLR is not compatible with an ecosystem-based management approach to this resource.[165] The Second Performance Review of CCAMLR, concluded in 2017, criticised the implementation of ecosystem-based management and recommended that the Commission develop an overall strategy for the CCAMLR area, including spatial management and structured ecosystem monitoring and management.[166] Among other recommendations, the Review also advocated the better integration of measures managing krill fisheries, toothfish fisheries and MPAs taking into consideration the wider ecosystem and climate change.[167]

Likewise, the Ross Sea MPA, whilst a critically important step in implementing ecosystem-based management of the toothfish fishery in the region, was hard won and subject to significant compromise.[168] Although the largest high seas MPA, the Ross Sea MPA was nevertheless reduced in scope from the original proposal and, crucially, is designated for only 35 years unless the Commission reaches a consensus decision to reaffirm or modify the Conservation Measure.[169] This period, as noted and critiqued by the Second Performance Review of CCAMLR, is shorter than the life span of many of the species the MPA is designed to protect and is arguably not in line with best practice.[170] These compromises were forced by states, such as China and Russia, which are sceptical to the use of MPAs to manage fisheries[171] and, in the case of

163 1980 CAMLR Convention, art. II(3)(c).

164 For a critical account of Southern Ocean resource management pre and post the adoption of the CAMLR Convention, see David G. Ainley and Daniel Pauly, "Fishing Down the Food Web of the Antarctic Continental Shelf and Slope," *Polar Record* 50 (2014): 92.

165 Cassandra M. Brooks and David G. Ainley, "Fishing the Bottom of the Earth: The Political Challenges of Ecosystem-based Management" in Klaus Dodds, Alan D. Hemmings and Peder Roberts, eds., *Handbook on the Politics of Antarctica* (Cheltenham: Edward Elgar Publishing, 2017), chap. 27, 423.

166 Second Performance Review of CCAMLR, [16–23], Recommendation 1.

167 Ibid, [33].

168 For background to the Ross Sea MPA negotiations, see Karen N. Scott, "Protecting the Commons in the Polar South: Progress and Prospects for Marine Protected Areas in the Antarctic" in Keyuan Zou, ed., *Global Commons and the Law of the Sea* (Leiden: Brill, 2018), chap. 16.

169 CCAMLR Conservation Measure 91-05, [20].

170 Second Performance Review of CCAMLR, [33(iii)].

171 *See* Nengye Liu and Cassandra M. Brooks, "China's Changing Position Towards Marine Protected Areas in the Southern Ocean: Implications for Future Antarctic Governance," *Marine Policy* 94 (2018): 189.

Russia, view MPAs as tools that could be used for pseudo-territorial purposes in Antarctica.[172] Tensions around the Ross Sea MPA have not abated to a significant extent since 2016, with a dispute between parties in 2017 as to whether the Research and Monitoring Plan (RMP) needed to be formally adopted. China and Russia asserted that formal adoption was necessary and, for various reasons, were not prepared to support its adoption.[173] The UK and Australia were happy for the RMP to be adopted in its current form[174] and the US was of the view that it did not need to be separately adopted and was already in effect.[175] The Commission decided that the RMP would be a "living document" and that it would facilitate the interaction of Members with respect to the activities it covered.[176] In relation to enforcement, China and Russia disagreed with a US proposal that all vessels involved in fishing and research would have to comply with an automated VMS alert when entering the Ross Sea MPA. Russia preferred the alert to apply to fishing vessels only, and China was of the view that the proposal was inconsistent with Conservation Measure 10-04 (2018) on Automated satellite-linked Vessel Monitoring Systems.[177] Worryingly, it was also reported at the 2017 CCAMLR meeting that since the designation of the Ross Sea MPA in 2016 there had been a significant number of vessels notified for toothfish fishing within Statistical Areas 88.1 and 88.2.[178] Progress in designating further MPAs has been slow, and disappointment was expressed that the revised proposal for East Antarctica, which has been reduced from 7 to 3 areas, and which has been in development since 2012, was not adopted in 2017, with China and Russia voicing the most significant reservations.[179] The Second Performance Review of CCAMLR strongly recommended that the Commission should make the designation of MPAs within the general framework of Conservation Measure 91-04 (2011) a priority.[180]

CCAMLR has similarly taken a pioneering position with respect to the impact of climate change and ocean acidification for its conservation and fisheries mandate within the Southern Ocean. Resolution 30/XXVIII, adopted in 2009,[181] urged the Commission to consider the impacts of climate change to

172 *See* V.V. Lukin, "Russia's Current Antarctic Policy," *The Polar Journal* 4 (2014) 199, 217, 220.

173 CCAMLR, *Report of the Thirty-sixth Meeting of the Commission*, [5.70–5.80].

174 Ibid, [5.72].

175 Ibid, [5.82].

176 Ibid, [5.74].

177 Ibid, Annex 6, [79–81].

178 Ibid, [3.72].

179 Ibid, [8.29–8.51].

180 Second Performance Review of CCAMLR, Recommendation 7.

181 CCAMLR Res. 30/XXVIII.

better inform Commission management decisions and encouraged Members to contribute to relevant science initiatives. An Intersessional Contact Group (ICG) on Climate Change was established in 2015,[182] co-facilitated by Australia and Norway, with the task of inter alia making recommendations of how the Commission can use scientific information in its decision-making, including to address climate change in accordance with Article II of the Convention and how the Commission can consider the impacts of climate change across its agenda.[183] As noted above, the Ross Sea MPA addresses climate change in its terms of reference, and CM 24-04 (2017) was adopted in order to establish Special Areas for Scientific Study in newly exposed marine areas following ice-shelf retreat or collapse owing to climate change. At the 2018 meeting of CCAMLR, the ICG proposed a Climate Change Response Work Program (CCRWP), which was supported by the Scientific Committee and by most members of the Commission.[184] However, owing to the objections of China and Russia, the Commission was not able to adopt the CCRWP or a set of terms of reference for an ICG to support its implementation.[185] In particular, China and Russia raised concerns about the overlap between the CCRWP and the work of other organisations.[186]

In contrast to the Antarctic Treaty where, despite a framework providing overt support for a strong ecosystem and integrated approach to environmental governance, party states have been relatively cautious in developing a bold agenda, CCAMLR has used its ecosystem-focused framework to become a pioneer in ecosystem-based management. However, that status is now under significant threat owing to consensus-based decision-making[187] and the consistent resistance of two states to ecosystem-focused measures: China and Russia. More generally, the Second Performance Review of CCAMLR, which reported in 2017, concluded that the Commission is

> rightly still widely recognized internationally as the pre-eminent regional conservation management organisation that also manages harvesting activities. However, because many of the pioneering conservation measures originally developed by CCAMLR had now been adopted by several

182 CCAMLR, *Report of the Thirty-fourth Meeting of the Commission* (Hobart, Australia, Oct. 19-30, 2015, Australia), [7.12].

183 Ibid, Annex 8.

184 CCAMLR, *Report of the Thirty-sixth Meeting of the Commission*, [7.1–7.6].

185 Ibid, [7.8].

186 Ibid, [7.7].

187 1980 CAMLR Convention, art. XII(1).

regional fisheries management organisations (RFMOs), this distinction was becoming less clear. The Panel noted that there was a sense that CCAMLR had become less focused on proactive precautionary ecosystem-based management measures, and more focused on responding to fisheries and fisheries research proposals submitted by its Members. The Panel observed that for CCAMLR to maintain its international reputation as a leading conservation-focused organisation, it needed to regain its proactivity on all aspects of its work.[188]

4.4 *Cooperation: Navigating the Southern Ocean Regime Complex*

The final lesson from Antarctica relates to cooperation and collaboration, within and beyond the Antarctic Treaty System: navigating the Antarctic regime complex. As noted above, the CAMLR Convention is an integral part of the Antarctic Treaty System and this has led to a unique level of cooperation between it and the equivalent of the regional seas regime for the Antarctic (the 1959 Antarctic Treaty and 1991 Environmental Protocol). This cooperation has been particularly evident in relation to the designation of marine MPAs. However, coordination across a range of areas could be improved. For example, the Second Performance Review of CCAMLR recommended the development of a work plan to identify issues of shared interest and opportunities for enhanced collaboration between the Commission and the CEP around climate change.[189] The Review also suggested that there could be benefit in developing common understanding between the Commission and the CEP around safety and environmental standards for fishing, tourist and scientific vessels operating in the Southern Ocean.[190]

Beyond the Antarctic Treaty System there has traditionally been a reluctance on the part of Treaty bodies to engage with other regimes and institutions, in part owing to the sensitive territorial dispute over the continent of Antarctica, but also connected to the view that Antarctic issues are a matter for the Antarctic Treaty only, to the exclusion of other organisations, including the UN; a view often described as "Antarctic exceptionalism."[191] This reluctance

188 Second Performance Review of CCAMLR, [21].

189 Ibid, [26], Recommendation 3.

190 Ibid, [18–19].

191 *See, e.g.*, Alan D. Hemmings, "From the New Geopolitics of Resources to Nanotechnology: Emerging Challenges of Globalism in Antarctica," *The Yearbook of Polar Law* 1 (2009): 55, 71; *see also* Alan Hemmings, "Re-justifying the Antarctic Treaty System for the 21st Century: Rights, Expectations and Global Equity" in Richard Powell and Klaus Dodds, eds., *Polar Geopolitics: Knowledges, Resources and Legal Regimes* (Cheltenham & Northampton MA: Edward Elgar Publishing, 2014), chap. 1, 1.

is a much stronger feature of the Antarctic Treaty than the CAMLR Convention although, as noted above, the ATCM has engaged with the IMO over the last decade on a range of important shipping issues, including the Polar Code, carriage of heavy fuel oil and ballast water.

CCAMLR also maintains relationships with a large number of RFMOs including (but not limited to) SPRFMO, SIOFA, SEAFO, CCSBT, WCPFC and the IWC as well as the Agreement for the Conservation of Albatrosses and Petrels. The parties to the 1973 CITES formally adopted Resolution 12.4, in 2002, supporting cooperation between CITES and CCAMLR and recommending CITES parties implement the CAMLR Convention catch documentation scheme for Dissosticus spp. (toothfish) as well as CCAMLR measures in relation to toothfish more generally.[192] At the 2016 Conference of the Parties to CITES, the Conference decided to direct the CITES Secretariat to issue a notification to parties involved in the harvest of toothfish and that are not cooperating with CCAMLR to submit a report to the Secretariat on their implementation of CITES Conf. 12.4 and for that information being passed onto the Commission.[193] Nevertheless, the Second Performance Review of CCAMLR, reporting in 2017, took the view that CCAMLR would benefit from more effective and proactive communication with the 1992 Biodiversity Convention, the UN, the IWC, RFMOs and CITES.[194]

The tension between the advantages of collaboration and the need to maintain regulatory control is not, however, entirely absent from the CAMLR Convention, although it is less overt as compared to the Antarctic Treaty. This tension was demonstrated recently in the context of a proposal developed by CCAMLR Members Chile, India, Namibia, South Africa and the Ukraine for an Antarctic Large Marine Ecosystem (ALME) and a funding application to the Global Environmental Facility (GEF). At the 2017 Commission meeting CCAMLR expressed concerns over the proposal, and noted that it raised questions as to the institutional independence of the Antarctic Treaty System, and the relationship between the Commission, the GEF and the United Nations

192 CITES Conf. 12.4, Cooperation Between CITES and the Commission for the Conservation of Antarctic Marine Living Resources Regarding Trade in Toothfish (2002, revised, Conference of the Parties 2018).

193 The Conference also adopted Decision 17.51 (2016) directing the Secretariat to consult with CCAMLR regarding the provisions of Resolution Conf. 12.4 relating to information exchange between CITES and CCAMLR and present its recommendations, including any proposals to amend the Resolution to the eighteenth COP. *See* CITES Dec. 17.50, Commission for the Conservation of Antarctic Marine Living Resources (2016).

194 Second Performance Review of CCAMLR, [63], Recommendations 14–15.

Development Programme in relation to the scientific, policy and administrative aspects of the proposal.[195]

The most significant contemporary opportunity for engagement of both the ATCM and CCAMLR is with the UN negotiations for an instrument under the 1982 UNCLOS on the conservation and sustainable use of marine biological diversity of areas beyond national jurisdiction (the BBNJ negotiations).[196] Under discussion are five areas comprising: conservation and sustainable use of biodiversity in areas beyond national jurisdiction (ABNJ); marine genetic resources including questions on the sharing of their benefits; area-based management tools including MPAs; environmental impact assessment; and capacity building and the transfer of technology.[197] To the extent that the Agreement may extend to areas beyond national jurisdiction in the Antarctic, it is clear that there is potential overlap between the Agreement and the Antarctic Treaty System in all of the negotiating areas, including marine genetic resources (MGRs) and area-based protection as discussed above. In order to manage its relationship with other components of the ABNJ regime complex, the Agreement is likely to contain a clause setting out the modality of its interaction with other instruments, frameworks and bodies. The President's Aid to Negotiations, released in December 2018,[198] provides for a number of options ranging from a direction that the Agreement "shall be interpreted and applied in a manner that does not undermine those instruments, frameworks and bodies"[199] to "due regard should be paid to useful and relevant ongoing work or practices under such international instruments and relevant international organizations, provided that they are supportive of and do not run counter to the objectives of the Convention and this instrument."[200] Even if the option most deferential to existing regional regimes were chosen, the term "undermine" is ambiguous and, more fundamentally, where the regional regime does not regulate an issue

195 CCAMLR, *Report of the Thirty-sixth Meeting of the Commission*, [4.14], Annex 7, [37–42].

196 G.A. Res. 72/249, Internationally Legally Binding Instrument Under the United Nations Convention on the Law of the Sea on the Conservation and Sustainable Use of Marine Biological Diversity of Areas Beyond National Jurisdiction. Statement of Financial Implications (Dec. 24, 2017).

197 G.A. Res. 66/321, Oceans and the Law of the Sea (Dec. 24, 2011), [167].

198 Intergovernmental Conference on an International Legally Binding Instrument Under the United Nations Convention on the Law of the Sea on the Conservation and Sustainable Use of Marine Biological Diversity of Areas Beyond National Jurisdiction, Second Session, New York, 25 March–5 April 2019, President's Aid to negotiations, U.N. Doc A/CONF.232/2019/1* (Dec. 3, 2018).

199 Ibid, 7.

200 Ibid.

(such as in the case of access and benefit sharing of MGRs), there would be no rules for the Agreement to defer to. It is beyond the scope of this chapter to explore the implications of the BBNJ Agreement to the Antarctic, but a failure of the ATS to engage in the process risks an inadvertent undermining of the values and interests of the ATS, particularly as some ATS states may find their ABNJ interests better served under a global rather than a regional regime.

5 Concluding Remarks

The Antarctic Treaty, when adopted in 1959, established a remarkably novel set of principles for governing an area of the commons. Their novelty was, in part, a consequence of the fact that at least a portion of the 'commons' was subject to a sovereignty dispute and, in part, that the Treaty itself responded directly to the conditions and rivalries of the Cold War. Nevertheless, the Antarctic Treaty provided the foundation for a suite of instruments managing resources and seeking to conserve and protect the environment, which were equally innovative and future-facing, in their own ways. As such, it is reasonable to ask what 'lessons' can be learned from the Antarctic regime for the commons more generally, a particularly pertinent question in light of the current negotiations for a global regime for the conservation of marine biodiversity in the commons. The four 'lessons' identified for the purposes of this chapter illustrate both the potential and the limits of the Antarctic regime as a model for commons governance.

The first two lessons emphasise transparency, openness and the role that scientific research can play in building a regime on the basis of principles other than territorial control or shared control through a mechanism such as common heritage of humankind. The regime for open inspection under the Antarctic Treaty and its associated instruments contribute to, but go well beyond, compliance and enforcement. The provisions under the 1959 Treaty in particular, are about building trust between the parties and, under the Protocol, provide an opportunity to share best practice. It might be suggested that this function is in fact more important than compliance per se given that there is no compliance mechanism under the Treaty or Protocol and oversight of the ATCM is weak. Despite these provisions supporting open inspection however, the process has been underused by the parties, with many states never having participated in an inspection. Nevertheless, it is recommended that the concept of transparency of facilities, vessels and activities in the commons and an open system of inspection available to any participating state are positive ways of building trust and can contribute to other objectives such as knowledge transfer and capacity building.

Similarly, the free dissemination of scientific information provides an important mode of sharing the benefits of commons resources and represents one starting point in the negotiations over additional benefit sharing of MGRs in the commons. The 'lesson' from the Antarctic demonstrates the challenges associated with sharing information where that information has potential commercial benefit, and it is notable that in twenty years of being a semi-regular agenda item, the parties to the Antarctic Treaty have failed to make meaningful progress in the regulation of bioprospecting in the region.

The third lesson—in ecosystem and integrated environmental management—is an approach which is now ubiquitous whether operating in the commons or in areas under the jurisdiction of states. Nevertheless, the Antarctic Treaty System provides an example of valuable practice in cooperation between the equivalent of a regional seas regime and the fisheries management arrangement, particularly in relation to MPAs. It also illustrates that even though the unique Antarctic Treaty System strongly facilitates a close level of collaboration, cooperation between the CEP and CCAMLR could be improved. Both the 1991 Environmental Protocol and the 1980 CAMLR Convention also demonstrate that being a pioneer in ecosystem-based management does not mean that it is easy to maintain that status. CCAMLR, in particular, has struggled owing to a process of consensus decision-making and consistent resistance from a minority of states to conservation measures that, in their opinion, are not compatible with the "rational use" component of conservation under Article II(2) of the CAMLR Convention. Managing diverse interests in conservation, sustainable use and the interaction between the BBNJ Agreement and RFMOs, particularly with respect to area-based protection, is going to be one of the many challenges for negotiators. Despite the difficulties encountered by CCAMLR, its work in relation to MPAs, in conjunction with the CEP, does provide useful practice for the negotiators to draw on.

The final lesson, rather than focusing on good practice, arguably draws on practice to be avoided in the broader commons context. Navigating the 'regime' complex in the Antarctic is something which the ATCM in particular has not done well. To a large extent, this has been a deliberate strategy on the part of the Antarctic Treaty parties in order to preserve and privilege the interests of parties in the governance and resources of Antarctica (at the expense of the wider international community more generally) as well as to protect the sovereignty compromise agreed under Article IV of the Treaty. The ATCM has been generally effective in this strategy by deliberately bringing states critical of the Treaty arrangement, such as Malaysia, within the Antarctic Treaty System as parties. Tensions over access to resources, particularly mineral resources, have been reasonably absent in recent years owing to the relative inaccessibility of these resources for physical and economic reasons. Whilst the ATCM has positively engaged with the IMO in recent years over shipping regulation in the Polar regions, this engagement has not been repeated in respect of other organisations such as the Biodiversity Convention and the 1992 UNFCCC. Currently, the ATCM appears relatively disengaged from the BBNJ negotiations, which is surprising given the potential level of overlap between the instruments. Whether states not party to the Antarctic Treaty will be content to allow the 53 states to continue to manage activities and, more significantly, access to genetic resources on an exclusive basis, remains to be seen. The BBNJ negotiators are undoubtedly alive to the issue of managing the relationship between the proposed instrument and a myriad of institutions and regimes with overlapping functions and appear to be developing a proactive and positive approach to that engagement.

Ultimately, the Antarctic Treaty System is, up until now, the most comprehensive and ambitious example of commons governance. Whilst far from perfect, and arguably under increasing pressure owing to the changing environmental and, more significantly, geopolitical landscape, it nevertheless has much to teach global commons governance more generally. It is likely that at least some of these lessons will be incorporated into the proposed BBNJ Agreement and be used as a basis to create a commons governance regime fit for the twenty-first century.

CHAPTER 4

Rethinking Governance for the Changing Arctic

A Perspective from China and South Korea

Young Kil Park[*]

1 Introduction

Professor Oran Young, a leading researcher on Arctic governance, defined "governance" as "a social function centered on steering societies toward socially desirable outcomes and away from socially undesirable outcomes."[1] As Professor Young says, to attain "socially desirable outcomes" governance requires adaptation to social changes. Although nowadays climate change caused by global warming affects every place, the Arctic suffers the most due to the characteristics of its natural environment. For this reason, the Arctic undergoes tremendous environmental, social, and economic changes. Non-Arctic countries are increasingly aware of the importance of Arctic resources, and engaged in vigorous Arctic-related activities. This paper aims to review the necessity and possibility of changes in Arctic governance, related especially to China and South Korea and connected with the environmental changes in the Arctic as well as increased activities in the region by non-Arctic countries.

For a long time, the Arctic was the most remote place known to human beings. Until 1991, when the Cold War ended with the collapse of the Soviet Union, human activities in the Arctic were mainly restricted to military operations.[2] However, with the advancement of traffic, communication, and scientific technologies, human interests and activities in the Arctic, such as travel and research, have increased progressively. In particular, the acceleration of ice melting in the Arctic due to climate change has increased the attention

* Director, Law of the Sea Research Division, Korea Maritime Institute.

1 Oran R. Young, "The Evolution of Arctic Ocean Governance: Challenges and Opportunities," in Oran R. Young *et al.* eds., *The Arctic in World Affairs: A North Pacific Dialogue on the Future of the Arctic* (*2013 North Pacific Arctic Conference Proceedings*), Korea Maritime Institute and East West Center (2013), 269.

2 In particular, the Arctic was used to deploy nuclear-armed submarines and long-range missiles. Oran R. Young, "Adaptive Governance for a Changing Arctic," in Leiv Lunde, Yang Jian, and Iselin Stensdal, eds., *Asian Countries and the Arctic Future* (Singapore: World Scientific, 2015), 16.

 | DOI:10.1163/9789004514218_006

of individuals, nongovernmental organizations (NGOs), businesses, and governments to Arctic scientific research, environmental protection, and economic values.

The Arctic is the area most vulnerable to climate change because of its unique environment—for much of the year, it is mostly covered with snow and ice. NASA reported that in 2019 at the end of summer the extent of the Arctic sea ice reached its second-lowest observed level since the late 1970s, when modern record-keeping began.[3] Claire Parkinson, a climate change scientist at NASA, pointed out that "the long-term trend for Arctic sea ice extent has been definitively downward."[4] The Intergovernmental Panel on Climate Change (IPCC) in its Special Report on the Ocean and Cryosphere in a Changing Climate also predicts that Arctic sea ice loss will continue through mid-century.[5] Melting of sea ice and thawing of the cryosphere in places like Greenland already have produced negative impacts on the Arctic's natural environment and human societies.[6] Melting of the sea ice threatens the lives of indigenous peoples and animals in the region; it also harms non-Arctic regions, causing sea level rise and weather fluctuations worldwide.[7]

On the other hand, the loss of sea ice causes an increased interest in economic development in the Arctic, not only in the Arctic coastal states but also in non-Arctic countries, including Northeast Asian states such as China and South Korea. The potential development of oil and gas resources in the Arctic and newly available Arctic Ocean shipping routes such as the Northern Sea Route (NSR), Northwest Passage, and Northeast Passage are the main areas of interest. States are also interested in tourism, fisheries, laying submarine cables, port development and modernization, and logistic connections between the Arctic Ocean and the inland.

Today, many problems related to the Arctic are no longer limited to the region and become global issues involving the interests of non-Arctic countries. As these problems globalize, it is natural for non-Arctic countries to want to join the governance discussion. There would be no problem if the existing

3 Maria-Jose Vinas, "2019 Arctic Sea Ice Minimum Tied for Second Lowest on Record," National Aeronautics and Space Administration (Sept. 23, 2019), https://www.nasa.gov/feature/goddard/2019-arctic-sea-ice-extent-fourth-lowest-on-record.

4 Ibid.

5 Intergovernmental Panel on Climate Change, *Ocean and Cryosphere in a Changing Climate: Summary for Policymakers* (Sept. 24, 2019), 42, available at: https://report.ipcc.ch/srocc/pdf/SROCC_FinalDraft_FullReport.pdf.

6 Ibid.

7 Ibid.

governance framework could cope with the changes in the Arctic; but if not, then the demand for governance change will increase.

2 Core Elements of Arctic Governance

Arctic governance involves complex activities of diverse multilateral treaties, bilateral treaties, international organizations, countries, and NGOs. Such treaties and international organizations do not ban non-Arctic countries from participation in Arctic activities. Among them, the UN Convention on the Law of the Sea (LOSC) is the treaty that has the greatest effect on the Arctic, and the International Maritime Organization (IMO) is the most influential organization.

2.1 *Multilateral Treaties: UN Convention on the Law of the Sea*

The UN Convention on the Law of the Sea (UNCLOS) plays the most important role among the international instruments that shape Arctic governance.[8] This convention regulates the scope and limits of rights and obligations of coastal states of the Arctic Ocean and all the countries that use the Arctic Ocean. By doing so, UNCLOS contributes to maintaining a peaceful maritime order of the Arctic Ocean. For instance, it states that coastal states have a territorial sea not exceeding 12 nautical miles and may claim an exclusive economic zone (EEZ) not exceeding 200 nautical miles and a continental shelf that extends to 200 nautical miles or beyond if approved by the UN Commission on the Limits of the Continental Shelf.[9] The development of petroleum and gas resources, fisheries, protection of the marine environment, navigation, execution of jurisdiction over ships, and activities in international waters must be carried out in accordance with UNCLOS.[10] Another important characteristic of UNCLOS is that a compulsory dispute settlement procedure applies to party states.[11]

---

8 As of December 2021, 168 countries are involved.

9 Russia, Denmark and Canada submitted information to extend their continental shelf beyond 200nm in the Arctic Ocean in 2001 (partial revised submission in 2015), 2014 and 2019 respectively.

10 The United States has not ratified the UN Convention on the Law of the Sea, but it regards core details of the convention as binding customary international law.

11 UN Convention on the Law of the Sea, Part 15, Section 2 (Compulsory procedures entailing binding decisions).

2.2 *Multilateral Treaties: Spitsbergen Treaty*

This treaty is a multilateral treaty on the Archipelago of Svalbard in the Arctic. The treaty acknowledges Norway's sovereignty over the Archipelago of Svalbard and grants equivalent commercial rights on this island to the countries concerned. Many non-Arctic countries, including South Korea, China, and Japan joined this treaty.[12] Currently, Norway and Russia have a dispute over the extent of Norway's EEZ around the island.

2.3 *International Organization: IMO*

Among many international organizations, the IMO engages in the activities that have the greatest impact on the Arctic. The IMO is a specialized organization of the UN with 175 member states responsible for ensuring safe shipping operations and preventing marine and air pollution caused by ships. The IMO has initiated 50 treaties or protocols to fulfill such responsibilities. Such treaties and protocols adopted by the IMO—including the International Convention for the Safety of Life at Sea (SOLAS), International Convention for the Prevention of Pollution from Ships and its Protocol (MARPOL), Convention on the International Regulations for Preventing Collision at Sea (COLEG), and International Convention on Maritime Search and Rescue (SAR)—play pivotal roles for the Arctic Ocean. The Polar Code, which came into effect on January 1, 2017, requires ships to meet high equipment standards for the safety of navigating and protection of the marine environment.[13] The Polar Code is binding for the member states pursuant to the SOLAS and MARPOL. GHG emissions and black carbon reduction regulations recently driven by the IMO also have a huge impact on shipping in the Arctic.

2.4 *Non-international Organization: Arctic Council*

The Arctic Council is an intergovernmental forum created in 1996 to facilitate cooperation, coordination, and interaction among the Arctic countries and Arctic natives aimed at the sustainable development and environmental protection of the Arctic.[14] The Arctic Council has eight member states[15] and six Arctic native organizations are permanent participants. The Arctic Council plays a key role in Arctic governance by providing a forum for discussion of

12 Spitsbergen Treaty (Signed on February 9, 1920, and entered into force on August 14, 1925). As of December 2021, 46 countries are involved.

13 International Code for Ships Operating in Polar Waters.

14 The Arctic Council, About, https://arctic-council.org/about.

15 Canada, Denmark, Finland, Iceland, Norway, Russia, Sweden, and the United States.

most Arctic affairs (with the exception of military security), with execution following through domestic action of the Arctic member states.

The Arctic Council deals with various topics, such as people who live in the Arctic region, biodiversity, climate, marine protection, pollution, and emergency response. Working groups under the Arctic Council conduct diverse projects on these topics, and legislative meetings create resolutions based on the results of the projects. These working groups play a very important role since they are the only organizations within the Arctic Council that analyze climate change and marine pollution in the Arctic and find solutions. Since the Arctic Council is not an international legal entity, individual countries can decide whether to follow the resolutions made by the Arctic Council.

Non-Arctic countries along with intergovernmental organizations and NGOs may participate in the Arctic Council as observers. In 2021, there are 13 non-Arctic observers, and all five East Asian observers (South Korea, China, Japan, India, and Singapore) were acknowledged as observers at the Kiruna Ministerial Meeting in 2013, where the Arctic Council clarified the roles of the observers by adopting the Arctic Council Observer Manual.[16] In this manual, the Arctic Council clarified that membership in the Arctic Council is "limited exclusively to" the eight Arctic states,[17] all decisions of the Arctic Council are the exclusive rights and responsibilities of the eight Arctic states,[18] and the primary role of observers is to observe the work of the Arctic Council.[19] The observers may participate in the meetings of the Arctic Council, but they do not have voting rights. In addition, the Arctic Council may decide to suspend or invalidate the qualifications of the observers.[20]

2.5 *Adaptive Governance for a Changing Arctic*

Global warming causes changes in the natural environment which is leading to increased economic activities. The permafrost melts, and the surface area of the sea ice continues to decrease. Such changes in the natural environment facilitate scientific research in the Arctic. Arctic governance tries to adapt to these changes.

---

16 Arctic Council, Arctic Council Observer Manual for Subsidiary Bodies, 2013, https://oaarchive.arctic-council.org/bitstream/handle/11374/939/EDOCS-3020-v1B-Observer-manual-with-addendum-finalized_Oct2016.pdf.

17 Ibid, 4.1. Membership.

18 Ibid, 5. Decision-making in the Arctic Council.

19 Ibid, 6. The role of observers.

20 Ibid, 4.3. Observers.

2.6 *Scientific Research*

The International Arctic Science Committee (IASC) is the representative organization for scientific research in the Arctic. The IASC is a non-governmental international scientific organization founded in 1990, and because the participating institutions represent their respective countries, its activities reflect the intentions of those countries. The IASC strengthens cooperation among the member institutions to raise scientific interest in the Arctic and cope with increases in research demands. The IASC was founded by the representative scientific institutions of the eight Arctic states in 1990, but it was later opened to the scientific institutions of non-Arctic states, and today scientific institutions from 15 non-Arctic states are members of the Board of Directors.[21] Regarding cooperation on Arctic research, Arctic and non-Arctic institutions are not differentiated within the IASC.

2.7 *Establishing the Arctic Economic Council*

The effects of global warming on the Arctic have paradoxically resulted in the expansion of the Arctic market. In other words, new business opportunities opened up in different areas, such as marine transportation, communications, aviation, energy resources, development of mineral resources, tourism, and the blue economy. In this context, the Arctic Economic Council (AEC) was founded in 2014 to facilitate business activities and secure sustainable development in the Arctic.[22] Membership is available to companies and indigenous groups economically interested in the Arctic, including companies from non-Arctic states.

The AEC is closely associated with the Arctic Council. The Arctic Council lacks the ability to respond to Arctic businesses because it mainly handles environmental protection and sustainable development. The Arctic Council recognized this at the Kiruna Ministerial Meeting in 2013 and asked Arctic businesses to create a forum to share ideas and exchange experiences. In September 2014, the AEC was founded in Iqaluit, Canada. The Secretariat of AEC and the Arctic Council are both located in Tromsø, Norway. In this sense, the AEC can be seen as a response of the Arctic Council to the economic changes in the Arctic. However, the AEC distinguishes legacy members with voting rights

21 The 15 States are: Austria, China, Czech Republic, France, Germany, Iceland, India, Italy, Japan, Netherlands, Poland, Portugal, South Korea, Switzerland, United Kingdom, https://iasc.info/about/organisation/council (last accessed Dec. 10, 2021).

22 See the Arctic Economic Council homepage, https://arcticeconomiccouncil.com/ (last accessed Dec. 10, 2021).

and members without voting rights, giving voting rights to the companies and organizations from the Arctic states only. That is, the AEC excludes non-Arctic states from its decision-making processes. It has 44 members overall, but companies from non-Arctic states are not participating, except for some shipping companies and resource development companies from Europe.

2.8 *The Arctic Council's Response to Change*

The Arctic Council's responses to Arctic changes can roughly be divided into two groups. The first is the strengthening of the internal response capabilities of the Arctic Council. The Arctic Council recognized the necessity to strengthen its capabilities in the Nuuk Declaration adopted in 2011,[23] and resolved to take various measures. One of them is to adopt a legally binding treaty with the help of the Arctic Council in response to reduced sea ice surface area due to global warming and increased economic activities. The reduced sea ice surface area leads to an increase in shipping operations in the Arctic Ocean, which can cause more accidents. The Arctic Ocean has an isolated natural environment with severely cold weather, and shipping accidents there cause enormous damages to nature. Rescue activities are far more difficult there than in any other region. Accordingly, the Arctic Council reinforced international cooperation on issues related to search and rescue, and marine oil pollution. Since 2011, the Arctic Council has also promoted adoption of the Agreement on Cooperation on Aeronautical and Maritime Search and Rescue in the Arctic (2011), Agreement on Cooperation on Marine Oil Pollution Preparedness and Response in the Arctic (2013), and Agreement on Enhancing International Arctic Scientific Cooperation (2017) to facilitate scientific cooperation in the Arctic. Although these agreements were signed by the Arctic states, they are different from previous agreements as legally binding international documents were adopted with the help of the Arctic Council. Another measure is to have a permanent secretariat of the Arctic Council. In January 2013, the Arctic Council founded its secretariat in Tromsø, Norway to provide administrative support. The existence of the secretariat does not imply that the council has become an international organization, but the secretariat clearly improved the

23 Nuuk Declaration, On the occasion of the Seventh Ministerial Meeting of the Arctic Council, 12 May 2011, Nuuk, Greenland: "Recognizing that rapidly changing circumstances, in particular the changing climate, have increased the challenges and opportunities facing the Arctic in both volume and complexity, and underscoring the importance of strengthening the Arctic Council to address this change."

ability of the Arctic Council to respond to external changes by strengthening its organizational foundation.[24]

The second group of responses is characterized by limited acceptance of the demand of non-Arctic countries to participate. Non-Arctic states that wished to join the Arctic Council were 'ad hoc' observers at first, becoming official observers in 2013. The attitude of the Arctic states toward non-Arctic observers was revealed most clearly through the Ilulissat Declaration issued in Greenland in 2008. Among the Arctic states, five countries[25] that have the Arctic Ocean as their coast adopted this declaration. The declaration confirmed that the five coastal countries of the Arctic Ocean have sovereignty, sovereign rights, and jurisdiction, that UNCLOS provides a legal framework regarding important rights and obligations related to the Arctic Ocean, and that there is "no need to develop a new comprehensive international legal regime to govern the Arctic Ocean."[26] Three non-coastal countries (Finland, Sweden, and Iceland) opposed this declaration, and there was a controversy over the roles of the Arctic Council, but this problem was solved when the eight Arctic states affirmed the primacy of the Council.[27] However, the attitude of the Arctic states toward non-Arctic states was maintained after this declaration. The Arctic Council admitted non-Arctic states like South Korea, China, Japan, India, and Singapore as observers in 2013, but the scope of activities of the non-Arctic states in the Arctic Council is extremely limited. Also, since the Arctic states explicitly denied the need to develop "a new comprehensive international legal regime," there is practically no possibility that the Arctic states would adopt a comprehensive treaty similar to those governing the Antarctic. So, the Arctic Council or the Arctic states are strengthening their capabilities by reinforcing the organization and adopting legally binding documents while allowing limited non-Arctic state participation.

---

24 The Arctic Council Secretariat plays many roles, including the facilitation of the information exchange between the Arctic States, permanent participants, and observers. https://arctic-council.org/about/secretariat/ (last accessed Dec. 10, 2021).

25 Canada, Denmark, Norway, Russia and The United States, Russia.

26 The Ilulissat Declaration, Arctic Ocean Conference, Ilulissat, Greenland, 27–29 May 2008.

27 Oran Young, "Informal Arctic Governance Mechanisms: Listening to the voices of non-Arctic Ocean governance," in Oran R. Young, Jong Deog Kim, Yoon Hyung Kim, *The Arctic in World Affairs: A North Pacific Dialogue on Arctic Marine Issues* (2012 North Pacific Arctic Conference Proceedings), Korea Maritime Institute and East West Center (2012), 281.

2.9 *Adoption of the Central Arctic Ocean Fisheries Agreement*

The adoption of the Agreement to Prevent Unregulated High Seas Fisheries in the Central Arctic Ocean[28] is very progressive from the Arctic governance perspective. The negotiations to adopt this legally binding agreement began when in June 2015 the five coastal countries of the Arctic Ocean adopted the Declaration Concerning the Prevention of Unregulated High Seas Fishing in the Central Arctic Ocean. The parties involved include the five coastal countries of the Arctic Ocean, EU, Iceland, South Korea, China, and Japan. It is significant that South Korea, China, and Japan, with their interest in commercial fishing in waters nearby the Arctic Ocean such as the Bering Sea, were involved in the early negotiation process. According to UNCLOS, all states have rights to operate in international waters of the Central Arctic Ocean if the sea ice of the Arctic Ocean continues melting. Countries of the Arctic Ocean invited major countries that can operate in the Central Arctic Ocean as partners for negotiation.

2.10 *Arctic Governance and Non-Arctic States: China and South Korea*

Since different regions around the world have interactive relationships regarding economic issues besides climate and environment, interest in the Arctic is not limited to Arctic states. The attention and desire of non-Arctic states to participate in Arctic affairs appears in various areas, including scientific research and economic activities. Non-Arctic states participate in Arctic activities through various intergovernmental and non-governmental organizations and bilateral cooperation with Arctic states. They are subject to international treaties, including UNCLOS. Therefore, no special restrictions apply when non-Arctic states engage in Arctic activities, as long as they observe existing international regulations.

Still, non-Arctic states are restricted from joining some NGOs or councils specific to the Arctic region. For example, the IASC, which is for scientific institutions related to the Arctic, does not discriminate against non-Arctic states, whereas the Arctic Economic Council, which is primarily for companies interested in running Arctic businesses, only accepts companies from non-Arctic countries as members without voting rights. Above all, the Arctic Council, a key forum of the Arctic states, strictly limits the rights of non-Arctic states and only grants them observer status. Given these circumstances, the standpoints of China and South Korea on the Arctic will be examined below.

28 This agreement was signed in Ilulissat, Greenland, on October 3, 2018, and came into effect on June 25, 2021.

2.11 *China and Arctic Governance*

China is the most noticeable country among non-Arctic states with Arctic activities. Arctic activities of China can be divided into scientific research and economic activities. China's scientific research activities are remarkable. The Polar Research Institute of China oversees its Arctic research program, including studies of the sea ice, glaciers, and atmospheric chemistry.[29] In 2003, China opened its Arctic Yellow River Station in Svalbard. Also, by the mid-1990s China converted its first icebreaker, MV Xue Long (Snow Dragon 1), from an Arctic cargo ship to a polar research and resupply vessel, extensively upgrading it in 2007 and 2013. China built a second icebreaking research vessel, MV Xue Long II (Snow Dragon 2), that entered operations in July 2019.[30] Notably, in 2013 China established the China-Nordic Research Center in Shanghai. The center aims to provide a platform for academic cooperation and to promote collaboration towards both the sustainable development of the Nordic Arctic and coherent development of China.[31] The research fields of the center include Arctic climate change and its impacts, Arctic resources, shipping, and economic cooperation, as well as Arctic policy-making and legislation.[32] The center is open to participation for Chinese and Nordic institutes, and has eight Chinese institutes and nine Nordic institutes as current members.[33]

China is at the forefront of the development race among non-Arctic states. China took part in Russia's oil and gas exploitation projects, including Russia's Yamal LNG Project, with the China National Petroleum Corporation and Silk Road Fund holding significant interests. China also participates in another of Russia's major Arctic natural gas projects, Arctic LNG 2, with 20% stakes.[34] In connection with the Yamal LNG project, Chinese companies provide a

29 Polar Research Institute of China (last accessed Feb. 10, 2020), http://www.pric.org.cn/.

30 Ice class of the vessel is Polar Class 3, indicating that the vessel is able to break up to 1.5 meters of thick ice. Available at: https://akerarctic.fi/en/reference/xue-long-2/ (last accessed Feb. 10, 2020).

31 China-Nordic Arctic Research Center (last accessed Feb. 10, 2020), https://www.cnarc.info/organization.

32 Ibid.

33 Nordic member institutes are Arctic Center at University of Lapland (Finland), Fridtjof Nansen Institute (Norway), Icelandic Center for Research (Iceland), Nord University, Nordic Institute of Asian Studies (Denmark), Norwegian Polar Institute (Norway), Swedish Polar Research Secretariat (Sweden), The Arctic University of Norway-UiT (Norway), and the University of Akureyri (Iceland). *See* "Member Institutions," China-Nordic Arctic Research Center (last accessed Feb. 10, 2020), https://www.cnarc.info/members.

34 The stakeholders of Arctic LNG 2 are Russia's Novatek (60%), France's Total (10%), China's CNPC (10%) and CNOOC (10%), and Japan's Mitsui and Jogmec (10%). Available at: https://www.novatek.ru/en/business/arctic-lng/.

substantial part of the equipment needed for the construction from China to Russia and are involved in the delivery of the products through the Northern Sea Route (NSR). In using the NSR, China has become the second most active player after Russia. Between its first voyage in 2013 and 2019, China Ocean Shipping Company (COSCO), a Chinese state-owned shipping and logistics services supplier company, navigated the NSR 31 times.[35] It has been gradually increasing the navigations: 1 in 2013, 2 in 2015 and 2016, 5 in 2017, 8 in 2018, and 14 in 2019.[36] Furthermore, China has actively been expanding bilateral economic cooperation with Russia. A recent result of the collaboration is the launch on December 2, 2019 of the China-Russia East-Route Natural Gas Pipeline. China planned to import 5 billion cubic meters of natural gas through the pipeline in 2020.[37] As such, it appears that China is expanding its economic footprint in the Arctic by cooperating with Russia.

China announced its Arctic policy in 2018 showing its position on Arctic governance. It has revealed a dual attitude. China emphasized that it respects the existing system rather than demands fundamental changes. It stresses words like "respect," "cooperation," and "sustainability" in its Arctic activities.[38] At the same time, China attaches conditions to this position. It says that "respect" must be reciprocal, meaning that all countries must respect the sovereignty, sovereign rights, and jurisdictions of the Arctic states, but the rights and freedom of non-Arctic states in the Arctic must be respected in return. China respects the existing Arctic governance, but it is ready to raise its voice for its benefits depending on the situation. In other words, China has shown its essential foreign strategy, called Gray Zone Strategy in its Arctic policy. The phrase "Near-Arctic state" symbolically reveals this strategy in the China's Arctic policy. Describing itself as an important stakeholder in the Arctic affairs, China defines itself as a "'Near-Arctic state,' one of the continental states that are the

35 Sun Yun, "Prospects and Limitations for China as a New Arctic Player," in Lawson W. Brigham et al., eds., *The Arctic in World Affairs: A North Pacific Dialogue on Will Great Power Politics Threaten Arctic Sustainability?* (2020 North Pacific Arctic Conference Proceeding), Korea Maritime Institute and East-West Center (2020), 181.

36 The NSR Transit statistics from 2013 to 2018 are available at Northern Sea Route Information Office, https://arctic-lio.com/cagetory/statistics.

37 China is going to gradually increase the volume of its natural gas imports to reach 38 billion cubic meters per year for 30 years. "China-Russia East-Route Natural Gas Pipeline in Operation," China National Petroleum Corporation (Dec. 5, 2019), http://www.cnpc.com.cn/en/nr2019/201912/8b6a25eea0ab4c18be40231cabb21e66.shtml.

38 *See* China's Arctic Policy, which was officially released in January 2018 by the State Council Information Office of the People's Republic of China. Available at: "Full Text: China's Arctic Policy," State Council, People's Republic of China (Jan. 26, 2018), http://english.www.gov.cn/archive/white_paper/2018/01/26/content_281476026660336.htm.

closest to the Arctic Circle."[39] It further explains that "the natural conditions of the Arctic and their changes have a direct impact on China's climate system and ecological environment, and on its economic interests."[40] This explanation implies that China regards itself as a country that has a legitimate right to take part in Arctic governance. Moreover, China wants to build a "Polar Silk Road" by developing new Arctic shipping routes along with all Arctic parties.[41] The Polar Silk Road is an Arctic version of the Belt and Road Initiative (BRI). The BRI is China's grand project to reinforce infrastructure, trade, and investment connections between China and countries in Asia, Africa, the Middle East, and Europe. Some scholars believe that China uses the BRI as a way to maximize its presence and influence at the global level and diffuse its own values, ideas, and norms.[42] In the 2000s, when it had the second largest economy in the world, China switched to the more openly aggressive so-called "rising China" policy, adopting many assertive policies such as the BRI and the establishment of the Asian Infrastructure Investment Bank. In addition, the assertive marine policy of China in the South China Sea makes trouble for countries like the Philippines and Vietnam, arousing concerns in the Arctic Ocean. In particular, China is not accepting the arbitral decisions on the South China Sea that have been issued pursuant to UNCLOS.

Can China's Arctic policy bring changes to Arctic governance? It seems difficult. The specific Arctic policy of China is mostly based on bilateral cooperation with Russia. Meanwhile, the Arctic states have clarified their unwillingness to change the Arctic Council's current governance or make a new international system. China would have difficulty modifying the existing governance or implementing a new system. Accordingly, the phrase "Near-Arctic state" used by China in the Arctic policy seems to have no gain because it caused unnecessary concerns and suspicions of the Arctic states.

2.12 *Korea and Arctic Governance*

Like China, South Korea has strengthened its Arctic research capacities since the 2000s. In 2002, South Korea joined the IASC and established the Dasan Research Station in Svalbard. In 2004, the Korea Polar Research Institute (KOPRI)[43] was created as an affiliate of the Korea Institute of Ocean Science

39 Ibid.

40 Ibid.

41 Ibid.

42 Laura-Anca Parepa, "The Belt and Road Initiative as continuity in Chinese foreign policy," *Journal of Contemporary East Asia Studies*, 9(2) (2020), 176.

43 Korean Polar Research Institute, http://www.kopri.re.kr/eng/ (last accessed Feb. 10, 2020).

and Technology. In 2009, the first Korean research icebreaker *Araon* began its maiden voyage. In 2011, KOPRI hosted the Arctic Science Summit Week. In 2015, South Korea established the Korea Arctic Research Consortium. In June 2021, the Korean government confirmed that a second research icebreaker will be constructed by 2027; it will have a capacity of 15,450 tons, twice as big as the existing icebreaker.[44] In 2021, the government also enacted the Polar Activities Promotion Act to ensure the sustainable development of Polar regions and support relevant activities in the region.[45]

On the other hand, South Korea's involvement in developing the Arctic is limited compared to China, despite the government support. In 2018, there were no Korean shipping companies among the 27 NSR transit voyages. In 2019, companies from other countries used the ports of South Korea five times as a point of departure, but none was used as a point of arrival.[46] This may imply that private companies in South Korea, unlike the Chinese state-owned companies, consider the NSR not ripe for competing against alternative routes such as the Suez Canal.

South Korea's Arctic policy is more moderate. South Korea's Arctic Policy Basic Plan, established in December 2013,[47] emphasizes the enforcement of international cooperation and strengthening of scientific research and studies in the Arctic. Although the government encourages South Korean companies to participate in the Arctic business,[48] their engagements are presently not as active as that of the Chinese companies, due to their limited resources and market economy system. Since becoming an observer in the Arctic Council in 2013, South Korea has expanded international cooperation with Arctic and non-Arctic countries, institutions, and indigenous peoples. It has actively participated in Working Groups of the Arctic Council and international forums such as Arctic Frontiers and Arctic Circle.[49] For example, on behalf of the government, the research institutes—including the Korea Maritime Institute (KMI)—conducted a research program with the Aleut International Association under the Arctic Council's Protection of the Arctic Marine

44 The Ministry of Oceans and Fisheries, Press Release, June 28, 2021.

45 The Polar Activities Promotion Act, enacted on April 13, 2021, and entered into force on October 14, 2021.

46 "Transit Statistics," Northern Sea Route Information Office, https://arctic-lio.com/wp-content/uploads/2019/02/Transits_2018.pdf.

47 Korea Maritime Institute, *Arctic Policy of the Republic of Korea* (2013), available at: http://library.arcticportal.org/1902/1/Arctic_Policy_of_the_Republic_of_Korea.pdf (last accessed Dec. 2021).

48 Ibid.

49 Ibid.

Environment working group. KMI has been hosting the Korea Arctic Academy in South Korea since 2015, where about twenty students—including indigenous people from the Arctic region universities—join Korean students in a study program related to Arctic issues. KMI also hosts an annual North Pacific Arctic Conference in Hawaii in cooperation with the East-West Center of the University of Hawaii. And every year in December the Korean government holds an Arctic Partnership Week, where members of the international community focused on Arctic affairs gather for collaborative discussions on such topics as Arctic policy, science, technology, shipping, energy, and resources. Finally, in 2018 South Korea participated in the negotiations leading to the adoption of the Agreement to Prevent Unregulated High Seas Fisheries in the Central Arctic Ocean.

As explained above, South Korea respects the existing Arctic governance framework while it tries to broaden the range of its activities. Therefore, the Arctic states hardly show adverse reactions to the activities of South Korea. On the one hand, perhaps such a moderate attitude of South Korea can be maintained because no conflict of interests in the Arctic surfaced. Except for scientific research, most South Korean activities in the Arctic are limited to bilateral cooperation between governments or private academic activities.

3 Conclusions

Rapid environmental changes in the Arctic caused by climate change led to an increase in the interests and activities of many non-Arctic states. Since Arctic issues are no longer just regional, to solve the problems, cooperation between the Arctic and non-Arctic states is crucial. The related governance structures need to naturally adapt to these changes. In particular, increased involvement of non-Arctic states in Arctic activities should be accepted adequately in Arctic governance.

Today, various multilateral treaties like UNCLOS, bilateral treaties, international organizations like the UN and IMO, and NGOs like the International Arctic Science Committee play their respective roles in Arctic governance. As such, non-Arctic states have already been participating in this governance, or are allowed to join. Conversely, the Arctic Council, an intergovernmental forum of the Arctic states that deals with key issues of the Arctic Ocean, is exclusive. The Arctic Council has taken actions to strengthen its internal organizational capability and admit non-Arctic states as observers in response to the changes in the global environment and the demands of non-Arctic states to participate. Nonetheless, the Arctic Council maintains its exclusive character limited to the Arctic states by blocking any discussion on new governance and restricting the rights of the observers.

Among non-Arctic states, China is the most active country in the Arctic. While respecting the existing Arctic governance framework, China does not hide its actual intentions to expand its influence in the Arctic. This intention can be found in China's Arctic policy announced in 2018, where China defines itself as a "Near-Arctic state" and actively promotes the Polar Silk Road. The Arctic states and many scholars have expressed concerns about this Chinese policy because of what they have learned from the assertive attitude shown by China in the South China Sea and while pursuing the BRI. Also, the view that sees an aggravating security threat to the Taiwan Strait between China and Taiwan in connection with the traffic security of the Bering Strait that acts as a gateway of the Arctic Route reflects the worries about the Chinese activities in the Arctic Ocean. Nonetheless, China has little chance to change Arctic governance to secure benefits other than increasing its cooperation with Russia. In this sense, China would do well to moderate promotion of its Arctic policy.

Unlike China, South Korea's Arctic policy aims to focus on scientific research while solidifying bilateral cooperation and actively engaging in forum activities, such as the Arctic Frontiers, Arctic Circle, and North Pacific Arctic Conference. South Korea has a low level of economic participation in the Arctic, such as resource development and the Arctic Route. Considering these factors and foreign policy in general, it is unlikely that South Korea will actively attempt to change Arctic governance.

Arctic governance can hardly be changed without the consent of the Arctic states. However, the Arctic states have been showing an attitude that would minimize the involvement of non-Arctic states while keeping their supremacy. Although the Arctic states allowed non-Arctic states such as South Korea, China, and Japan to take part in the Central Arctic Ocean Fishing Agreement in 2018, this just means that it is difficult for the Arctic states to ignore non-Arctic states that have fishing rights in the international waters according to UNCLOS. The agreement would have been somewhat ineffective if adopted without these non-Arctic countries, as they are the major distant water fishing countries that operate in the Bering Strait near the Central Arctic Ocean.

Accordingly, the Arctic states need to take measures to ease their exclusiveness by opening matters of interest, such as the fisheries issue, to non-Arctic states. For example, the three treaties adopted by the Arctic Council may permit the participation of the non-Arctic states because they do not infringe the fundamental rights of the coastal countries and are related to the non-Arctic states.

PART 3

Managing Fish as a Common Resource

CHAPTER 5

The "Commons" Discourse on Marine Fisheries Resources, and the Problematic of Hardin's "Tragedy" Concept

Harry N. Scheiber[*]

1 Introduction[**]

The historical significance of Garrett Hardin's paper, "The Tragedy of the Commons," resides in the way that it has become "a pivotal trope in the environmental movement."[1] And it has continued to maintain its stature as an icon of environmental thought and discourse throughout the fifty years of debates since 1968 as they have addressed issues of law, policy, and moral values. As happens when the mists of passing time close in and obscure the full original meaning or context of intellectual events of even such extraordinary influence, however, it has too often been forgotten that Hardin's paper was essentially a narrowly focused polemic advocating a Malthusian position on unregulated human "freedom to breed." Paradoxically, the principal initial responses to the paper, and its longer-term impact, were most prominently concerned with the exposition he offered on the inherent problem of open access for users of common resources. Hardin contended that to head off disastrous depletion of natural resources, as the consequence of this problem, it was necessary to accept a coercive regime to curb birth rates, however repulsive the concept might be to the liberal *mentalité*; it must be recognized, he declared, that uncontrolled access to common resources would lead to continuously rising pressure on, and ultimately disaster for, those resources in counterpoint with the increasing demand for resources generated by unregulated human reproduction.

* Riesenfeld Professor of Law and History, Emeritus; and Director, Law of the Sea Institute, Emeritus, School of Law, University of California, Berkeley.

** The author is grateful to Profs. Carol Rose and Daniel Schorr, and to his wife and research collaborator Jane L. Scheiber, for critical readings and suggestions for revisions. An earlier version of this Chapter appeared in a symposium issue of THEORETICAL INQUIRES IN LAW, 19 (2018).

1 PAUL SABIN, THE BET: PAUL EHRLICH, JULIAN SIMON, AND OUR GAMBLE OVER EARTH'S FUTURE 36 (2013). Reference is to Garrett Hardin, *The Tragedy of the Commons*, 162 SCI. 1243, 1244 (1968).

DOI:10.1163/9789004514218_007

2 The Problem of the Commons through a Malthusian Lens

An essential element in Hardin's argument was his depiction of the way in which regimes of commons (in contrast to private property rights) had been used by communities in earlier periods of history, with their smaller population numbers and their smaller-scale, less destructive tools for resource exploitation. Famously, he cited the example of the destructive overpressure on the grazing commons of traditional societies: there was an inherent disincentive for any individual with an acknowledged right of access to exercise any self-restraint in the intensity of that individual's use of the "free" resource that the commons area offered. Once having pointed to the relevance of that metaphor (whatever the degree to which he oversimplified and overgeneralized the facts regarding traditional societies' management of commons resources), Hardin proceeded to concentrate his polemical fire on the comparable licentiousness, as he saw it, with which uncontrolled population growth had placed modern society inevitably on the path to tragic Malthusian consequences.

In only a few brief passages—they were submerged, as it were, in the rhetorical tidal wave of the main argument about "breeding"—did Hardin provide substantive content to his concession that "the logic of the commons has been understood for a long time, perhaps since the discovery of agriculture or the invention of private property in real estate." He immediately qualified this statement, asserting that it had been understood "only in an approximate way" and "mostly only in special cases which are not sufficiently generalized." A special case in point that he mentioned in a few lines concerned how private cattle-raising firms were placing demands on the U.S. federal government to increase constantly the allowable count of their cattle permitted to graze on the publicly owned lands (i.e., the commons)—"to the point where overgrazing produces erosion and weed-dominance."[2]

3 The Example of the Oceans Commons

The only other significant reference in which Hardin's text deviated from his focus on population was with respect to the contemporary resource-use problem represented by exploitative pressures that were damaging living marine resources, a vital source of protein food and other products important to human activities. With regard to whales, he noted specifically, certain

2 Garrett Hardin, *The Tragedy of the Commons*, 162 SCI. 1243, 1244 (1968).

species were close to extinction already; and, in a passing additional phrase, Hardin suggested that marine fisheries were being subjected to devastating exploitation because the philosophy of the commons prevailed: maritime nations, he contended, were committed to "the shibboleth of the 'freedom of the seas,'" and on that basis were resisting any coercive restraint on their fishing and whaling operations at sea. Compounding the problem, he declared, was the way in which these marine nations (and presumably fishing industry interests generally) held to a persisting belief in the myth of "the inexhaustible resources of the oceans."[3] Consequently, they were reinforced in their opposition to effective legal curbs on fishing or whale hunting on the high sea. In sum, they were fecklessly set on a course toward bringing many species of fish and whales closer and closer to extinction.

The sole citation in Hardin's "Tragedy" that provided supportive empirical evidence with regard to the oceans issues was a then-recent article in *Scientific American* on the failures of the International Whaling Commission (IWC) to protect Antarctic whales from destructive levels of harvests.[4] The author, Scott McVay, was not a scientist, let alone an expert on cetology or on international resource regimes; rather, he was a brilliant generalist and gifted writer, a liberal arts graduate then employed as a special assistant to the president of Princeton University. He brought together in his article (illustrated with portraits of the various species of whales being hunted) a summary of the abundant data on hunting effort and impacts on stocks that were readily available in the IWC reports. These data constituted a record of dismal failure on two counts, since the commission's founding in 1946: first, its failure to agree upon reliable scientific standards for setting goals on annual whale kills, allocating the harvest quotas to individual member whaling nations on a basis that would protect the most obviously endangered species; and second, its failure to command trustworthy compliance with the rules (whatever their value) that it promulgated. McVay's article was not an original scientific report; it was, rather, a well-written summary popularization of information on a resource crisis that was already very well recognized in the research fields and in the larger professional community in biology to which one might reasonably think Hardin was connected and of whose scientific work he ought to have been aware.[5] In

3 *Id.* at 1244.

4 Scott McVay, *The Last of the Great Whales*, 216 SCI. AM. (1966).

5 The immediate background to McVay's writing of his 1966 article, and his subsequent career as an activist in the campaign for whale conservation, are discussed in D. GRAHAM BURNETT, THE SOUNDING OF THE WHALE: SCIENCE AND CETACEANS IN THE TWENTIETH CENTURY 628–35 (2012).

fact, the crisis of the whale stocks and the scandalous failures of the IWC—its regime routinely derided by knowledgeable critics as a "whalers club" at best, and as a "fiasco" at worst—had long been well recognized, and deeply concerning, to biological oceanographers, marine zoologists, international lawyers, and resource conservation specialists.[6] The considerable literature that they had produced in their respective professional fields was either unknown to Hardin or apparently of no interest to him, being perhaps too far beyond the boundaries of his purpose to sound his alarm regarding the Malthusian disaster that he believed was unfolding.

Recent scholarly studies have refuted definitively any notion that Hardin's pronouncements on the problem of the commons represented originality of thought; for, as Professor Banner contends, this thesis "was of course not invented by Hardin. It is a very old one."[7] Well-known writings, from the era of the ancients to the time that the "Tragedy" was published, had explicitly recognized and devoted systematic study to the problematic of uncontrolled access to a common resource.

In the same light, I submit, one ought to give close scrutiny to Hardin's strictures about what he alleged was a widespread acceptance in ocean affairs of the dual "shibboleths," freedom of the sea and the inexhaustibility of marine resources. His assertions on these points cannot be taken as a well-informed judgment, let alone a fully credible portrayal of how the commons issue in marine fisheries had in reality been defined, debated, and addressed by marine scientists, international lawyers and diplomats, and resource specialists throughout much of the twentieth century—the basic issues having been set out by Grotius in the 17th century, and having been analyzed with new intensity of focus and sense of urgency in the decade immediately prior to publication in 1968 of the "Tragedy" article.[8] Hardin was content with reiterating

6 *Ibid.*; MALGOSIA FITZMAURICE, WHALING AND INTERNATIONAL LAW (2015); KURKPATRICK DORSEY, WHALES AND NATIONS: ENVIRONMENTAL DIPLOMACY ON THE HIGH SEAS (2013); JOHAN N. TØNNESSEN AND ARNE O. JOHNSEN, THE HISTORY OF MODERN WHALING (R. I. Christophersen trans., 1982).

7 Stuart Banner, *The Banality of the Commons*, 19 THEORETICAL INQUIRIES L. 395 (2018). *Cf., contra,* Nathaniel Wolloch, *The Early Modern Prehistory of the Tragedy of the Commons*, 19 THEORETICAL INQUIRIES L. 409 (2018) (arguing that the tragedy of the commons is a modern concept). Of course, much depends on the meaning that one gives to "very old."

8 Ironically, Hugo Grotius—credited with being the founder of ocean law as it prevailed for over two centuries, having set in place the theoretical and moral foundations of "freedom of the seas" in the early 17th century—wrote in his revered treatise *The Free Sea* that land is a resource that must be subjected to division into property rights holdings, because a commons holding would be depleted by the selfish actions of individuals (a concise expression of the "tragedy" as Hardin reiterated it); Grotius distinguished from property

McVay's message on the whaling crisis and with what amounts to only a few throwaway lines on the nature of the general problem of the ocean commons. He assumed no obligation to provide his readers with a sense of even the rudiments—let alone the rich complexities—that had characterized prior debates in ocean resource discourse. The following brief discussion seeks to recapture the main content and historic importance of that prior discourse, as they reveal a major problematic of Hardin's article, whatever the influence it has had for environmental studies since its publication.

4 Prior Discourses on the Commons Issue

First of all, there is the matter of terminology. It has been suggested that one reason why Hardin's article gained such immediate (and perdurable) attention is that he invented an effective name—"tragedy of the commons"—for a long-familiar phenomenon. In fact, in the debates of ocean resources law, science and policy, a term of art of the same meaning, *viz.*, "*the dilemma of the commons*," was already being deployed routinely. It is especially relevant to note that in a widely noticed 1966 symposium of oceans experts from several academic fields, law, and industry, the phrase was applied not only by presenters who addressed the issue of high-seas fisheries' sustainability, but also by others who warned that the "dilemma" applied in a variant way to any future regime for seabed mining that failed to vest property rights in mining enterprises. They argued that open access would at best discourage investments, and that even if investments were mobilized the foreseeable consequence of open access would be resource depletion wrought by firms with no incentive in sustaining the resource itself for the future.[9]

---

on land the high-seas oceans, which were too vast for their resources to be subject to effective control of any asserted property rights in them, hence, must be considered legally, at least beyond the marginal sea (of varying width, by the 19th century most commonly three miles offshore of coastal nations), as rightfully belonging to all but, equally, being owned by none. HUGO GROTIUS, THE FREE SEA, 20–38 (Davis Armitage ed., Richard Haklyut trans., 2004); HUGO GROTIUS, THE RIGHTS OF WAR AND PEACE 420–29, 462 (Richard Tuck ed., A. C. Campbell trans., 2005) (citing Ulpian: "The Sea is by Nature open and free for all, and is common as the Air itself").

9 The reference is to papers and panel discussions in the 1966 and 1967 Law of the Sea Institute conferences, proceedings of which were published in THE LAW OF THE SEA: OFFSHORE BOUNDARIES AND ZONES (Lewis M. Alexander ed., 1967); THE LAW OF THE SEA: THE FUTURE OF THE SEA'S RESOURCES (Lewis M. Alexander ed., 1968). For full analysis of the 1966 and 1967 papers, see HARRY N. SCHEIBER, OCEAN LAW

Second, regardless of when the specific phrase "dilemma of the commons" had come to be used routinely, the dilemma itself had long been a central subject of debate among experts in relevant fields of study and policy. At one time, to be sure, there had been wide acceptance of the notion that fish stocks in the high seas were an "inexhaustible" resource, so that "overfishing" was a misguided concept. This perception began to change in the early decades of the 20th century, with the advent of trawler technology, linked with the supplanting of wind power by coal-fueled engine power and the larger vessels and trawls that it permitted. This twin development, often termed the "industrialization of marine fishing," fuelled ever-larger-scale and increasingly efficient fishing operations in the early twentieth century. This was followed in the 1930s by the introduction in high-seas fishing of even larger-scale factory vessels—ships that were driven by diesel power, working the fishing grounds with fleets of small motorized catcher boats and with refrigeration capacity that permitted greater distances ranges of operations. These developments largely put to rest the traditional "inexhaustibility" concept, as its implausibility was demonstrated by a flood of reported data on volume of catch, and more especially the data on "catch per unit of effort" for various commercial species, which indicated that significant, and increasingly alarming, levels of reductions of biomass were occurring in some intensively fished marine stocks.[10]

By the mid-1950s, fishery science experts had recognized almost universally that fishing intensity was certainly a key factor, if not the only one, as a cause of the observed declines. The rare but sensational occurrences of a complete

---

DEBATES: THE FIFTY YEAR LEGACY AND EMERGING ISSUES (Harry N. Scheiber, Nilufer Oral, & Moon Sang Kwon eds., 2018).

10 Even in the sailing ship era, before the 19th century, some whale stocks in the Barents Sea had been decimated and the whaling fleets were diverted to other ocean regions to conduct their operations; in the twentieth century, there was a widely noted collapse of the halibut fishery offshore of British Columbia and the State of Washington, impelling negotiation of a treaty creating a joint regime, whose commissioners closed down the fishery altogether and thereby successfully achieved a resurgence of the stock's population so as to permit a resumption of fishing (closely regulated) at a future time; and after World War II, the most famous collapse of a commercial fishery, the sardine fishery based in Monterey, California, drew worldwide notice and occasioned the establishment of a major scientific consortium, known in later years as the California Cooperative Oceanic Fisheries Investigations (CalCOFI) headquartered at Scripps Institution of the University of California, which won fame for its basic scientific work on the ecology of the fishery while, however, failing to solve definitively the mystery of the fishes' "disappearance" or to produce a new basis for sustainable management. *See* Harry N. Scheiber, *Pacific Ocean Resources, Science, and the Law of the Sea: Wilbert M. Chapman and the Pacific Fisheries, 1945–70*, 13 ECOLOGY L.Q. 383, 417–27 (1986).

collapse of a long-established and once-profitable commercial fishery—the result of the target stock having declined so drastically as to render operations financially insupportable for individual fishing firms or units—further impelled the already manifest concerns about the threats to sustainability of fish stocks globally. Those concerns extended not only to the comprehensive threat of unregulated entry and fishing operations on the high seas (where "freedom of the seas" doctrine continued to be dominant), but also to the open-access commons regimes of many nations' coastal fisheries within the limits of their jurisdiction, being for most countries and their possessions the "marginal sea" ocean waters out to a distance of three miles offshore.[11]

Third, once the notion of "inexhaustibility" had become discredited, fishery scientists and managers—together with a few mathematicians—began to focus on how best to address the dilemma of the commons. The problem became a major theme of scientific study, policy debate, and efforts at practical reform of both national regimes and international fisheries law. One of its important manifestations was the founding of the International Council for the Exploration of the Seas (ICES), an organization that enjoyed major support from marine nations and was devoted to the scientific study of the biology and population dynamics of marine fisheries; various applied uses of its investigations were expected to be valuable in the designing of more effective fisheries management regimes that addressed the dilemma of the commons.[12]

Another line of study was directed at resolving the quintessentially practical "management" issue: devising the methodology for determining the point in a fishery's harvest at which an increase in "effort" would no longer produce an increase in "yield" (volume of the catch). When that point was reached, it meant that the "commons dilemma" had become operative. The data for calculating CPUE (catch per unit of effort) in a given fishery were collected season by season, with "catch" being the aggregate weight of landings of the target species; the "unit of effort" was calculated from whatever the authorities determined as its basis (usually the number of boats, their aggregate time on the

11 *See ibid.; see also* Arthur McEvoy & Harry N. Scheiber, *Scientists, Entrepreneurs and the Policy Process: A Study of the Post-1945 California Sardine Depletion*, 44 J. ECON. HIST. 393 (1984); ARTHUR MCEVOY, THE FISHERMAN'S PROBLEM: ECOLOGY AND LAW IN THE CALIFORNIA FISHERIES, 1880–1980, at 198–203 (1986); Harry N. Scheiber, *California Marine Research and the Founding of Modern Fisheries Oceanography: CalCOFI's Early Years, 1947–64*, 31 CALCOFI REP. 63 (1990).

12 *See, inter alia,* HELEN M. ROZWADOWSKI, THE SEA KNOWS NO BOUNDARIES: A CENTURY OF MARINE SCIENCE UNDER ICES (2002).

water, and the number of crew members).[13] And the CPUE data became the empirical justification for identifying the critical point at which "effort" should be subjected to some kind of effective regulation, so as to ensure (as was hoped) the conservationist goal of the fish stock's sustainability at the optimum level. This critical point came to be designated Maximum Sustainable Yield (MSY).[14]

In regard to the theoretical literature analyzing the validity of MSY—and also in regard to the evidence coming to light from the applications of MSY in the regulatory efforts actually deployed in various fishery management regimes—there was ample material for Hardin (had he been interested) to provide a fuller, more nuanced, and withal more accurate portrayal of the responses (whatever their strengths or weaknesses) to the unfolding "tragedy" that Hardin regarded as being irreversible unless population increases were stopped and coercive measures on resource use were imposed. We need not rehearse here the details of a heated controversy over MSY and its applications that was taking place in the years before Hardin's "Tragedy" appeared, except to underline Hardin's puzzling failure to recognize, even in a passing way, how prominent a place was being given by the community of oceans scholars to the issue of how best to address the dilemma of the commons.[15]

There is a special irony in the fact that one of the most eminent figures in fishery management design, including analysis of the MSY model and its variants, and equally prominent in the marine biological research in this field was Milner Schaefer, a University of California colleague of Hardin's. Schaefer held his professorship at the university's Scripps Institution of Oceanography,

13 The above protocol for data evaluation seldom included the differences in type, scale, and efficiency of harvest gear, although they were recognized prior to the 1950s as relevant to profitability for the individual fishing operator, and indeed became of central interest in economic studies later on, yet they were difficult to quantify. In any case, their quantification was not necessary for a calculation of CPUE, which was a measure of aggregative fishing effort by vessels, gear, and other equipment of all kinds.

14 John A. Gulland, The Concept of the Maximum Sustainable Yield in Fishery Management, FAO Fisheries Tech. Papers No. 70, U.N. Doc. FRS/T70 (1968); John A. Gulland, Fisheries Management and the Limitation of Fishing, FAO Fisheries Tech. Papers No. 92, U.N. Doc FRS/T92 (1969).

15 The MSY concept long continued to attract scholarly attention as a matter of substantive importance and lively debate in resources management, and persists as a central concept in fisheries and whaling management, on which see Ellen Hey, *The Persistence of a Concept: Maximum Sustainable Yield*, 27 INT'L J. MARINE & COASTAL L. 763 (2012). *See also* Marc B. Mangel et al., *Requiem for Ricker: Unpacking MSY*, 70 BULL. MARINE SCI. 763 (2002). For historical perspectives, see TIM D. SMITH, SCALING FISHERIES: THE SCIENCE OF MEASURING THE EFFECTS OF FISHING, 1855–1955 (1994); STUART M. KAYE, INTERNATIONAL FISHERIES MANAGEMENT 62–75 (2000).

located only a few hours' drive south from the Santa Barbara campus, where Hardin was based. Schaefer's research on fishery dynamics had become a powerful influence in the scientific study of MSY determination; and when the United Nations, recognizing the critical nature of the overfishing threat globally, convened a fishery science specialists' conference on the subject, held in Rome in 1955, Schaefer's paper on the scientific issues in fisheries management was given a featured role.[16]

Closer to home, in 1964 (four years prior to the appearance of Hardin's article), Schaefer, then heading the university's Institute of Marine Research, was organizer and director of a symposium commissioned by the state's governor, Edmund Brown, that sponsored papers by leading researchers and policy analysts on a broad range of issues subsumed under the title "California and the World Ocean." The papers, widely noticed by scientists and others in the ocean resources community, were presented at a public event in Los Angeles in 1964 and published in revised form the following year.[17] Here again, Hardin made no reference to some important papers providing contemporary experts' perspectives on the ocean commons.

5 Economists' Perspectives on the Commons Dilemma

An additional aspect of the commons debate antedating Hardin's paper was a concerted attack on the conventional wisdom in fisheries management that was launched by a group of economists, sparked mainly by the appearance in 1954 of an article on the dilemma of the commons written by Scott Gordon.[18]

16 Milner B. Schaefer, *The Scientific Basis for a Fisheries Management Program*, Report of the Int'l Tech. Conf. on the Conservation of the Living Res. of the Sea, A/CONF.10/6/Corr.1 (1955). On Schaefer's scientific research, see SMITH, *supra* at 14. On Schaefer's creative roles as research director of two major fishery research and management projects during the period of post-World War II initiatives, the Pacific Oceanic Fisheries Investigations, and the Inter-American Tropical Tuna Convention, together with the large strategy of fisheries diplomacy and scientific management that Wilbert Chapman championed, see Harry N. Scheiber, *Pacific Ocean Resources, Science, and Law of the Sea*, 13 ECOLOGY L.Q. 464 (1986); John L. Kask, *Dedication: Wilbert McLeod Chapman, 1910–70*; *Milner Baily Schaefer, 1912–70*, *in* WORLD FISHERIES POLICY: MULTIDISCIPLINARY VIEWS i-xi (Brian J. Rothschild ed., 1972).

17 California Museum of Science and Industry, *California and the World Ocean: Conference Proceedings* (Los Angeles 1964).

18 Scott H. Gordon, *The Economic Theory of a Common-Property Resource: The Fishery*, 62 J. POL. ECON. 124 (1954). In the prefatory section of his article, Gordon credited earlier analyses that applied economic efficiency criteria, one of which, by Robert Nesbit, published more than a decade previously, had sparked a controversy between him and the prominent

This study inspired empirical research on specific management regimes, conducted by James Crutchfield (a University of Washington economics professor) and Giuliu Pontecorvo (professor of business administration at Columbia). Other economists, most notably Francis Christy, Jr, and Anthony Scott, were severely critical of MSY or its variants, which were aimed at preservation of maximum levels of the fish stock; they contended, instead, that the objective of management regimes should be achieving efficiency—not only efficiency of fishing operations (i.e., the cost and benefit in profit to the individual fishing entity), but more comprehensively, efficiency in terms of the economy (so that the aggregate expenditure of funds to harvest the fish produced a net gain in returns—the capture of "net rent"—to the economy as a whole). The dilemma of the commons—that "no individual fisherman will restrict his effort or rate of output unless all others take the same measures, for, to the individual, restraint means loss of harvest [and] not deferment"—should be addressed, they contended, by persuading the fishing operators to accept the coercive measures necessary to engage them in "collective action" that would produce a "surplus value [rent] of the annual catch over total costs of labor and capital used in the fishery."[19] The MSY standard, the economists regularly asserted, was a "socially meaningless" objective;[20] its widespread acceptance by fishery managers and most scientists was thus, they argued, a sadly misguided practice that militated against fish stock conservation in the long run. They argued that the optimum level of harvest effort should be signaled by the point of maximum economic yield, which is to say the level of fishing beyond which the rate of increase in product was lower than the additional rent from a continued increase in

federal fisheries biologist and management expert William C. Herrington, as to the adequacy of MSY as a standard. *Id.* at 124, citing Robert A. Nesbit, Fishery Management, U.S. Fish and Wildlife Service, Special Scientific Rep, No. 18 (mimeographed, Chicago, 1943). Nesbit contended for vesting in fishing operators specific property rights in harvest quotas, linked with limits on entry such as the State of Maryland had introduced by freezing the issuance of new licenses in one of the State's major fisheries. Detailed analysis of this predecessor debate to the ITQ (individual transferable quota) proposals of the 1960s onward, is provided in Harry N. Scheiber & Christopher Carr, *From Extended Jurisdiction to Privatization: International Law, Biology, and Economics in the Marine Fisheries Debates, 1937–1976*, 14 BERKELEY J. OF INT'L L. (1998).

19 FRANCIS T. CHRISTY JR. & ANTHONY SCOTT, THE COMMON WEALTH IN OCEAN FISHERIES: SOME PROBLEMS OF GROWTH AND ECONOMIC ALLOCATION 219–21 (1965). For an insightful overview of the literature and major theoretical arguments of the economists' critique of MSY, see Anthony Scott, *Development of Economic Theory on Fisheries Regulation*, 36 J. FISHERIES RES. BOARD CANADA 724 (1979).

20 CHRISTY & SCOTT, *supra* note 18, at 65.

fishing effort. This point would appear, in an equilibrium model, at an effort level below what the MSY model would justify.[21]

The economists who spearheaded this attack on MSY augmented their critiques with a range of policy options (e.g., vesting of property rights in quotas, the licensing of fishing rights, tax incentives, and others) that they asserted would advance the goal of maximizing social rents from fisheries, as being superior to the instruments (such as gear restrictions, or reduced length of seasons for fishing) that were used by existing management regimes governed by the MSY principle while maintaining open access.

Taken from our own perspective today, however, the economists' signal contribution was to promote the idea of abandoning open access, substituting for it in one form or another the overarching alternative of limited entry. For at least ten years prior to the publication of Hardin's "Tragedy" article, proposals for limited entry were featured in a sequence of notable academic and industry-oriented conferences on fisheries management, beginning in 1956 with The United Nations Food and Agriculture Organization international symposium, "The Economics of Fishing," in which the proceedings were dominated by the views of Gordon and Scott. The views of Jens Warming of Denmark, another economist seeking to introduce efficiency criteria in fisheries regimes by means of limiting entry, also had an influence on the direction and content of the discussions.[22] In 1959 the University of Washington hosted a conference on the theme "Biological and Economic Aspects of Fisheries Management," in which Crutchfield, who edited the proceedings for publication, set the tone by denouncing even the Canadian-U.S. halibut management regime, which had brought back the stocks from virtual collapse eighteen years earlier to a sustainable level—yet one that was achieved by a confessedly "inefficient" policy of allowing the fishing units to operate for only a few weeks each season, until the MSY catch level, as calculated by the regime's scientists, was achieved. Defenders of the halibut commission countered that the biological objective of conservation, and the "social values" associated with preservation of the fishers' way of life, more than offset the shortfall in "efficiency" or "social rent" that was involved.[23]

In Canada, meanwhile, a heated controversy was initiated by the publication in 1960 of a government-sponsored study by the economist Sol Sinclair,

---

21 *Id.* at 6–16, 221–25.

22 The Economics of Fisheries, FAO Roundtable, (Int'l Econ. Ass'n, Rome, 1956), http://www.fao.org/docrep/011/ai761e/ai761e00.htm.

23 JAMES A. CRUTCHFIELD, BIOLOGICAL AND ECONOMIC ASPECTS OF FISHERIES MANAGEMENT 79, 84 (1959).

who had been charged with making recommendations as to regulations that would "permit [more efficient] economic operations" in the halibut and salmon grounds of British Columbia. Sinclair rejected some of his fellow economists' recommendations for achieving limited entry through taxes by volume on the catch or privatization of ownership of quotas; he contended instead for a licensing scheme that over time would transition into an annual auction for licenses. The fishermen's unions coalesced in a powerful political campaign to defeat adoption of Sinclair's proposal. Ironically, the British Columbia provincial government actually did institute a limited entry program in 1969, after salmon harvests had experienced a decline that seemed to portend the danger of a complete commercial collapse.

In subsequent years, other conferences and journal publications—all in print prior to the 1968 appearance of the "Tragedy" article—debated the terms of how open-access commons in fisheries might best be supplanted by "rational exploitation" maximizing operations by the economists' efficiency standards. Also relevant to the ocean resources debate, as an antecedent, is the fact that in counterpoint to the controversy over the purposes and technical calculation of the optimal point in fishing effort, the principal scientific researchers in the field were also cognizant of the problem of rising population. Taking into account the then-current rate of population increase, they sought to predict the volume of food fish and other resources (such as krill) in the marine biomass that could be processed for fertilizer and for aquaculture-feeding in relation to the estimated volume of demand from rising consumer market volume.[24]

In sum, advocacy for limited entry, based on recognition of the "dilemma of the commons," was anything but a quiet, behind-the-scenes academic

---

24 These conferences featuring economists' reformist arguments included another FAO meeting on the economics of fisheries, held in Ottawa in 1961, at which arguments for allocating "sole ownership" rights as a way of limiting fishing intensity were first put forward in a systematic analysis by Scott, foreshadowing the later movement for "individual transferable quotas" as the instrument for full privatization (albeit under the aegis of regulatory authorities imposing total limits on the harvest as well as allocating individual quotas). See the discussion of the several conferences and their key papers in Scheiber & Carr, *supra* note 17, at 30–50. For discussions expressing concern about future capacity of aggregate marine fisheries to meet the nutritional needs of rising population, see, e.g., papers and commentary by Wilbert Chapman, Donald McKernan, Milner Schaefer et al., *The Future Development of World Fisheries*, *in* THE LAW OF THE SEA: THE FUTURE OF THE SEA'S RESOURCES 121–42 (Lewis M. Alexander ed., 1968). For discussion of the various estimates of maximum potential food fish harvests, and implications as to adequacy in meeting human needs, see John A. Gulland, *Fishery Management and the Needs of Developing Countries*, *in* WORLD FISHERIES POLICY 25–51 (B. J. Rothschild ed., 1972).

movement, waiting for Hardin to step forward as discoverer or originator. Furthermore, practical applications of the limited entry principle were already in operation. In the northeastern quadrant of the Pacific Ocean, in the rich salmon grounds offshore of Alaska, Canada and the State of Washington, for example, a tripartite treaty of Canada, the United States, and Japan placed in operation the policy of “abstention”—an agreed regime limiting altogether entry of Japanese distant-water fishing vessels into the prescribed ocean area, which was reserved to Canadian and U.S. fishing—with exclusion contingent upon periodic scientific investigations demonstrating that the salmon and several other species stocks in that prescribed area were found to be at maximum sustainable yield.[25] In Japan's own domestic policy for coastal fisheries, meanwhile, a 1949 New Fisheries Law (enacted during the Occupation, when all legislation was under “guidance” and in fact required approval from General Douglas MacArthur's command) established a system of property rights for fishing operators' collectives, together with licensing that limited intensity of effort.[26] In 1958, the second UN Conference on the Law of the Sea, held in Geneva, produced four new conventions, one of which was on fishing and conservation of living resources of the high seas, and another on the extent of a newly defined “contiguous area beyond the limit of territorial seas” (i.e., limit of complete sovereignty). Both these agreements impelled still further movement, dramatically debated in diplomatic forums but also in the scientific and legal arenas, in international ocean law.

The well-known “ocean enclosure” movement, in which coastal nations began declaring exclusive control over fishing, barring entry by other nations' distant-water fishing vessels, gained impetus when the enhanced powers of coastal states in their declared contiguous zones (as stated in the Contiguous Zone Convention) were interpreted—at first arbitrarily, by unilateral actions, then as a matter of emerging customary law, including the power to exercise full control over fishing. The Fishing Convention, on the other hand, addressed the vexed issue of maximum sustainable yield, opting for the alternative designation of Optimal Sustainable Yield (which implicitly incorporated the

25 Harry N. Scheiber, *Origins of the Abstention Doctrine in Ocean Law: Japanese-US Relations and the Pacific Fisheries, 1937–1958*, 16 ECOLOGY L.Q. 23 (1989). On the longer-term influence of the doctrine, see Harry N. Scheiber, *Reflections on the Abstention Doctrine in the Diplomatic History of Modern Ocean Law*, *in* LAW OF THE SEA: FROM GROTIUS TO THE INTERNATIONAL TRIBUNAL FOR THE LAW OF THE SEA 64 (Lilian del Castillo ed., 2015).

26 W. Neville, Supreme Commander of the Allied Powers, Fisheries Programs in Japan 1945–1951 (Natural Resources Section Rep. No. 152, (1951)); Harry N. Scheiber, INTER-ALLIED CONFLICTS AND OCEAN LAW, 1945–1953: THE OCCUPATION COMMAND'S REVIVAL OF JAPANESE WHALING AND MARINE FISHERIES 64–67 (2001).

relevance of the "efficiency" standard, albeit without systematically defining it operationally).[27]

Neither of these developments that were given new salience by the 1958 UN Conventions resolved the dilemma of the commons, to be sure. Whatever the lack of full clarity in either of the two conventions, the process of limiting entry by declarations of offshore fishing zones went forward rapidly in the ensuing decade. By 1966, so many coastal nations, including the great fishing powers Japan, the United States, and Canada, had issued proclamations establishing twelve-mile fishing zones, that as a matter of "state practice" the twelve-mile zone was close to attaining the status of an embedded feature of international law.[28]

6 Conclusion

Long before 1968 the dilemma of the commons and the enclosure of the oceans that was taking place at a pivotal moment in ocean resources history were widely recognized and given intensive attention by experts in all the professions, including biology, concerned with ocean resources management. There was no informational gap that warrants one's viewing Hardin's article as a breakthrough in that regard, whatever its other merits. Moreover, in the years immediately following publication of his article, as confirmation of where his real interest lay, Hardin's further engagement with the general topic of the "Tragedy" was focused entirely on population control, manifested especially in an alliance with Paul Ehrlich and others

27 Kaye, *supra* note 14, at 68–75; Scheiber, *supra* note 9. A cautiously optimistic appraisal of the 1958 agreement was written in 1966 by the State Department officer who was instrumental in advancing the U.S. position on the abstention doctrine. William C. Herrington, *The Convention on Fisheries and Conservation of Living Resources: Accomplishments of the 1958 Geneva Conference, in* THE LAW OF THE SEA: OFFSHORE BOUNDARIES AND ZONES 26–35 (Lewis M. Alexander ed., 1967).

28 Shigeru Oda (then a senior professor of international law, and later a long-serving and revered judge on the International Court of Justice), though he remained in 1963 a determined opponent of ocean enclosure, conceded in 1960 that "no one can ignore ... the trend" toward incorporation of the twelve-mile fishing zone into the corpus of accepted law. SHIGERU ODA, INTERNATIONAL CONTROL OF SEA RESOURCES 136–37 (1989). On the trend of fishery law development after 1958, see WILLIAM T. BURKE, THE NEW INTERNATIONAL LAW OF FISHERIES: UNCLOS 1982 AND BEYOND (1994); FRANCISCO ORREGO VICUÑA, THE CHANGING INTERNATIONAL LAW OF HIGH SEAS FISHERIES (1999).

in polemical writings and in the activities of the Zero Population Growth movement.[29]

From the 1960s to the present day, however, the dilemma of the commons has continued to be a subject of enormous concern in the development of ocean resources law and policy, at both the national and international levels.

The issues and complex debates in this area of environmental concerns, identified here for the years antedating Hardin's article, have continued to dominate the ocean science, law, and policy literature. The definitions both of problems and of potential solutions have been newly reconfigured as to the basic legal framework with the signing of the UN Convention on the Law of the Sea in 1982 and its entering into force in 1994. The limited entry and MSY controversies have become interwoven with a set of varying concepts of "ecosystem management." The "precautionary approach" has taken on new force as a requirement validated in multinational agreements for high-seas fisheries regimes, and in a decision of the International Tribunal for the Law of the Sea. Most recently, the UN has authorized a series of potentially transformative negotiations for the protection of biodiversity in the high-seas areas beyond national jurisdiction. Among other already accepted changes in the structure of ocean governance and the expansion of legally endorsed environmental and resource protections, changes such as these in the last fifty years have imposed in environmental debates not only a transformed legal context but also an enriched scientific agenda and vital changes in moral context.[30]

---

29 Sabin, *supra* note 1, at 36–41. Sabin also points out that Hardin's "Tragedy" was in the tradition of an already established line of writings warning of Malthusian consequences from unrestrained population growth; he refers especially (*supra* note 1, at 16–18, 116) to FAIRFIELD OSBORN, OUR PLUNDERED PLANET (1948). Of equal importance in establishing the ideology of the modern environmentalist movement, especially its Malthusian premises, was the book by William Vogt, ROAD TO SURVIVAL, also published in 1948. Vogt's influence is analyzed in CHARLES C. MANN, THE WIZARD AND THE PROPHET: TWO REMARKABLE SCIENTISTS AND THEIR DUELING VISIONS TO SHAPE TOMORROW'S WORLD (2018).

30 An incisive overview is provided by Tullio Treves, *Historical Development of the Law of the Sea*, in OXFORD HANDBOOK OF THE LAW OF THE SEA 1–23 (Donald R. Rothwell, Alex G. Oude Elferink, Karen N. Scott, & Tim Stephens eds., 2015); and numerous other entries, on individual topics, ibid.; *also*, OCEAN LAW AND POLICY: 20 YEARS UNDER UNCLOS (Carlos Espósito, James Kraska, Harry N. Scheiber & Moon-Sang Kwon eds., 2016); THE LAW OF THE SEA: PROGRESS AND PROSPECTS (David Freestone, Richard Barnes & David Ong. eds., 2006); THE WORLD OCEAN IN GLOBALISATION: CLIMATE CHANGE, SUSTAINABLE FISHERIES, BIODIVERSITY, SHIPPING, REGIONAL ISSUES (Davor Vidas ed., 2011). Innovations in both hard law and soft law, together with the emergence of the newly accepted ecosystem management paradigm, and with further advances in technologies for resource location and assessment, came into play even as early as the last

Looking back at Hardin's "Tragedy" article today, the challenges of population pressure on resources that have persisted and grown since 1968 may well justify its seemingly fixed place in the discourses on environmental policy. But such recognition of Hardin's contribution requires one's attaching, in the interests of candor and accuracy, a set of appropriate caveats that recognize the actual historical context in which Hardin's writing was embedded.

---

two decades of the twentieth century, on which see Harry N. Scheiber, *Ocean Governance and the Marine Fisheries Crisis: Two Decades of Innovation—and Frustration*, 20 Va Envt'l L. Jnl.. 119–137 (2001).

CHAPTER 6

Sustaining Wild Salmon in the North Atlantic

Progressions and Tribulations

David L. VanderZwaag

1 Introduction*

Sustaining wild Atlantic salmon continues to be a great "ocean commons" challenge. Salmon populations are spread across over 2,000 rivers in North America and Europe[1] with each river needing conservation measures. Salmon populations have shown serious declines, including in Canada and the United States. Atlantic salmon in U.S. rivers are listed as endangered under the U.S. Endangered Species Act.[2] Atlantic salmon in inner Bay of Fundy rivers have been listed as endangered under Canada's Species at Risk Act.[3] All commercial fisheries for North Atlantic salmon in the two countries are closed.[4]

Salmon are not "home bodies" but are anadromous.[5] They spend early life stages in rivers and estuaries and later may migrate long distances, including into the high seas and into waters of non-origin countries.[6]

The United Nations Convention on the Law of the Sea (LOSC)[7] only sets very general governance coordinates for anadromous stocks through Article 66.

* The chapter seeks to be accurate as of 1 August 2019. The author wishes to acknowledge the research support of the Social Sciences and Humanities Research Council of Canada (SSHRC) through the Ocean Canada Partnership; the Marine Environmental Observation Prediction and Response (MEOPAR) network; and the Ocean Frontier Institute (OFI) through the Canada First Research Excellence Fund.

1 "Working Group on North Atlantic Salmon," ICES, http://www.ices.dk/community/groups/pages/WGNAS.aspx.

2 16 U.S.C. § 1531 (2019).

3 S.C. 2002, c. 29 (2020).

4 *Report of the ICES Advisory Committee*, NASCO Council doc. (19)08 (2019), § 3.1.

5 Eva B. Thorstad et al., "Aquatic Nomads: The Life and Migrations of the Atlantic Salmon," in Øystein Aas et al., eds., *Atlantic Salmon Ecology*, 2nd ed. (Chichester, West Sussex, UK: Wiley—Blackwell, 2011), chap. 1.

6 Ibid.

7 United Nations Convention on the Law of the Sea, *opened for signature* Dec. 10, 1982, 1833 U.N.T.S 3 (entered into force Nov. 16, 1994) [hereinafter LOSC].

 | DOI:10.1163/9789004514218_008

States in whose rivers anadromous stocks originate have the primary interest in and responsibility for such stocks.[8] The State of origin must ensure conservation by the establishment of appropriate regulatory measures for fishing in all waters landward of the outer limits of its exclusive economic zone (EEZ),[9] while fishing on the high seas is to be prohibited except where that would result in economic dislocation for a State other than the State of origin. Consultations are called for between or among States concerned with high seas fishing[10] and regulatory enforcement regarding anadromous stocks on the high seas shall be by agreement between the State of origin and other States concerned.[11] Where anadromous stocks migrate into or through the EEZ of a State other than the State of origin, such State must cooperate with the State of origin regarding conservation and management of such stocks.[12] Finally, the State of origin and other States fishing anadromous stocks must make conservation arrangements where appropriate, through regional organizations.[13]

Two words help capture how Atlantic salmon governance has fared in the wake of the general LOSC directions: progressions and tribulations. International cooperation in sustaining Atlantic salmon has progressed post-LOSC through the adoption of the Convention for the Conservation of Salmon in the North Atlantic Ocean (NASCO Convention) in 1982[14] and through numerous implementation efforts pursuant to it. However, four governance tribulations also stand out. They include: difficulties in controlling the harvest of salmon at West Greenland; problems in getting all salmon jurisdictions aboard the NASCO Convention; challenges in getting an effective grip on salmon aquaculture development and management; and deciphering what is causing severe population declines. A review of these progressions and tribulations follows.

8 Ibid, art. 66(1).
9 Ibid, art. 66(2).
10 Ibid, art. 66(3)(a).
11 Ibid, art. 66(3)(d).
12 Ibid, art. 66(4).
13 Ibid, art. 66(5).
14 Convention for the Conservation of Salmon in the North Atlantic Ocean, Mar. 2, 1982, 1338 U.N.T.S. 34 (entered into force Oct. 1, 1983) [hereinafter NASCO Convention].

2 Progressions in Atlantic Salmon Governance

2.1 *Adoption of the NASCO Convention*

Entering into force on 1 October 1983, the NASCO Convention set out the geographical, regulatory and institutional coordinates for conserving Atlantic salmon. The Convention seeks to conserve and enhance salmon stocks throughout their migratory range, including the high seas areas of the Atlantic Ocean, north of 36° N latitude.[15]

The Convention places strict limitations on where salmon fishing may occur. It prohibits fishing of salmon on the high seas beyond national jurisdiction.[16] Harvesting of salmon in waters beyond the 12 nautical mile territorial sea of Contracting Parties is also prohibited with two exceptions: fishing is allowed off West Greenland up to 40 nautical miles from the territorial sea baselines and within waters under the fisheries jurisdiction of the Faroe Islands.[17]

The NASCO Convention also promotes salmon conservation by providing for the establishment of the North Atlantic Salmon Conservation Organization (NASCO) and its institutional components. The NASCO Council is the overall coordinating and decision-making body of the organization,[18] and is authorized to make recommendations regarding scientific research to NASCO members and other scientific and fisheries organizations.[19] Up to three representatives from each Party can serve on the Council with each Party accorded one vote.[20] NASCO's Secretariat is responsible for all the administrative functions of the Council. The Secretariat helps organize annual meetings of the Council and the regional commissions. The Secretariat also maintains the NASCO website.[21]

Three regional commissions serve as forums for cooperation and consultation in addressing management of transboundary salmon resources. The North American Commission (NAC), composed of representatives from Canada and the United States, addresses salmon-related issues within the fisheries jurisdiction of its members off the East Coast of North America.[22] The West Greenland Commission (WGC), which includes Canada, the United States, the European

15 Ibid, art. 1(1).
16 Ibid, art. 2(1).
17 Ibid, art. 2.
18 Ibid, art. 4.
19 Ibid, art. 4(e).
20 Ibid, art. 5–6.
21 NASCO, http://nasco.int/.
22 NASCO Convention, art. 7.

Union and Denmark in respect of the Faroe Islands and Greenland, deals with a designated area of fisheries jurisdiction off the West Coast of Greenland.[23] Finally, the North-East Atlantic Commission (NEAC), composed of representation from Denmark in respect of the Faroe Islands and Greenland, the European Union, Norway and the Russian Federation, is responsible for the maritime waters to the east of the WGC's area.[24]

The regulatory power of the Commissions is substantially constrained. The Commissions may only propose regulatory measures for salmon fisheries under the jurisdiction of a member which involves harvesting of salmon originating from the rivers of another member.[25] Unanimous agreement among voting members is required for a Commission to determine regulatory measures affecting fisheries in its area.[26] A Party in whose waters a proposed regulatory measure would apply has the option of lodging an objection to the regulatory measure within 60 days.[27]

2.2 *Implementation Progressions Pursuant to the NASCO Convention*

NASCO's actual regulatory efforts have been very limited. Only the West Greenland Commission continues to set annual quotas.[28] NEAC has not imposed quotas for Faroe Island fisheries since 2000 and the commercial fishery remains closed.[29] NAC does not impose regulatory measures and neither Canada nor the USA allows a commercial Atlantic salmon fishery.[30]

NASCO has been successful in ensuring high seas salmon fishing does not occur by States not party to the NASCO Convention. A 1990 Council resolution highlighted that there were a number of illegal high seas fishing reports and called on all Contracting Parties to put pressure, through diplomatic channels, on those countries allowing high seas fishing to occur.[31] A Protocol for signature by States not parties to the NASCO Convention was adopted in 1992, which pledged signatories to prohibit their registered vessels from fishing for Atlantic

23 Ibid, art. 8.

24 "North-East Atlantic Commission," NASCO, http://www.nasco.int/neac.html.

25 NASCO Convention, art. 7–8.

26 Ibid, art. 11(3).

27 Ibid, art. 13(3).

28 "West Greenland Salmon Fishery Measures," NASCO, http://nasco.int/wgc_measures.html.

29 "Faroese Salmon Fishery Measures," NASCO, http://www.nasco.int/neac_measures.html.

30 *Report of the ICES Advisory Committee* (2019), § 3.1.

31 *Resolutions of the Council of NASCO at Its Seventh Annual Meeting Helsinki, 12–15 June 1990*, NASCO Council doc. CNL (90)49 (1990).

salmon on the high seas.[32] A further NASCO Resolution on Fishing for Salmon on the High Seas, also adopted in 1992, urged NASCO Parties to encourage non-contracting parties fishing salmon on the high seas to comply with the 1992 Protocol and requested greater sharing and collection of information on high seas fishing activities.[33] These Protocols appear to have been quite effective—there have been no reported high seas fisheries since the early 1990s.[34]

NASCO has made progress on encouraging national approaches and actions on three main fronts: fisheries management, minimizing the impacts from aquaculture, and encouraging habitat protection and restoration. The following subsections detail each of these in turn.

2.2.1 Fisheries Management

NASCO has sought to strengthen management of Atlantic salmon fisheries in all jurisdictions through six main "paper progressions." First, the 1998 Agreement on Adoption of a Precautionary Approach[35] urges a long list of precautionary measures. They include, among others: giving priority to conserving salmon stocks in the face of uncertainties regarding resource use; identifying undesirable outcomes and the actions necessary to correct or avoid them prior to authorizing fishing; implementing corrective measures immediately when required; demonstrating consideration of the needs of future generations by avoiding irreversible changes; setting conservation limits and management targets for each river; and maintaining all salmon stocks in the Convention Area above their conservation limit.

Second, an Action Plan for Application of a Precautionary Approach was added in 1999.[36] The Action Plan calls for various measures to be undertaken by the Contracting Parties, including establishing a Standing Committee on the Precautionary Approach; developing river specific conservation limits for the North-East Atlantic Commission Area as an immediate priority; and identifying stocks requiring rebuilding programmes followed by developing stock specific rebuilding programmes.

---

32 *Protocol Open for Signature by States Not Parties to the Convention for the Conservation of Salmon in the North Atlantic Ocean*, NASCO Council doc. CNL (92)53 (1992).

33 *Resolution of the Council of NASCO at its Ninth Annual Meeting Washington DC, 9–12 June 1992, Fishing for Salmon on the High Seas*, NASCO Council doc. CNL (92)54 (1992).

34 "Background," NASCO, http://www.nasco.int/background.html.

35 *Precautionary Approach Agreement*, NASCO Council doc. CNL (98)46 (1998).

36 *Action Plan for Application of the Precautionary Approach*, NASCO Council doc. CNL (99)48 (1998).

A third progression was the NASCO Council's adoption of a Decision Structure for Management of North Atlantic Salmon Fisheries in 2002.[37] The Decision Structure urges management decisions to be based upon risk assessments, such that, in the face of uncertainty, there is a low risk to abundance and diversity of the stock(s). The document calls upon Parties to report annually to NASCO on their experiences in applying the Decision Structure with details on items such as reference points used to define adequate abundance of the exploited stock(s); threats to the stock(s) by factors other than fisheries, such as habitat degradation and diseases/parasites and management actions to be taken; management measures to control harvest and measures to be followed in case of any failure or trend in abundances or diversity; and monitoring programmes in place to assess the effect of management measures.

A fourth step forward was adoption of Guidelines for Incorporating Social and Economic Factors in Decisions under the Precautionary Approach in 2004.[38] The Guidelines urge social economic impact assessments to be undertaken to inform management of salmon fisheries and suggest that the regulatory option with the highest social, economic and environmental benefits should normally be chosen and implemented.

A fifth progression was the adoption, in 2009, of NASCO Guidelines for the Management of Salmon Fisheries.[39] These Guidelines aimed to further clarify previous NASCO guidance documents relating to salmon fisheries management and to identify further necessary interventions. For example, the Guidelines provide that fishing on stocks that are below conservation limits (CLs) should not be permitted, but if a decision is made to allow such fishing on the basis of socio-economic factors, fishing should clearly be limited to a level that will still permit stock recovery within a stated timeframe. For mixed-stock fisheries, management actions should aim to protect the weakest of the contributing stocks.

Finally, NASCO has adopted Guidelines on Catch and Release.[40] These Guidelines suggest various ways to decrease mortality of Atlantic salmon

37 *Decision Structure for Management of North Atlantic Salmon Fisheries.* NASCO Council doc. CNL 31.332 (2002).

38 *Guidelines for Incorporating Social and Economic Factors in Decisions Under the Precautionary Approach*, NASCO Council doc. CNL (04)57 (2004).

39 *NASCO Guidelines for the Management of Salmon Fisheries*, NASCO Council doc. CNL (09)43 (2009).

40 NASCO, *Guidelines on Catch and Release* (2014), available at http://www.nasco.int/pdf/agreements/C&R_guidelines_eng%20.pdf.

caught in recreational fisheries, such as requiring small, barbless hooks; encouraging large landing nets; and keeping fish in the water during release.

2.2.2 Minimizing Aquaculture Impacts

Two main NASCO guidance documents have been issued to address potential aquaculture impacts on wild salmon. The first and primary guidance document is the Williamsburg Resolution to Minimise Impacts from Aquaculture, Introductions and Transfers, and Transgenics on the Wild Salmon Stocks, adopted in 2003.[41] The Resolution text urges application of the precautionary approach in various ways. Each Party is urged to place the burden of proof on proponents of activities to demonstrate the activities will not have a significant adverse input on wild salmon stocks or lead to irreversible change.[42] Parties are also encouraged to develop and apply risk assessment as an integral component of precaution.[43] The Resolution suggests that the use of transgenic salmonids should be considered a high-risk activity in light of the lack of scientific knowledge and advocates a strong presumption against any such use.[44]

The Williamsburg Resolution calls for various measures to minimize impacts of aquaculture and introductions/transfers of aquaculture species. For example, Parties are urged to minimize the escape of farmed salmon to a level as close to zero as practicable through the development and implementation of action plans.[45] Parties are also encouraged not to introduce non-indigenous fish into a river containing Atlantic salmon unless a thorough examination of the potential adverse impacts on the Atlantic salmon populations demonstrates there is no unacceptable risk of adverse ecological introductions.[46]

Annexes to the Williamsburg Resolution provide further guidance with respect to aquaculture best practices. Annex 3 provides general directions on how to prevent escapes of farmed salmon by, for example, siting aquaculture operations in areas where environmental conditions are not harsh on nets or moorings and adopting preventive net inspection and repair procedures. Annex 4 seeks to place controls on introducing salmon, for example, from hatcheries. Parties are urged to apply the precautionary approach to stocking proposals whereby proponents would have to provide all information necessary to demonstrate that stocking would not have a significant adverse impact

41 NASCO Council doc. CNL (06)48 (2003, amended 2004, 2006).

42 Ibid, art. 3.

43 Ibid, art. 4.

44 Ibid, art. 7.

45 Ibid, art. 5.

46 Ibid, art. 6.

on wild salmon populations or an unacceptable impact on the ecosystem. Parties are also urged to prohibit the release of Atlantic salmon of European, including Icelandic, origin into the NAC Area, and of Atlantic salmon of North American origin in the NEAC Area. Finally, Annex V sets out Guidelines for Action on Transgenic Salmon. They call on Parties to confine the use of transgenic salmonids to secure, self-contained, land-based facilities. Parties are requested to inform the NASCO Council of any proposal to permit the rearing of transgenic salmonids.

In 2009, the NASCO Council adopted a second document, the Guidance on Best Management Practices to Address Impacts of Sea Lice and Escaped Farmed Salmon on Wild Salmon Stocks.[47] This document sets international goals for 100% of farms to have effective sea lice management and 100% of farmed fish to be retained in all production facilities. Suggested best management practices for sea lice include integrated pest management, fallowing, risk-based site selection, trigger levels for treatment and regulated fish health programs. Suggested best management practices for containment include codes of containment, technical standards for equipment and mandatory reporting of escape events.

2.2.3 Encouraging Habitat Protection and Restoration

The NASCO Council has adopted two sets of guidelines to address habitat issues. First, a Plan of Action for the Application of the Precautionary Approach to the Protection and Restoration of Atlantic Salmon Habitat was agreed to in 2001.[48] The Plan urges each Party and its relevant jurisdictions to establish salmon river inventories and to develop national salmon habitat and restoration plans. Second, NASCO Guidelines for the Protection, Restoration and Enhancement of Atlantic Salmon Habitat were adopted in 2010.[49] The 2010 Guidelines urge a precautionary approach in decision-making processes related to habitat protection. In particular, they call for protecting salmon habitat from a wide range of activities, including siltation, loss of shelter, stocking of competitors, creating physical barriers and deteriorations of water quality. The Guidelines also encourage designation of key habitats for restoration and improvement.

47 NASCO doc. SLG (09)5 (2009, amended 2010).

48 *NASCO Plan of Action for the Application of the Precautionary Approach to the Protection and Restoration of Atlantic Salmon Habitat*, NASCO Council doc. CNL (01)51 (2001).

49 NASCO Council doc. CNL (10)51 (2010).

3 Tribulations in Atlantic Salmon Governance

3.1 *Controlling the Harvest of Salmon off West Greenland*

One of the most troubling NASCO challenges has been to effectively control the harvest of Atlantic salmon at West Greenland, which is a mixed-stock fishery with about 83% of North American origin and 17% of European origin.[50] The International Council for the Exploration of the Sea (ICES) in its scientific advice to NASCO has consistently recommended against authorizing a fishery off West Greenland since some contributing populations are in weak states and below their conservation limits.[51] However thousands of Greenlanders rely on salmon catches for subsistence and cultural identity.[52]

NASCO has struggled over the years to appropriately address this fishery challenge. From 1998 to 2012, the management waters were relatively calm, with the West Greenland Commission in all but two years restricting the fishery for internal consumption only alongside a commercial export ban that has been in place since 1998.[53] In 2012, however, Parties could not agree on a quota and Greenland proceeded to unilaterally set them, including specific factory quotas of 35 tonnes for 2012 and 2013 and 32 tonnes in 2014.[54] In 2015, Greenland unilaterally committed to limit the total annual catch for all components of its fisheries to no more than 45 tonnes in 2015, 2016 and 2017, with any overharvest to be deducted from the following year's catch limit.[55]

In 2018, the West Greenland Commission was again able to reach an agreement on regulatory measures.[56] Denmark on behalf of Greenland agreed to restrict the total allowable catch for all components of the West Greenland salmon fishery to 30 tonnes for 2018, 2019 and 2020. In addition, landings and sales of Atlantic salmon to fish processing factories will be prohibited and all fishers for Atlantic salmon will be required to have a license to fish and to provide a full account of fishing activity and harvest. Only licensed full-time

50 *Report of the ICES Advisory Committee* (2019), 78.

51 Ibid, 77.

52 *The Management Approach to the West Greenland Salmon Fishery—Fairness and Balance in the Management of Distant-water Fisheries (Tabled by Denmark in Respect of the Faroe Islands and Greenland)*, NASCO Council doc. CNL (14)44 (2014).

53 "West Greenland Salmon Fishery Measures," NASCO, http://nasco.int/wgc_measures.html.

54 *Report of the ICES Advisory Committee* (2019), 77.

55 *Multi-Annual Regulatory Measure for Fishing for Salmon at West Greenland for 2015, 2016 and 2017*, WGC doc. (15)21 (2015).

56 *Multi-Annual Regulatory Measure for Fishing for Atlantic Salmon at West Greenland*, WGC doc. (18)11 (2018).

harvesters and fishers will be authorized to sell Atlantic salmon, and only at open air markets in communities.

The Greenland Government's acceptance of a commercial export ban has been facilitated by private conservation agreements. The Atlantic Salmon Federation (ASF), the North Atlantic Salmon Fund (NASF) and the Association of Hunters and Fishers in Greenland (KNAPK) have entered into four such agreements: the first signed in 1993; a continuation agreement concluded in 1994; a third stretching from 2002–2010; and the fourth agreed to in May 2018 for a 12-year period (2018–2029).[57] In exchange for the no commercial salmon fishing commitment by KNAPK, ASF and NASF have agreed to financially support alternative economic development, scientific research and education activities in Greenland. The texts of the agreements and the exact monetary commitments have not been made public.

International tensions over management of the Atlantic salmon harvest off West Greenland seem likely to continue. An unregulated harvest of Atlantic salmon is estimated to be about 10 tonnes per year,[58] while the United States has emphasized that the 30 tonne quota agreed to in 2018 is still above the sustainable limit for the stock complex.[59] For the 2018 fishery season Greenland reported a total salmon catch of 40.5 tonnes, well above the agreed to quota.[60] While Greenland has set the 2019 quota at 19.5 tonnes to account for the over-harvest,[61] it remains to be seen how effective the regulatory measures will be.

3.2 *Getting (and Keeping) All Salmon Jurisdictions aboard the NASCO Convention*

The success of NASCO depends on the participation of all salmon jurisdictions. An ongoing sore point is the refusal by France to become a Party on behalf of its St. Pierre and Miquelon territory located off Newfoundland. St. Pierre and Miquelon fishers continue to harvest salmon of North American origin with nine professional and 80 recreational permits issued in 2018.[62] A total catch of 1,286.2 kg was reported in 2018 compared to catches of 2,816 kg in 2017 and

57 Atlantic Salmon Federation, *ASF-NASF International Conservation Agreements* (n.d.), available at https://www.asf.ca/assets/files/03-asf-greenland-backgrounder.pdf.

58 *Report of the ICES Advisory Committee* (2019), 77.

59 *Report of the Activities of the North Atlantic Salmon Conservation Organization in 2018*, NASCO Council doc. CNL (19)07 (2019), 12.

60 *Report of the West Greenland Commission on the Evaluation of the Salmon Fishery in Greenland in 2018 and Measures for the 2019 Salmon Fishery*, WGC doc. (19)05 (2019).

61 Ibid.

62 *Management and Sampling of the St Pierre and Miquelon Salmon Fishery*, NASCO Council doc. CNL (19)19 (2019).

4,727 kg in 2016.[63] NASCO has tried to coax France into joining the Convention on behalf of St. Pierre and Miquelon for almost 20 years through a series of letters.[64] France has consistently refused, referring to the low overall catches at St. Pierre and Miquelon of North American salmon, and instead maintains a preference to participate as an observer which includes providing annual fisheries management and sampling information.[65]

Keeping all relevant jurisdictions aboard the NASCO Convention has also been troublesome. Following a severe economic crisis, Iceland withdrew from NASCO effective December 31, 2009.[66] Subsequently a number of letters have been sent by the President of NASCO to the Icelandic Ministry for Fisheries and Agriculture encouraging Iceland to re-accede to the Convention,[67] but that invitation has yet to be taken up. Iceland has been involved in ranching salmon, and bycatch of salmon in the Icelandic mackerel fishery is a continuing concern.[68]

3.3 *Getting an Effective Grip on Aquaculture*

NASCO faces large challenges in trying to ensure national aquaculture operations do not adversely affect wild salmon populations.[69] NASCO has no regulatory powers over aquaculture and thus has not developed common regulatory standards. Only soft guidelines have been adopted to steer national aquaculture laws and policies.[70]

---

63 Ibid.

64 *Management and Sampling of the St Pierre and Miquelon Salmon Fishery*, NASCO Council doc. CNL (18)17 (2018).

65 Ibid.

66 David L. VanderZwaag and Emily J. Pudden, "The North Atlantic Salmon Conservation Organization (NASCO): Surpassing a 25 Year Voyage in Transboundary Cooperation but Still Confronting a Sea of Challenges," in Dawn A. Russel and David L. VanderZwaag, eds., *Recasting Transboundary Fisheries Management Arrangements in Light of Sustainability Principles: Canadian and International Perspectives* (Leiden: Martinus Nijhoff, 2010), chap.11, 340.

67 *Report on Progress in Implementing the 'Action Plan' for Taking Forward the Recommendations of the External Performance Review and the Review of the 'Next Steps' for NASCO*, NASCO council doc. CNL (18)16 (2018), 16.

68 *Revised Report of the ICES Advisory Committee*, NASCO Council doc. CNL (18)08rev. (2018), 5, 12.

69 Irene Dahl, "Regional Approaches to Aquaculture and a Case Study of the North Atlantic Salmon Conservation Organization," in Nigel Bankes, Irene Dahl and David L. VanderZwaag, eds., *Aquaculture Law and Policy: Global, Regional and National Perspectives* (Cheltenham, UK: Edward Elgar, 2016), 103–129.

70 *See supra*, Minimizing Aquaculture Impacts (discussing NASCO guidelines with respect to aquaculture management).

Direct engagement with the aquaculture industry has been very limited. For nearly a decade, NASCO convened a Liaison Group with the Salmon Farming Industry to discuss impacts of aquaculture on wild salmon, but following major confrontations between NGOs and industry representatives, NASCO in 2013 decided to discontinue the Liaison Group.[71] Instead NASCO has retained an item on its annual agenda, "Liaison with the Salmon Farming Industry," where a representative from the International Salmon Farmers' Association (ISFA) can be invited to participate and share information.[72]

NASCO has also attempted to improve aquaculture management by advancing discussions and understandings of the possible effects of salmonid aquaculture on wild Atlantic salmon populations. For example, in 2016, NASCO's Council held a theme-based special session on the impacts of salmon farming and issued a report highlighting understanding of the impacts of sea lice on wild salmon and the impacts of escaped farmed salmon on the genetic integrity of wild Atlantic salmon.[73] NASCO has also asked ICES to advise on possible effects of salmonid aquaculture. A 2016 ICES report showed that the expanding scale of salmon aquaculture in the North Atlantic, estimated at about 1.5 million tonnes in 2013, exceeded the nominal wild catch in the North Atlantic by over 1,900 times.[74] The report emphasized the widespread introgression of farmed salmon genomes, especially in Norway,[75] and reviewed the varying scientific estimates on marine mortality attributable to sea lice which range from 1% to 20% loss of adult salmon abundance.[76] The ICES report also identified the substantial uncertainties remaining and the knowledge gaps needing to be further addressed.[77]

NASCO has instituted an implementation planning and annual reporting process to pressure Parties to carry out their commitments under the various NASCO agreements and guidelines, including those on aquaculture, but with limited success. Implementation plans have been required over three five-year periods (2007–2012, 2013–2018 and 2019–2024) and the Implementation Plan/ Annual Progress Report Review Group that reviews annual progress reports

71 *Explanatory Memorandum on the Agenda*, NASCO doc. CNL (19)03 (2019), 4.

72 Ibid.

73 *Addressing Impacts of Salmon Farming on Wild Atlantic Salmon: Challenges to and Developments Supporting, Achievement of NASCO's International Goals, Report of a Theme-based Special Session of the Council of NASCO*, NASCO Council doc. CNL (16)60 (2016).

74 ICES, "North Atlantic Salmon Stocks," in *Report of the ICES Advisory Committee 2016*, ICES Advice (2016), book 10, § 10.1.8.

75 Ibid.

76 Ibid.

77 Ibid.

has continually lamented the problem of vague and general reporting on how international goals for sea lice and farmed fish containment are being met.[78] NGOs continue to accuse NASCO parties with major salmon farming industries of prioritizing further expansion of salmon farming at the expense of wild salmon and of giving lip service to NASCO principles.[79]

3.4 *Deciphering the Causes of Severe Population Declines*

An array of threats, besides fishing, are likely at play in Atlantic population declines. Those threats include dams, habitat degradations, disease and predation, water quality deteriorations, aquaculture, artificial propagation, climate change, and competition from other fish species.[80] Low marine survival has been a special concern.[81] The mortality of migrants in saltwater is typically high, ranging from 90% to more than 99%.[82] NASCO has promoted research cooperation into the causes of marine mortality of Atlantic salmon through the establishment of an International Atlantic Salmon Research Board (IASRB) in 2001[83] and its subsequent Salmon at Sea (SALSEA) research program adopted in 2005.[84] However, uncertainties continue to abound over the causes of high marine mortalities, although links to altered trophic dynamics and warming climate have been identified.[85] The latest phase of SALSEA, referred to as SALSEA-Track, is attempting to advance the use of telemetry, such as the use of

78 *See, e.g.*, *Report of the Meeting of the Implementation Plan/Annual Progress Report Review Group for the Review of Annual Progress Reports under the Second Cycle of Reporting (2013–2018)*, NASCO Council doc. CNL (19)12 (2019); *Report of the Meeting of the Implementation Plan/Annual Progress Report Review Group*, NASCO Council doc. CNL (18)13 (2018).

79 *Salmon Farming: NGOs Demand that Governments Honour the Williamsburg Resolution Commitments*, NASCO Council doc. CNL (19)43 (2019); *Salmon Farming: NGOs Demand that Governments Honour the Williamsburg Resolution Commitments*, NASCO Council doc. CNL (18)20 (2018).

80 National Marine Fisheries Service and U.S. Fish and Wildlife Service, *Recovery Plan for the Gulf of Main District Populations Segment of Atlantic Salmon* (Salmo salar), *Final Plan for 2009 ESA Listing* (2019), ix-x.

81 Ibid., ix.

82 Thorstad et al., "Aquatic Nomads," 4.

83 "Scientific Advice & Research," NASCO, http://www.nasco.int/scientificadvice.html.

84 "The SALSEA Programme," ISARB, http://www.nasco.int/sas/salsea.htm.

85 Mark D. Renkawitz et al., "Changing Trophic Structure and Energy Dynamics in the Northwest Atlantic: Implications for Atlantic Salmon Feeding at West Greenland," *Marine Ecology Progress Series* 538 (2015): 197–211; North Pacific Anadromous Fish Commission, *Report of the Proceedings for the IYS Workshop: Toward Effective Coupling of the Science of a Changing Climate with Salmon and People, Santa Barbara, CA, USA, June 27–29, 2018*, NPAFC Technical Rep. 12 (2019), 5–6.

acoustic tags, and to identify key mortality points and the factors causing the mortality.[86]

Another major concern is the impacts of climate change. In May 2017, the ICES Advisory Committee responded to a NASCO special request for advice on the potential future impacts of climate change on salmon stock dynamics with a report highlighting both positive and negative impacts, but again emphasizing the numerous uncertainties.[87] On the positive side, climate change may result in increased growth and production in northern areas[88] and even a range expansion on the northern, western and eastern parts of the range of salmon.[89] On the negative side, the southern range of salmon might be markedly altered with a disappearance of species in the river basins of Portugal, Spain and Southern France.[90] Changes in water temperatures and stream flows may create a mismatch between juvenile emergence and environmental conditions with increased level of early juvenile mortality.[91] Prevalence and virulence of parasites and pathogens might be increased.[92] Expanded competition from non-native species, such as smallmouth bass, might also be expected.[93] The report concluded by emphasizing the many scientific uncertainties, with the greatest uncertainty being the inability to predict sudden large phase-shifts in climate, marine or terrestrial systems.[94]

4 Conclusion

As discussed above, the NASCO story might be described as "mixed" regarding NASCO's ability to ensure the sustainability of wild Atlantic salmon populations. NASCO has demonstrated progress on many fronts including stopping high seas fisheries and encouraging precautionary approaches to fisheries management, aquaculture and habitat protection and restoration. However, NASCO continues to face difficult challenges which include controlling the

86 NASCO, *SALSEA-Track: Innovative Research to Solve the Mystery of Atlantic Salmon Mortality at Sea* (2016), available at http://www.nasco.int/sas/pdf/archive/other_reports/SALSEA_TrackBrochure.pdf.

87 *Report of the ICES Advisory Committee*, NASCO Council doc. CNL (17)8 (2018), § 1.5.

88 Ibid, 107.

89 Ibid, 116.

90 Ibid.

91 Ibid, 108.

92 Ibid, 101.

93 Ibid, 115.

94 Ibid, 117.

harvest of salmon at West Greenland, getting and keeping all the relevant salmon jurisdictions aboard the NASCO Convention, getting an effective grip on aquaculture operations, and deciphering the causes of severe salmon population declines.

Various trends in regional resource management stand out from the NASCO experience.[95] There is a preference for moving incrementally and softly to implement a principled approach to governance. There is a hesitancy to amend the founding Convention even though a 2012 external performance review set out many advantages to be had in modernizing the NASCO Convention and agreeing on a clear legal basis for the evolving obligations and activities under the Convention.[96] There are continuing tensions between national sovereign interests and the appropriate functions and powers for a regional organization. There is a growing recognition of the wide array of human causes and impacts beyond fisheries that need to be addressed.

Various "tweakings" to NASCO efforts and approaches have recently been suggested through a Symposium on Managing Atlantic Salmon in a Rapidly Changing Environment held in Tromsø, Norway in June 2019, ahead of NASCO's annual meeting. The report from the Symposium Steering Committee made 11 recommendations for NASCO, which included: developing a renewed strategy to respond to the challenges facing wild Atlantic salmon and specifically identifying strategic activities to deal with climate change and its cascading effects; updating its 2010 Salmon Habitat Guidelines to better address water quality issues such as toxic substances and diffuse aquaculture pollution; updating its 2004 Social and Economic Factors in Decisions Guidelines to enhance the incorporation of traditional and local knowledge and Indigenous perspectives; strengthening compliance with the agreed international goals of 100% farmed fish containments and 100% of farms to have effective sea lice management; establishing a new goal to prevent the spread of disease pathogens from fish farms; and continuing to support and encourage research on mortality for Atlantic salmon in estuaries and near coastal areas as well as on the high seas.[97]

Some rough voyaging likely lies ahead of NASCO and its efforts to sustain wild Atlantic salmon. NASCO has limited abilities to counter the powerful political and economic currents pushing aquacultural expansions around the

95 VanderZwaag and Pudden, "The North Atlantic Salmon Conservation Organization," 345–46.

96 *NASCO External Performance Review*, NASCO Council doc. CNL (12)11 (2012).

97 *Report of the Tromsø Symposium on the Recommendations to Address Future Management Challenges*, NASCO Council doc. CNL (19)16 (2019).

North Atlantic and coastal developments within national jurisdictions.[98] Even the most valiant fisheries conservation measures may not be able to counter the threats of climate change and ocean acidity to wild salmon where international and national responses to date are still lagging.[99]

Two realities are clear. First, NASCO does not "swim alone" in the quest for sustainable seas and salmon—global and national governance responses are also essential. Second, NASCO, like other regional fisheries management organizations confronting a fast-changing ocean,[100] remains a "work in progress."

98 VanderZwaag and Pudden, "The North Atlantic Salmon Conservation Organization," 346.

99 Cecilia Engler, David L. VanderZwaag and Katja Fennel "Ocean Acidification Post-Paris: Gauging Law and Policy Responses in Light of Evolving Scientific Knowledge," *Ocean Yearbook* 33 (2019): 207–49.

100 Brian Pentz et al., "Can Regional Fisheries Management Organizations (RFMOs) Manage Resources Effectively During Climate Change?" *Marine Policy* 92 (2018): 13–20; Brian Pentz and Nicole Klenk, "The 'Responsiveness Gap' in RFMOS: The Critical Role of Decision-making Policies in the Fisheries Management Response to Climate Change," *Ocean & Coastal Management* 145 (2017) 44–51.

PART 4

Managing Biodiversity as a Common Resource

CHAPTER 7

The Evolution of the Sargasso Sea Regime in International Law

David Balton and David Freestone

This paper looks at the background to the establishment of the Sargasso Sea Commission pursuant to the 2014 Hamilton Declaration on Collaboration for the Conservation of the Sargasso Sea. It reviews the impact of the work of the Sargasso Sea Commission and the Signatory Governments on this unique high seas ecosystem and then reviews some of the possible options for strengthening the role of "Stewardship" which the Hamilton Declaration gives to the Commission. It considers and assesses the advantages and disadvantages of two possible models: the Commission for the Conservation of Antarctic Marine Living Resources (CCAMLR) and the Commission for the Protection of the Marine Environment of the North-East Atlantic (OSPAR). It then considers and assesses a new or hybrid model.

1 Introduction

The Sargasso Sea is a unique and extraordinary ecosystem.[1] Located in the North Atlantic Ocean near Bermuda, the Sargasso is the only sea with no land boundaries, surrounded only by ocean currents.[2] The Sargasso Sea is named for the *Sargassum* seaweed endemic to its waters, which provides exceptional habitat for a rich array of marine species.[3] So biodiverse is the Sargasso that it has been called the "golden floating rainforest of the ocean."[4]

1 This chapter is an updated and expanded version of a report prepared by David Balton in collaboration with the Sargasso Sea Commission Secretariat that was published as David A. Balton "Strengthening the Stewardship of the Sargasso Sea" in *Frontiers in International Environmental Law: Oceans and Climate Challenges. Essays in Honour of David Freestone* (Richard Barnes and Ronán Long, eds.) Leiden and Boston, Brill Nijhoff, 2021, 490–512. The authors are grateful to the publishers for allowing them to republish that chapter in this expanded format.

2 Sargasso Sea Commission, *About the Sargasso Sea* (last accessed Jan. 28, 2020), http://www.sargassoseacommission.org/about-the-sargasso-sea.

3 Ibid.

4 Ibid.

 | DOI:10.1163/9789004514218_009

In 2014, five governments—the Azores, Bermuda, Monaco, the UK and the US—signed the Hamilton Declaration on Collaboration for the Conservation of the Sargasso Sea,[5] which created the Sargasso Sea Commission ("the Commission") to act as a steward of this extraordinary part of the ocean. To date, five additional governments have signed the Declaration, and others may follow.[6] The Commission and the Government Signatories to the Declaration have undertaken a number of steps to promote conservation of the Sargasso Sea, including through interactions with other regional bodies, such as regional fisheries management organizations, and sectoral organizations, such as the International Seabed Authority.

In the few years since the establishment of the Commission, the international community has significantly increased its attention to the serious, interrelated challenges facing the ocean, including unsustainable fisheries, marine pollution, and a range of climate-related threats to the marine environment. The 2017 United Nations Oceans Conference on implementation of Sustainable Development Goal 14, the Our Ocean Conference series,[7] and similar high-level events, have prompted unprecedented commitments from world leaders, philanthropies, the private sector, intergovernmental organizations and civil society groups to enhance the protection of ocean space. This movement will almost certainly continue despite the disruptions caused to public events by the global pandemic. The United Nations Ocean Conference due to reconvene in 2020 will now meet in 2022 in Lisbon "as soon as public health conditions allow".[8] Similarly, the Our Ocean Conference scheduled for Palau in 2020 was postponed but is likely to occur perhaps virtually in 2021 or 2022.[9]

After almost a decade of preliminary discussions, negotiations have also begun on an international legally binding agreement on the conservation and sustainable use of biodiversity in marine areas beyond national jurisdiction (BBNJ).[10] Although the outcome of these negotiations may not become clear

5 Hamilton Declaration on Collaboration for the Conservation of the Sargasso Sea (Mar. 11, 2014), http://www.sargassoseacommission.org/storage/Hamilton_Declaration_with_signatures_April_2018.pdf; *see also* David Freestone & Kate K. Morrison, "The Signing of the Hamilton Declaration on Collaboration for the Conservation of the Sargasso Sea: A new paradigm for high seas conservation?," *International Journal of Marine and Coastal Law* 28 (2014): 345, 354.

6 Ibid.

7 United Nations Ocean Action, https://oceanconference.un.org/oceanaction.

8 https://www.un.org/en/conferences/ocean2022.

9 https://www.ourocean2020.pw/.

10 G.A. Res. 72/249, Intergovernmental Conference on an international legally binding instrument under the United Nations Convention on the Law of the Sea on the conservation

for some time, they nevertheless demonstrate a seriousness of purpose by the international community to address the challenges facing the ocean more effectively.[11]

In this context, the time may be ripe to build on the success of the Hamilton Declaration and the Commission it created with a view to strengthening the stewardship of the Sargasso Sea. This paper outlines a number of possible approaches to achieve this objective, each of which would entail reestablishing the Sargasso Sea Commission as an international organization based on a binding international agreement that confers on the Commission a more robust mandate and international legal personality. One possible model of such an organization is the Commission on the Conservation of Antarctic Marine Living Resources (CCAMLR).[12] Another possible model is the OSPAR Commission.[13] This paper will examine each of these models in turn. It will also consider the possibility of reestablishing the Sargasso Sea Commission based on a hybrid model, or even a completely new model, tailored to the unique circumstances of the Sargasso Sea.

This initiative to strengthen stewardship of the Sargasso Sea is intended to complement, not undermine, the ongoing BBNJ negotiations at the United Nations. Indeed, a successful initiative relating to the Sargasso Sea could provide useful lessons on how to implement ecosystem-based management, how to use environmental impact analyses, and how to develop and apply spatial and temporal measures in a specific ocean area beyond national jurisdiction. It may also have lessons to teach in relation to marine genetic resources, and regional marine science capacity building.

---

and sustainable use of marine biological diversity of areas beyond national jurisdiction (Dec. 24, 2017); *see generally* David Freestone, ed., *Conserving Biodiversity in Areas beyond National Jurisdiction* (Boston & The Hague: Brill Nijhoff, 2019).

11 The Fourth (and final) Session of the Intergovernmental Conference scheduled for 2020 was postponed because of the pandemic and will now take place in 2022. It seems likely that at least one extra session may be necessary to finalize the text of the international legally binding instrument.

12 1980 Convention on the Conservation of Antarctic Marine Living Resources, May 20, 1980, 1329 U.N.T.S. 47, entered into force Apr. 7, 1982.

13 1992 Convention for the Protection of the Marine Environment of the North-East Atlantic, Sept. 22, 1992, 32 I.L.M. 1069, entered into force Mar. 25, 1998 (OSPAR Convention). OSPAR owes its name to the fact that its founding agreement represented a merging of two agreements from the 1970s, the Oslo Convention for the Prevention of Marine Pollution by Dumping for Ships and Aircrafts, and the Paris Convention for the Prevention of Marine Pollution from Land-Based Sources. *See* OSPAR Commission, *About OSPAR* (2020), https://www.ospar.org/about.

2 The Hamilton Declaration and the Sargasso Sea Commission

The Sargasso Sea project began more than a decade ago with the Sargasso Sea Alliance promoting the protection and management of the Sargasso Sea, the "Golden Floating Rainforest of the Atlantic Ocean." The Science Case produced by the Alliance[14] demonstrated that the Sargasso Sea constitutes a unique marine ecosystem, home to numerous endemic species and essential habitat for countless others, including endangered sea turtles, whales and other marine mammals, seabirds and invertebrates, as well as commercially valuable fish such as billfish and tunas.[15] It is also the only known spawning ground of the critically endangered European eel (*Anguilla anguilla*) and the endangered American eel (*A. rostrata*).[16]

The 2011 Science Case identified various threats to the ecosystem, including possible overfishing and destructive fishing practices, shipping-related impacts, pollution, potential sea-bed mining and commercial extraction of *Sargassum*.[17] A variety of organizations have mandates to address some of these threats. While some have taken action, others have not. Moreover, actions by individual organizations are also not taking account of cumulative impacts from all human activities affecting the Sargasso Sea. Indeed, significant gaps exist in the ways in which the mandates of these organizations relate to the Sargasso Sea. These include the lack of any international regime for managing fisheries in most of the Sargasso Sea, with the exception of tuna and tuna-like species managed by the International Commission for the Conservation of Atlantic Tunas (ICCAT),[18] and for fisheries managed by the Northwest Atlantic Fisheries Organization in a small Northern area of the Sargasso Sea above 35°N.[19] Gaps also exist in the regulation of shipping impacts on the marine

14 *See* Dan d'A Laffoley et al., *The Protection and Management of the Sargasso Sea: The Golden Floating Rainforest of the Atlantic Ocean. Summary Science and Supporting Evidence Case* (Washington, DC: Sargasso Sea Alliance, 2011) (Science Case).

15 Ibid.

16 Ibid. For a more recent discussion, see Michael J. Miller et al., "Spawning by the European Eel Across 2000 Km of the Sargasso Sea," *Biology Letters* 15 (2019): 1.

17 Laffoley et al., *Science Case*, 33–36.

18 1966 International Convention for the Conservation of Atlantic Tunas, May 14, 1966, 673 U.N.T.S. 63, entered into force Mar. 21, 1969, available at: https://www.iccat.int/Documents/Commission/BasicTexts.pdf.

19 1979 Convention on Future Multilateral Cooperation in the Northwest Atlantic Fisheries, Oct. 24, 1978, 1285 U.N.T.S. 129, entered into force Mar. 17, 1982. NAFO was founded in 1979 as a successor to the International Commission of the Northwest Atlantic Fisheries (1949–1978) and applies to most fishery resources of the Northwest Atlantic. *See* Northwest Atlantic Fisheries Organization, *History of the Northwest Atlantic Fishery* (2020), https://www.nafo.int/About-us/History.

environment in the Sargasso Sea, including on the *Sargassum* and the habitat protection it provides for many fish and marine mammal species. Also lacking are specific mitigation measures to address the impacts of shipping in the Sargasso Sea.

The idea to develop and sign a political declaration on the conservation of the Sargasso Sea arose in the early days of the Sargasso Sea project in 2010. After the development of a preliminary text by a working group, two negotiating meetings were held in Tarrytown, New York, in November 2012 and December 2013.[20] The choice of a declaration, rather than a binding international agreement, was essentially pragmatic, in that it was seen as a more effective way of developing initial support from concerned governments than attempting a treaty negotiation. Binding agreements can take a long time to negotiate and to enter into force. Moreover, governments may tend to negotiate softer language to reflect their commitments in a text that will be legally binding. Those involved in the early days of the Sargasso Sea project also recognized that it might be possible to start with a political declaration and move to a binding agreement in the future, a scenario that has worked well in other contexts.[21]

Having chosen to develop a political declaration rather than a binding agreement, those involved next turned their attention to the *content* of what was to become the Hamilton Declaration. Once again, they chose to begin with

20 For a more detailed account of these meetings, see David Freestone, "Governance of Areas beyond National Jurisdiction: An Unfinished Agenda?" in Jill Barrett & Richard Barnes, eds., *Law of the Sea: UNCLOS as a Living Treaty*, (London: British Institute of International and Comparative Law, 2016), 231, 259–60. Representatives of 14 governments, plus the Canadian Senate and the EU Commission, as well as of seven international organizations attended one or more of the meetings.

21 For example, governments concerned with marine environmental issues in the Northeast Atlantic first developed and signed declarations in the 1980s and early 1990s regarding the North Sea which were a precursor to the Convention for the Protection of the Marine Environment of the North-East Atlantic, which established OSPAR. The Bremen, London, and Hague Declarations which preceded negotiation of OSPAR can all be found at https://www.ospar.org/about/international-cooperation/north-sea-conferences/ministerial-declarations. Similarly, in the 1990s, governments concerned with reducing the mortality of dolphins in the tuna purse seine fisheries in the Eastern Pacific first developed the Panama Declaration before negotiating the Agreement on the International Dolphin Conservation Program. Rachel C. Hampton, "Of Dolphins and Tuna: The Evolution to an International Agreement," *Fordham Environmental Law Journal* 10 (1998): 99, 139–40. More recently, several governments signed the 2015 Oslo Declaration as a first step toward negotiating the 2018 Agreement to Prevent Unregulated High Seas Fisheries in the Central Arctic Ocean. Valentin A. Schatz et al., "The 2018 Agreement to Prevent Unregulated High Seas Fisheries in the Central Arctic Ocean: A Critical Analysis," *International Journal of Marine and Coastal Law* 34 (2019): 195.

a gentle approach, in hopes of attracting maximum support from relevant governments. This approach emphasized voluntary cooperation among governments in protecting the Sargasso Sea, working within the accepted framework of the 1982 United Nations Convention on the Law of the Sea, and engaging with existing regional and sectoral regimes such as OSPAR, the Cartagena[22] and Abidjan[23] Conventions, regional fisheries management organizations, and the International Seabed Authority, among others. The Hamilton Declaration would not establish a new international organization with the authority to adopt binding measures, nor would it include mandatory financial commitments. The Commission to be created would have an essentially custodial and educative role, would operate under national law rather than international law, and would receive support solely through voluntary contributions.[24]

This approach attracted initial support of five governments that signed the Hamilton Declaration in 2014: the Azores, Bermuda, Monaco, the United Kingdom and the United States. Five additional governments have signed the Declaration subsequently: the British Virgin Islands, the Bahamas, Canada, the Cayman Islands, and the Dominican Republic. The Hamilton Declaration is the first non-binding instrument to establish a framework for its signatory governments to work together through existing international organizations and other partners to minimize the adverse effects of human activities in an ecosystem that lies in an area beyond national jurisdiction (ABNJ).[25]

The Declaration envisages a light institutional structure with a regular Meeting of Signatories,[26] a Commission[27] and a Secretariat "to assist the Commission and the Signatories."[28] The Hamilton Declaration structure is unusual in that not all the Signatory governments represent autonomous States

22 Convention for the Protection and Development of the Marine Environment of the Wider Caribbean Region, available at http://cep.unep.org/cartagena-convention/text-of-the-cartagena-convention.

23 Convention for Co-operation in the Protection and Development of the Marine and Coastal Environment of the West and Central African Region, available at https://www.informea.org/en/treaties/abidjan-convention/text.

24 Sargasso Sea Project Inc is a not-for-profit US 501(c)(3) company registered in New York and Sargasso Sea Commission was registered as a Bermudian Charity in 2015.

25 *See* David Freestone & Faith Bulger, "The Sargasso Sea Commission: An Innovative Approach to the Conservation of Areas Beyond National Jurisdiction," *Ocean Yearbook* 30 (2016): 80.

26 Hamilton Declaration, ¶ 5.

27 Ibid., ¶ 6 ("The Commission would, at the outset, be established under Bermudian law."). Pursuant to this provision, the Commission is now a charitable company established in Bermuda. http://www.sargassoseacommission.org/support-our-work/charitable-status.

28 Ibid., ¶ 6.

and that the Sargasso Sea Commission is not composed of representatives of the participating governments. Instead it provides that the Government of Bermuda, after consultation with the Signatories and Collaborating Partners, will establish the Commission "composed of distinguished scientists and other persons of international repute committed to the conservation of high seas ecosystems that would serve in their personal capacity."[29] Not only do the Commission members not represent the Signatory governments, they do not even need to hold their nationality.[30] The role of the Commission members, as set out in Annex II of the Declaration, is to "exercise a stewardship role for the Sargasso Sea and keep its health, productivity and resilience under continual review."[31] The Commissioners serve three-year renewable terms, although the terms of the first Commissioners were staggered to ensure regular rotation. The first five Commissioners were appointed by the Bermuda Cabinet in August 2014[32] and appointments have been made annually since then.

3 The Work of the Sargasso Sea Commission

The technocratic commission-based approach described above has yielded significant early benefits.[33] The Sargasso Sea initiative has gained widespread recognition of the need to protect and preserve "the golden floating rainforest of the Atlantic." For example, in successive years since 2012, the United Nations General Assembly has included references to the Sargasso Sea and, since 2017, the Commission, in its annual resolutions on the Oceans and Law of the Sea.[34]

29 Hamilton Declaration, ¶ 6.

30 For example, Professor Dire Tladi of South Africa—which is not a Signatory Government —was a member of the first Commission appointed in August 2014. Greenrock.org, Appointment of the Sargasso Sea Commission, Aug. 18, 2014, https://www.greenrock.org/news/82-bermuda/528-sargasso-sea-commission.

31 Hamilton Declaration, 361.

32 The first Commissioners were: Dr Billy Causey (US), Professor Howard Roe (UK), Professor Ricardo Serrão Santos (Azores), Professor Dire Tladi (South Africa) and Dr Tammy Trott (Bermuda). *See* Royal Gazette, *Local biologist appointed to Sargasso Sea Commission* (Aug. 6, 2014), http://www.royalgazette.com/article/20140806/NEWS/140809882.

33 For a comprehensive review of the work of the Commission see Kristina M. Gjerde and Ole Varmer, "The Sargasso Sea: An Innovative Approach to Governance in Areas beyond National Jurisdiction" in *Frontiers in International Environmental Law: Oceans and Climate Challenges. Essays in Honour of David Freestone* (Richard Barnes and Ronán Long, eds.) Leiden and Boson Brill Nijhoff, 2021, 446–489.

34 *See, e.g.*, G.A. Res 67/78, Oceans and the Law of the Sea, at ¶ 199 (Dec. 11, 2012) (proposed by the United Kingdom, the United States and South Africa); G.A. Res 68/70, at ¶ 215 (Dec. 9, 2013) (proposed by the United Kingdom, the United States and the Bahamas); G.A. Res

The Sargasso Sea received a dedicated chapter—the only named ecosystem chapter in the volume—in the first United Nations Ocean Assessment in 2015. Commissioner Howard Roe, the lead author of that chapter,[35] coordinated an updated contribution to the Second Assessment, published in 2021.[36]

The Commission's first major achievement came in 2012. At the Wider Caribbean and Western Mid-Atlantic Regional Workshop on Ecologically and Biologically Significant (Marine) Areas (EBSAs) held in Recife, Brazil in February/March of 2012, the Government of Bermuda, on behalf of the Sargasso Sea project, put forward a proposal for the "description" of the Sargasso Sea as an Ecologically or Biologically Significant Marine Area (EBSA) under the Convention on Biological Diversity (CBD). The case was discussed and adopted by the scientists at the workshop, then forwarded as part of the Workshop Report to the CBD Subsidiary Body on Scientific, Technical and Technological Advice (SBSTTA) meeting in April 2012, and, ultimately, the Eleventh Session of the Conference of Parties (COP 11) in Hyderabad in October 2012, where it was officially described as an EBSA.[37]

The Commission has also established a network of bilateral links with key organizations with related competencies or similar objectives. The Commission has formal Observer status with the Northwest Atlantic Fisheries Organization (NAFO), with the International Seabed Authority (ISA)—with which it signed an MOU in 2020, the Western Central Atlantic Fisheries Commission (WECAFC) and the Inter-American Convention for the Protection and Conservation of Sea Turtles (IAC). It has a Collaboration Arrangement with OSPAR dating from 2011, which is being updated, and a 2017 MOU with the UN Environment Programme in relation to the West African Abidjan and the Wider Caribbean Cartagena

69/245, at ¶ 231 (Dec. 29, 2014) (proposed by South Africa and the Bahamas, supported by the United Kingdom, the United States and Monaco); GA Res 70/235, at ¶ 302 (Dec. 23, 2015) (proposed by South Africa and the Bahamas, supported by the United Kingdom, the United States and Monaco); GA Res 71/257, at ¶ 329 (Dec. 23, 2016) (proposed by the Bahamas, supported by the United Kingdom, the United States and Monaco); GA Res 72/73, at ¶ 342 (Dec. 5, 2017) (proposed by the Bahamas, supported by the United Kingdom, the United States and Monaco); Sargasso Sea Commission, *Our Work: United Nations General Assembly*, http://www.sargassoseacommission.org/about-our-work/relevant-organizations/united-nations-general-assembly.

35 United Nations, The First Global Integrated Marine Assessment: World Ocean Assessment I (2016), Chapter 50, available at https://www.un.org/depts/los/global_reporting/WOA_RPROC/Chapter_50.pdf.

36 Chapter 7Q in https://www.un.org/regularprocess/sites/www.un.org.regularprocess/files/2011859-e-woa-ii-vol-i.pdf.

37 CDB Dec. XI/17, Marine and coastal biodiversity: ecologically or biologically significant marine areas (Dec. 5, 2012), item 13, at 23.

Conventions—its closest Regional Seas Programmes. The Commission is in the process of negotiating MOUs with both NAFO and ICCAT. In addition, the Commission also has more than 30 formal Collaborating Partners (envisaged by ¶ 11 of the Hamilton Declaration),[38] as well as a number of Programmatic Partners.[39]

Since 2010, representatives of the Sargasso Sea project and the Sargasso Sea Commission have attended the annual round of meetings of ICCAT and its scientific bodies. Nearly twenty major research papers have been contributed to the ecosystem subcommittee of the Standing Committee on Research and Statistics (SCRS or the Science Body), and the government of Bermuda—with Commission support—has proposed two resolutions relating to the Sargasso Sea, both of which were adopted after some amendment in the Commission plenary sessions.[40]

The most recent Resolution, 16–23, provided that the Science Body would "examine the available information" on pelagic ecosystems important to ICCAT species, such as the Sargasso Sea.[41]

The Commission ICCAT team is currently working on extending the indicator-based ecosystem report card developed by the Science Body's ecosystem sub-committee to the Sargasso Sea.[42]

The Commission has also established itself as a leader in Anguillid eel conservation. The International Union for the Conservation of Nature (IUCN) Red List categorizes the American eel (*Anguilla rostrata*) as endangered and the European eel (*A. anguilla*) as critically endangered.[43] Both species are

38 Sargasso Sea Commission, *About the Commission: Collaborating Partners* (last accessed Jan. 28, 2020), http://www.sargassoseacommission.org/about-the-commission/collaborating-partners.

39 Sargasso Sea Commission, *About the Commission: Programmatic Partners* (last accessed Jan. 28, 2020), http://www.sargassoseacommission.org/about-the-commission/programmatic-partners.

40 ICCAT Res. 12–12, Resolution by ICCAT on the Sargasso Sea (2012); ICCAT Res. 16–23, Resolution by ICCAT on Ecosystems that are Important and Unique for ICCAT Species (2016).

41 ICCAT Res. 16/23, which continues:

1. As part of advancing the work of Ecosystem Based Fisheries Management, the SCRS will examine the available information on the trophic ecology of pelagic ecosystems that are important and unique for ICCAT species in the Convention Area.
2. The SCRS will provide an update on the progress of this work in 2018 and report back to the Commission with available findings in 2019, if possible.

42 L.T. Kell & B.E. Luckhurst "Extending the Indicator-Based Ecosystem Report Card to the Whole Ecosystem; a Preliminary Example Based on the Sargasso Sea," *Collective Volumes of Scientific Papers, ICCAT*, 75 (2018): 258–275; L.T.Kell, B.E. Luckhurst & A. Leach, "Toward Ecosystem-Based Fisheries Management in the Sargasso Sea," SCRS/2019/055.

43 The Red List can be found at https://www.iucnredlist.org/.

catadromous, spending most of their life stages in fresh or brackish waters but returning to the North Atlantic Subtropical Gyre around the Sargasso Sea to spawn. In 2014, the Sargasso Sea project commissioned a science report to support the listing of the European Eel under Appendix II to the Convention on Migratory Species (CMS).[44] Such a listing is appropriate if the species has an "unfavourable conservation status" and if its conservation status "would significantly benefit from the international cooperation that could be achieved by an international agreement."[45] The Government of the Principality of Monaco, as a signatory to the Hamilton Declaration in March 2014, put forward the report on behalf of the Commission, first to the CMS Science Council, and subsequently to the CMS 11th Conference of the Parties (COP 11) in Quito in November 2014, where it was approved.[46]

Since the report was approved, the SSC Secretariat in collaboration with the CMS Secretariat has hosted three Range States Workshops on the European Eel: in Galway, Ireland in October 2016; and in Malmo, Sweden in May 2018 and June 2019.[47] At the June 2019 workshop, Range States supported the development of a Single Species Action Plan for the European Eel, while remaining open to the idea of extending the scope of any conservation initiative to other Anguillid species, such as the American Eel (*Anguilla rostrata*). A proposal to this effect was presented by the government of Monaco to the CMS COP 13 in Gandhinagar, India, 16–22 February, 2020 where it was approved.[48]

---

44 Prepared by Dr. Matthew Gollock and Dr David Jacoby of the Zoological Society of London. Dr Gollock is chair of the IUCN Anguillid specialist group. Their report is attached to the Monaco proposal at http://files.ctctcdn.com/dc8f5ce3201/1bd104b6-95a3-4804-9e23-762a3e50a562.pdf.

45 Convention on the Conservation of Migratory Species of Wild Animals, Art. IV, ¶ 1, June 23, 1979, 19 I.L.M. 15, 1651 U.N.T.S. 28,395.

46 Convention on Migratory Species, 11th Meeting of the Conference of the parties, Agenda Item 24.1.1: Proposal for the Inclusion of the European Eel (*Anguilla Anguilla*) on CMS Appendix II (Quito, Ecuador, Nov. 4-9, 2014), available at: https://www.cms.int/sites/default/files/document/Doc_24_1_18_Prop_II_12_Rev.1_Anguilla_anguilla_%28European_eel%29_MCO_E.pdf.

47 In November/December 2017 in Stockholm, the SSC co-hosted a Regional Workshop on Eel and the Baltic Sea, see Helsinki Commission, *HELCOM Workshop on Eel and the Baltic Sea* (last accessed Jan. 28, 2020), https://portal.helcom.fi/meetings/fish-m%205-2017-492/default.aspx, and, in April 2018, the SSC also hosted a Workshop of Range States of the American Eel, in Santo Domingo, Dominican Republic. *See* Sargasso Sea Commission, *About Our Work: American Eel Range State Workshops* (last accessed Jan. 28, 2020), http://www.sargassoseacommission.org/about-our-work/workshops/american-eel-range-states-workshop.

48 UNEP/CMS/COP13/Doc.26.2.9.

In September 2012, shortly after the CBD EBSA description, the NAFO Scientific Council was formally asked, on behalf the Sargasso Sea project, to comment and advise on whether the Sargasso Sea provides forage area or habitat for living marine resources that could be impacted by different types of fishing, and on whether there is a need for any closure to protect this ecosystem. After some considerable internal discussion, in late 2016 NAFO agreed to the closure of seamounts (including those in the Sargasso Sea EBSA) to deep sea bottom fishing through 2020 and included restrictions on the use of certain types of mid-water trawling gear in the areas near those seamounts.[49] This decision by NAFO is the first legally binding measure that the Sargasso Sea initiative has achieved. Or, to put it in a less positive way, after nearly a decade of work the project has secured only this one binding measure to protect the Sargasso Sea.

In the meantime, however, the threats to the Sargasso Sea have not diminished, nor has the Sargasso Sea Commission been able to mitigate the major sources of those threats. Since the publication of the 2011 Science Case, human activities have continued to adversely affect the Sargasso Sea. Satellite surveillance using Automatic Identification System (AIS) records has found increases in fishing activity, primarily in the northeastern part of the Sargasso Sea, and marked increases in shipping frequency, primarily in the southern part.[50]

The Sargasso Sea will also likely feel the effects of a previously rare form of *Sargassum* (*natans VIII*) that has created huge inundations on beaches in

49 At the NAFO 37th Annual Meeting in Halifax, the NAFO members agreed, with effect from 2017, to: "(1) prohibit the use of attachments of mid-water trawling gear that could damage or touch the seabed, and required all Vulnerable Marine Ecosystem indicator species caught during mid-water trawling be reported; (2) agreed to close completely all seamounts in the NAFO area to bottom trawling activities until the end of 2020 by prohibiting bottom trawling exemptions for exploratory fishing." Kristina M. Gjerde and Ole Varmer, "The Sargasso Sea," in Richard Barnes and Ronán Long (eds.), *Frontiers in International Environmental Law: Oceans and Climate Challenges* (Leiden: Koninklijke Brill 2021), 446, 462. According to Daniela Diz, "[t]his is an important development in international environmental law and the law of the sea, as it brings together two biodiversity concepts, namely the FAO's vulnerable marine ecosystems (VMEs) and the Convention on Biological Diversity's (CBD) ecologically or biologically significant marine areas (EBSAs)." Daniela Diz, "The Seamounts of the Sargasso Sea: Adequately Protected?," *International Journal of Marine and Coastal Law* 31 (2016): 359.

50 Paul Woods, Global Fishing Watch, "Monitoring Human Activities in the Sargasso Sea," Presentation at the Sargasso Sea Commission Bermuda Conference (Mar. 13, 2019), available at http://www.sargassoseacommission.org/storage/GFW_-_Sargasso_Sea_Commission_March_2019_2_1.pdf.

the Caribbean, the United States, West Africa and South America since 2011.[51] While this form of *Sargassum* remains rare in the Sargasso Sea, inundations in nearby areas are likely to affect the Sargasso Sea by, for example, preventing endangered sea turtles that spend part of their life cycle in the Sargasso Sea from nesting on the affected beaches. These new inundations highlight the importance of maintaining conservation over as wide an area as possible.[52]

The Sargasso Sea Commission has also been unable to prevent the continued decline of the European and American eels, two of the most iconic species in the Sargasso Sea. While recent research has confirmed the importance of the North Atlantic Gyre and the Sargasso Sea for spawning,[53] both species remain endangered, both have suffered major drops in recruitment, and both show marked declines in numbers of larvae in the Sargasso Sea.[54] The causes of these declines are complex, involving factors within and outside the Sargasso Sea. As currently configured, the Sargasso Sea Commission lacks the mandate to develop and implement conservation measures within the spawning area of these species in the Sargasso Sea, which could complement conservation measures elsewhere and greatly enhance protection of both species.

The other marked change in recent years is increased pollution, particularly the level of plastic pollution in the Sargasso Sea. Plastic is now ubiquitous in the ocean. Because of the concentrating effect of ocean circulation patterns, it accumulates particularly in the ocean gyres, including the Sargasso Sea. An estimated 56,000 tons of floating plastic were found in the Sargasso Sea in 2014.[55] Almost certainly there is more now.[56] The impacts of plastics, especially microplastics, on oceanic ecosystems are not fully understood, but

---

51 Linda A. Amural-Zettler et al., "Comparative Mitochondrial and Chloroplast Genomics of a Genetically Distinct Form of Sargassum Contributing to Recent "Golden Tides" in the Western Atlantic," *Ecology and Evolution* 7 (2017): 516.

52 Taylor Sehein et al., "Connectivity in the Slender Sargassum Shrimp (*Latreutes fucorum*) : Implications for a Sargasso Sea Protected Area," *Journal of Plankton Research* 36 (2014): 1408; C. L. Huffard et al., "Pelagic Sargassum community change over a 40-year period : temporal and spatial variability," *Marine Biology* 161 (2014): 2735.

53 Miller et al., "Spawning by the European Eel," 1.

54 R. Hanel et al., "Low Larval Abundance in the Sargasso Sea: New Evidence About Reduced Recruitment of the Atlantic Eels," *The Science of Nature* 101 (2014): 1041; Michael J. Miller et al., "Did a 'Perfect Storm' of Oceanic Changes and Continental Anthropogenic Impacts Cause Northern Hemisphere Anguillid Recruitment Reductions?" *ICES Journal of Marine Science* 73 (2016): 43.

55 Marcus Eriksen et al., "Plastic Pollution in the World's Oceans: More than 5 Trillion Plastic Pieces Weighing over 250,000 Tons Afloat at Sea," *PLOS One* 9 (2014): 1.

56 Jenna R. Jambeck et al., "Marine pollution. Plastic waste inputs from land into the ocean," *Science* 347 (2015): 768.

their effect on already reduced eel populations and other sensitive species is unlikely to be positive.

In light of these persistent and growing threats, the limitations of the Hamilton Declaration, and the limited mandate of the Sargasso Sea Commission, are becoming more obvious. The Commission's lack of authority to adopt binding decisions means that it cannot truly act as a steward of the Sargasso Sea directly, as more robust international regimes, such a CCAMLR or OSPAR (discussed below), have done for other areas of the ocean. The Commission can only seek to influence other organizations that do have such authority, organizations that, by their own terms, have missions that do not focus on the stewardship of the Sargasso Sea. Hence, it seems likely that the ability of the Commission to broker comprehensive solutions working in partnership with existing organizations would be strengthened if it had a legally binding mandate. A new mandate could also address the gaps not covered by other organizations.

A number of changes to the legal structure and mandate of the Commission might well be needed to make it a more effective vehicle for stewardship of the Sargasso Sea. The most significant would entail replacing the Hamilton Declaration with a legally binding agreement that would give its Parties, acting through the Commission, authorities that are presently lacking.

An opportunity to review the current Hamilton Declaration arrangements will arise in the near future. In June 2020 the GEF Council approved a proposal, as part of the FAO "Common Ocean" Program, for a four-year grant of $3 million dollars to the Sargasso Sea Commission to conduct a comprehensive Ecosystem Diagnostic Analysis (EDA) of the whole Sargasso Sea ecosystem. This EDA will be followed by and inform the development of a Strategic Action Programme (SAP) for future collective action. The objective of the SAP that will need to be formally approved by all the partners will be to develop a future framework for the sustainable conservation and governance of the Sargasso Sea. This project is the first to be focused on a high sea ecosystem to be financed by the GEF.[57] Part of the project will be to explore any existing

57 The GEF project is also supported by a parallel project financed by the French Global Environment Fund (*Fonds Francais pour l'Environnement Mondial*—FFEM) which is looking at hybrid systems of governance for high seas areas. The Sargasso Sea and the Central American Thermal Dome are the areas under investigation in that project. See further David Freestone, "The Sargasso Sea Commission: An Evolving New Paradigm for High Seas Ecosystem Governance?" in "Challenges and Opportunities in Regional Governance of Ocean Ecosystems" *Frontiers in Marine Science* (2021) 8:668253. doi: 10.3389/fmars.2021.668253 1-10.

deficiencies in the existing governance of the ecosystem and to consider alternatives for the future.

The discussion below explores three options for recasting the Sargasso Sea Commission as a more robust body through which to strengthen stewardship of the Sargasso Sea. Others may, of course, also exist.

4 Options for Strengthening Stewardship of the Sargasso Sea

Several different types of international bodies exist through which States jointly govern some uses of some parts of the world's oceans, including some areas beyond national jurisdiction. Some of these bodies—regional fisheries management organizations (RFMOs)—have mandates focused on fisheries management. Others are devoted to marine environmental protection, marine scientific research or capacity building for developing States. This section will focus on two organizations that offer particularly attractive models, the Commission for the Conservation of Antarctic Marine Living Resources (CCAMLR) and the Commission for the Protection of the Marine Environment of the North-East Atlantic (OSPAR), before considering possibilities for novel or hybrid structures.

5 CCAMLR as a Possible Model

CCAMLR was established by international convention that entered into force in 1982.[58] Its objective is to conserve Antarctic marine life.[59] The ocean space that is within the purview of CCAMLR, known as the CAMLR Convention Area, covers more than 35 million square kilometers—roughly 10 percent of all ocean space on the planet. The definition of the Convention area refers to the Antarctic Convergence as one of its limits—making it the first to be defined by a moveable ecosystem.[60]

58 The Convention on the Conservation of Antarctic Marine Living Resources was adopted at the Conference on the Conservation of Antarctic Marine Living Resources, which met at Canberra, Australia, 7–20 May 1980. Convention on the Conservation of Antarctic Marine Living Resources, Aug. 1, 1980, 1329 U.N.T.S. 48 (entered into force Apr. 7, 1982). The Convention has 33 articles and an Annex concerning the resolution of disputes through an arbitral tribunal.

59 Ibid., Art. II, ¶ 1.

60 Specifically, the CAMLR Convention applies to the Antarctic marine living resources of the area south of 60° South latitude and to the Antarctic marine living resources of

CCAMLR currently has 26 Members.[61] Additional States may join CCAMLR by acceding to the Convention.[62] CCAMLR Members meet at least annually to consider and adopt conservation measures for the CCAMLR Convention Area, based on the best available scientific information.[63] The primary focus of CCAMLR relates to fisheries conservation and management, particularly fisheries for krill and toothfish, but CCAMLR differs from traditional RFMOs in that it has a mandate to conserve a wide array of marine living resources—and the marine ecosystem as a whole—within its Convention Area.[64] Using its broad authority, CCAMLR has on more than one occasion established marine protected areas (MPAs), including the Ross Sea Marine Protected Area—the largest MPA in the world.[65]

Although the CCAMLR Convention was adopted as a distinct treaty, it constitutes part of a suite of treaties and other arrangements and understandings that, together, form the Antarctic Treaty System.[66] The Convention establishes

---

the area between that latitude and the Antarctic Convergence which form part of the Antarctic marine ecosystem. Ibid., Art. I, ¶ 1.

61 CCAMLR's current Members are Argentina, Australia, Belgium, Brazil, Chile, China, the European Union, France, Germany, India, Italy, Japan, the Republic of Korea, Namibia, the Netherlands, New Zealand, Norway, Poland, the Russian Federation, South Africa, Spain, Sweden, Ukraine, United Kingdom, United States, and Uruguay. Commission for the Conservation of Antarctic Marine Living Resources, Members, https://www.ccamlr.org/en/organisation/members.

62 CCAMLR, Art. XXIX, ¶ 1.

63 Ibid., Art. XIII, ¶ 2; Art. IX, ¶ 1(f).

64 Art I, ¶ (3) of CAMLR provides that "[t]he Antarctic marine ecosystem means the complex of relationships of Antarctic marine living resources with each other and with their physical environment." CCAMLR has authority to manage all Antarctic populations of finfish, mollusks, crustaceans and seabirds within the Convention Area. Ibid., Art. I, ¶ 2. Its authority does not include the management of whales or seals, ibid., Art. VI, or other human activities, such as shipping or seabed mining. As part of the Antarctic Treaty System, CCAMLR contributed to efforts to secure a ban on the use and carriage of heavy fuel oil by ships sailing in waters south of 60° adopted by the IMO in 2011, but has otherwise not had much interaction with the IMO. Unlike the Sargasso Sea, the Southern Ocean has very little vessel activity unrelated to fishing (managed by CCAMLR) or tourism (managed under the Antarctic Treaty). Also unlike the Sargasso Sea, there is little near-term prospect for deep seabed mining in the CCAMLR Convention Area. The ISA has granted three exploration contracts on the Mid-Atlantic Ridge adjacent to the Sargasso Sea, see https://www.isa.org.jm/exploration-contracts.

65 Commission for the Conservation of Antarctic Marine Living Resources, *CCAMLR to create world's largest Marine Protected Area* (Feb. 24, 2017), https://www.ccamlr.org/en/news/2016/ccamlr-create-worlds-largest-marine-protected-area.

66 International Science Council, Scientific Committee on Antarctic Research, The Antarctic Treaty System, https://www.scar.org/policy/antarctic-treaty-system/.

the Commission under Article VII,[67] and authorizes the Commission, *inter alia*, to:

- engage in scientific research on Antarctic marine living resources and the Antarctic marine ecosystem;
- collect and disseminate relevant data;
- identify conservation needs and analyze the effectiveness of its conservation measures;
- adopt conservation measures on the basis of the best scientific evidence available; and
- implement a system of observation and inspection.[68]

In practical terms, CCAMLR has succeeded in developing and adopting science-based measures to manage Antarctic fisheries and to protect the affected ecosystems from illegal, unreported and unregulated (IUU) fishing and other unsustainable fishing practices. It has advanced approaches to ecosystem-based management and, as noted above, created several marine protected areas, including the world's largest MPA.

CCAMLR has created a series of Working Groups, including on ecosystem monitoring and management, fish stock assessment, statistics and modeling, and incidental mortality. CCAMLR adopts conservation measures and other substantive decisions by consensus, often on the recommendation of one or more of its Working Groups. CCAMLR members must implement adopted measures, although the Convention does permit individual members to "opt out" of specific decisions (a right that CCAMLR members have rarely exercised).[69]

---

67 CCAMLR, art VII, ¶ 2 provides:

Membership in the Commission shall be as follows:

(a) each Contracting Party which participated in the meeting at which this Convention was adopted shall be a Member of the Commission;

(b) each State Party which has acceded to this Convention pursuant to Article XXIX shall be entitled to be a Member of the Commission during such time as that acceding Party is engaged in research or harvesting activities in relation to the marine living resources to which this Convention applies;

(c) each regional economic integration organisation which has acceded to this Convention pursuant to Article XXIX shall be entitled to be a Member of the Commission during such time as its States members are so entitled; (d) a Contracting Party seeking to participate in the work of the Commission pursuant to sub-paragraphs (b) and (c) above shall notify the Depositary of the basis upon which it seeks to become a Member of the Commission and of its willingness to accept conservation measures in force. The Depositary shall communicate to each Member of the Commission such notification and accompanying information.

68 Ibid., art. IX.

69 CCAMLR art IX, ¶ 6 provides:

The Convention also establishes a Scientific Committee as a forum for consultation and cooperation concerning the collection, study and exchange of information with respect to Antarctic marine living resources.[70] The Scientific Committee has a mandate, *inter alia*, to:

- assess the status and trends the populations of Antarctic marine living resources;
- analyze data concerning the effects of harvesting on those populations;
- assess the effects of proposed changes in the harvesting and other proposed conservation measures;
- transmit assessments, analyses, reports and recommendations to the Commission; and
- formulate proposals for the conduct of programs of research into Antarctic marine living resources.[71]

CCAMLR members share the costs of the Secretariat and other elements of the CCAMLR budget in accordance with a formula based in part on the value of living marine resources each member harvests and in part on equal sharing among all Members. The annual budget for CCAMLR in 2021 was just over 4 million USD.

Conservation measures adopted by the Commission in accordance with this Convention shall be implemented by Members of the Commission in the following manner:

(a) the Commission shall notify conservation measures to all Members of the Commission;

(b) conservation measures shall become binding upon all Members of the Commission 180 days after such notification, except as provided in subparagraphs (c) and (d) below;

(c) if a Member of the Commission, within ninety days following the notification specified in sub-paragraph (a), notifies the Commission that it is unable to accept the conservation measure, in whole or in part, the measure shall not, to the extent stated, be binding upon that Member of the Commission;

(d) in the event that any Member of the Commission invokes the procedure set forth in sub-paragraph (c) above, the Commission shall meet at the request of any Member of the Commission to review the conservation measure. At the time of such meeting and within thirty days following the meeting, any Member of the Commission shall have the right to declare that it is no longer able to accept the conservation measure, in which case the Member shall no longer be bound by such a measure.

70 Ibid., art. XIV.

71 Ibid.

6 Comparing the CCAMLR and Sargasso Sea Contexts

The CCAMLR and Sargasso Sea contexts have important similarities. Both ocean spaces are highly productive ecosystems that are particularly vulnerable to degradation through human activity. CCAMLR, like the Sargasso Sea Commission, operates within the international framework of the 1982 UN Convention on the Law of the Sea and interacts with other international bodies whose mandates extend into the Convention Area, such as the International Maritime Organization. In addition, two of the governments that signed the Hamilton Declaration—the United Kingdom and the United States—are also involved in CCAMLR.[72]

As noted above, CCAMLR has broad legal authority to act as a steward for almost all living marine resources in its Convention Area, and in a sense for Antarctic marine ecosystems as a whole, authority that the Sargasso Sea Commission presently lacks. Mostly, however, CCAMLR exercises its authority by engaging in fisheries management. In doing so, CCAMLR does not face any challenge from other entities with responsibilities for living marine resources, as it is the only international body in its region with a mandate for fisheries management.

The circumstances of the Sargasso Sea are quite different in this regard. At least two existing RFMOs—ICCAT and NAFO—already have responsibility for fisheries management in some or all of the waters within the Sargasso Sea.[73] Were the Sargasso Sea Commission to become a "CCAMLR for the Sargasso Sea" and seek to manage fisheries in those waters, its mandate might be likely to come into conflict, or at least overlap, with the mandates of ICCAT and NAFO.

One solution to this overlap would be to limit the fisheries management authorities of an enhanced Sargasso Sea Commission to those that are outside the respective mandates of ICCAT and NAFO—i.e., to fill the "gap" in fisheries management left open by the respective mandates of ICCAT and NAFO. For example, if the fisheries management responsibilities of the Sargasso Sea Commission were restricted to fisheries for species other than tunas and tuna-like species, there would be no conflict with ICCAT, at least in principle.[74]

72 Canada has also attended CCAMLR meetings as an observer.

73 In theory, the North Atlantic Salmon Conservation Organization has responsibility for managing salmon resources in the North Atlantic north of 36 degrees north latitude, which covers a portion of the Sargasso Sea. However, there are no actual salmon fisheries taking place within the Sargasso Sea.

74 Amendments to the ICCAT Convention approved in 2019, assuming they enter into force, will marginally broaden ICCAT's mandate, giving it express authority to manage fisheries

Similarly, if the enhanced Sargasso Sea Commission had responsibility for managing fisheries only in the waters south of the NAFO Convention Area, once again there would be no conflict with NAFO, at least in principle.

In any event, the CCAMLR model could prove useful in the Sargasso Sea context inasmuch as an enhanced Sargasso Sea Commission could take on the other aspects of CCAMLR's role. For example, the Commission could assume more robust authorities to:

- engage in scientific research on all marine living resources in the Sargasso Sea and on the Sargasso Sea ecosystem as a whole;
- collect and disseminate relevant data;
- identify conservation needs and analyze the effectiveness of conservation measures;
- except as noted above in relation to ICCAT and NAFO, adopt conservation measures with respect to human activities, including the establishment of marine protected areas, on the basis of the best scientific evidence available; and
- implement a system of observation and inspection.

An enhanced Sargasso Sea Commission could have a number of subsidiary bodies similar to the Working Groups of CCAMLR. It could also have a formal Scientific Committee and a larger Secretariat to deal with the additional administrative matters that its broader mandate would entail.

7 Implementing the CCAMLR Model

To transform the Sargasso Sea Commission into an international organization similar to CCAMLR, governments concerned would need to negotiate a binding international agreement with at least the following basic elements:

Objective. The objective of the agreement should be broad enough to provide a mandate for the strengthened Commission to fill current gaps in protection and management of marine resources and species (e.g., for fisheries taking place south of the NAFO Convention Area and for species not within ICCAT's mandate, such as dorado, wahoo and most sharks; also for non-fish

for tuna and tuna-like species as well as for elasmobranchs that are oceanic, pelagic, and highly migratory (mostly certain sharks and rays). ICCAT will also have a mandate to promote the conservation of other species that are associated with, or dependent on, tuna and tuna-like species and the covered elasmobranchs. ICCAT, Doc. No. PLE_108 / 2019, Nov. 7, 2019.

species such as turtles and marine mammals), and to deal with cumulative impacts of other human activities.[75] One approach would be to borrow language from the CCAMLR Convention, which has as its object "the conservation of Antarctic marine living resources."[76] Another approach would be to use even broader language, e.g., an objective "to protect and preserve the marine ecosystem(s) of the Sargasso Sea."

Agreement Area. Many international agreements establishing regional organizations contain specific language identifying the area in question. For the Sargasso Sea, such language could draw from Annex I of the Hamilton Declaration. At present, the Hamilton Declaration defines the Sargasso Sea to exclude any area under national jurisdiction, including around Bermuda. In negotiating a new international agreement to replace the Hamilton Declaration, one issue would be whether the agreement would also apply to waters under national jurisdiction around Bermuda and/or other areas under national jurisdiction.

Establishment and Mandate of the Sargasso Sea Commission and Possible Subsidiary Bodies. The agreement could formally reestablish the Commission as an international organization with legal personality under international law. The Commission could have a precise mandate, along the lines discussed above, set forth in the agreement. The agreement could also establish one or more subsidiary bodies, such as a Scientific Committee with its own mandate, or simply authorize the Commission to establish such subsidiary bodies as the Parties may agree in the future. The agreement could also formally establish a Secretariat.

Commitments of the Parties. The agreement would presumably commit its parties to attend regular meetings, implement agreed measures, share in the financing of the Commission and its Secretariat, and settle any disputes amicably through agreed means.

Relationship with Other International Bodies. Given the complex relationships that the enhanced Commission could expect to have with other existing (and possibly future) organizations, the agreement could contain provisions outlining the nature of those relationships.

Final Clauses. Like other international agreements, provisions would be necessary to identify eligible parties and to address issues concerning signature

75 As noted immediately above, the ICCAT Convention is in the process of being amended, and will include some sharks and rays, in its mandate, but not all species. These amendments may take some time to come into force.

76 CCAMLR, art. II, ¶ 1.

and entry into force, amendment, withdrawal and/or termination, and identification of a depositary, among other things.

8 Advantages of Pursuing the CCAMLR Approach

The primary advantage of using CCAMLR as a model arises from the general recognition that CCAMLR is one of the most successful ocean governance regimes in existence today.[77] CCAMLR's actions in conserving the marine environment around Antarctica based on sound science deserve very significant credit. CCAMLR also boasts the creation of the world's largest marine protected area, and pioneered certain fisheries management approaches (such as catch documentation schemes) that States have later adopted through RFMOs covering other ocean areas.

9 Disadvantages of Pursuing the CCAMLR Approach

The primary disadvantage of using CCAMLR as a model has to do with the reality that, due to the pressing need to manage growing fisheries in its Convention Area, CCAMLR has developed primarily into a fisheries management organization, albeit one with broader responsibilities. If the governments concerned with strengthening the stewardship of the Sargasso Sea wish to start with a different premise—that an enhanced Sargasso Sea Commission should not focus primarily on fisheries management but rather on the full range of human activities affecting the Sargasso Sea—the CCAMLR model may prove less than fully satisfactory or fitting.

Like RFMOs, the CCAMLR Commission is composed entirely of State representatives (who under Art VIII (3) "may be accompanied by alternate representatives and advisers"). This is a significant distinction from the unique, expert-driven composition of the Sargasso Sea Commission, whose members serve in their personal capacity. Although innovative approaches could be considered to address this issue, it seems likely that States agreeing to give international authority to such a body would want it to be comprised of their representatives.

77 Jessica A. Nilsson et al., "Consensus Management in Antarctica's High Seas—Past Success and Current Challenges," *Marine Policy* 73 (2016): 172.

10 OSPAR as a Possible Model

Beginning in the 1970s, nations concerned with particular areas of the ocean started to create "Regional Seas Programmes" through which to collaborate. Many of these programmes operate under the auspices of the United Nations Environment Programme (UNEP), but others exist outside—or largely outside—the UNEP framework. The activities of these programmes vary considerably, as a consequence of the different challenges facing particular regions and due to differing levels of available resources, both financial and human.[78]

One of the more successful Regional Seas Programmes is the OSPAR Commission, which focuses on the North-East Atlantic region. More specifically, its area of responsibility includes the internal waters, territorial seas and other maritime zones over which its Contracting Parties exercise sovereign rights and jurisdiction in parts of the Baltic Sea, the Mediterranean Sea and the North-East Atlantic, as well as the high seas portions of that region.[79]

OSPAR has at present sixteen Contracting Parties.[80] Other States may join OSPAR by acceding to the OSPAR Convention. The basic obligation of an OSPAR Contracting Party is to take steps to prevent and eliminate marine pollution and to protect the OSPAR area against the adverse effects of human activities.[81] The OSPAR Commission, which is composed of representatives of the Contracting Parties,[82] includes a variety of Committees and serves as the venue through which the Contracting Parties agree on programmes and measures preventing and eliminating pollution and for controlling activities that may adversely affect the OSPAR area. The Commission has the authority to

78 A brief description of the Regional Seas Programme and links to all the existing examples, can be found at UN Environment Programme, Why Does Working With Regional Seas Matter?, https://www.unenvironment.org/explore-topics/oceans-seas/what-we-do/working-regional-seas/why-does-working-regional-seas-matter.

79 Convention for the Protection of the Marine Environment of the North-East Atlantic, Sept. 22, 1992, 2354 U.N.T.S. 67.

80 The OSPAR Contracting Parties are: Belgium, Denmark, Finland, France, Germany, Iceland, Ireland, Luxembourg, The Netherlands, Norway, Portugal, Spain, Sweden, Switzerland and United Kingdom, as well as the European Union. OSPAR Commission, Contracting Parties, https://www.ospar.org/organisation/contracting-parties.

81 Specifically, the OSPAR Contracting Parties have the obligation to "take all possible steps to prevent and eliminate pollution and shall take the necessary measures to protect the maritime area against the adverse effects of human activities so as to safeguard human health and to conserve marine ecosystems and, when practicable, restore marine areas which have been adversely affected." Ibid., art. 2, ¶ 1(a).

82 Ibid., art. 10, ¶ 1 ("A Commission, made up of representatives of each of the Contracting Parties, is hereby established.").

adopt binding decisions, as well as recommendations and other non-binding decisions. Contracting Parties may "opt out" of binding decisions, though this rarely happens.[83] The Commission also issues numerous publications about the state of the marine environment, many of which result from evaluations or assessments based on reports of its Contracting Parties.

Within this framework, OSPAR has six general "work areas":
- Biological Diversity & Ecosystems
- Hazardous Substances & Eutrophication
- Human Activities
- Offshore Industry
- Radioactive Substances
- Cross Cutting Issues

In each area, the Commission operates on the basis of four principles:
- the ecosystem approach
- the precautionary principle
- the polluter pays principle
- best available techniques (BAT) and best environmental practices (BEP)

OSPAR has been on the cutting edge of efforts to protect the marine environment. It served as an early forum in which to develop and implement marine protected areas, undertook innovative studies on water quality, established standards for environmental impact assessments, and issued groundbreaking guidelines relating to submarine cables. For these and other accomplishments, OSPAR has earned a reputation as an effective and proactive international body.

OSPAR exists essentially outside the UNEP framework. The OSPAR Commission nevertheless engages very actively with other international bodies, often through memoranda of understanding or cooperative agreements. The ocean area within the purview of OSPAR is essentially the same as the Convention Area of an RFMO known as the North-East Atlantic Fisheries Commission, necessitating a close collaboration between the two organizations. In 2014, the two organizations established what is known as a "Collective Arrangement" which is "a formal agreement between legally competent authorities managing human activities in the Areas beyond National Jurisdiction

83 Ibid, art 13(2) ("A decision shall be binding on the expiry of a period of two hundred days after its adoption for those Contracting Parties that voted for it and have not within that period notified the Executive Secretary in writing that they are unable to accept the decision, provided that at the expiry of that period three-quarters of the Contracting Parties have either voted for the decision and not withdrawn their acceptance or notified the Executive Secretary in writing that they are able to accept the decision …").

(ABNJ) in the North-East Atlantic."[84] In addition, OSPAR regularly interacts with the International Council for the Exploration of the Sea, other regional seas programmes that cover adjacent ocean areas, and the Arctic Council, and has an extended network of MOUs and other collaboration arrangements.[85]

OSPAR members share the costs of the Commission and its Secretariat through a formula set forth in the OSPAR Financial Regulations, which takes account of the members' GNP and other factors. The current annual budget for OSPAR is approximately 2 million USD.

11 Comparing the OSPAR and Sargasso Sea Contexts

At first blush, the OSPAR and Sargasso Sea contexts seem quite similar. Both are large and essentially adjacent areas of the North Atlantic Ocean. Two major oceanic features—the Gulf Stream and the North Atlantic Gyre—carry water, living marine resources, nutrients and pollutants through both regions. The world's largest mountain range—the mid-Atlantic ridge—also runs through the OSPAR region and an area adjacent to the Sargasso Sea.

But the two regions also differ in some significant respects. One difference is that the coastal States of the OSPAR region are all Organization for Economic Cooperation and Development (OECD) members—wealthy nations with considerable human and financial resources. By contrast, the States with territory in or nearby the Sargasso Sea are more heterogeneous, some wealthy and some not. There are of course other regions where States participating in such programmes have similar inequalities, such as the Mediterranean and the Caribbean. A Regional Seas Programme for the Sargasso Sea could be adapted to accommodate this difference in a number of ways. For example, it might need to devote some of its efforts to capacity building and technology transfer to assist members who are developing States in implementing their commitments.

One other significant difference between OSPAR and the Sargasso Sea Commission as currently configured is that the former includes marine areas

---

84 North-East Atlantic Fisheries Commission & OSPAR Commission, OSPAR Agreement 2014-09, A Collective Arrangement between competent international organisations on cooperation and coordination regarding selected areas in areas beyond national jurisdiction in the North-East Atlantic (2014); *see also* OSPAR Commission, *Collective Arrangement* (2020), https://www.ospar.org/about/international-cooperation/collective-arrangement.

85 OSPAR Commission, *Memoranda of Understanding & Cooperation Arrangements* (2020), https://www.ospar.org/about/international-cooperation/memoranda-of-understanding.

under national jurisdiction, while the latter does not. This is a significant difference as the OSPAR mandate includes the issue of control of marine pollution.[86] OSPAR's ability to take effective action on this issue is predicated on the assumption that much marine pollution—even in the ABNJ zones of its area of competence—emanates from land-based sources in the littoral states. If the Sargasso Sea Commission were to be given a similar mandate to reduce pollution, then, in order to allow it to be able to address this mandate effectively, the governments concerned with the Sargasso Sea would need to consider whether to amend the current "Geographical Area of Collaboration" reflected in the Hamilton Declaration.[87]

12 Implementing the OSPAR Model

To replace the Sargasso Sea Commission with an international organization similar to OSPAR—or to transform the Commission into such an organization—the governments concerned would need to negotiate a binding international agreement similar in many respects to the hypothetical agreement described above, ("Implementing the CCAMLR Model"). The primary differences of using OSPAR as a model rather than CCAMLR stem from the fact that OSPAR's main purpose and mandate—controlling marine pollution—differs from CCAMLR's main purpose and mandate—managing fishing activities. Accordingly, an international agreement to create a Regional Seas Programme for the Sargasso Sea modeled on OSPAR would presumably have an objective primarily relating to the control of marine pollution and would establish a related mandate, and possibly geographical area of competence also, for the new international organization to be created.[88]

But many of the other aspects of the international agreement might be the same as, or at least similar to, the hypothetical CCAMLR-modeled agreement described above, including the need for an Agreement Area, some of the basic

86 OSPAR Convention, art. 2, ¶ 1(a).

87 *See* Hamilton Declaration, annex I.

88 Like OSPAR, most other Regional Seas Programmes focus on marine pollution issues. Some programmes, such as the Caribbean Environment Programme, have broader authorities, e.g., to identify "specially protected areas and wildlife." Specially Protected Areas and Wildlife Protocol, available at http://cep.unep.org/content/about-cep/spaw/spaw. See further David Freestone, "Specially Protected Areas and Wildlife in the Caribbean: the 1990 Kingston Protocol to the Cartagena Convention," *International Journal of Estuarine and Coastal Law*, 5 (1990): 396.

commitments of the Parties, relationships with other international bodies, and final clauses.

One fundamental question that would arise in pursuing this approach would be whether to establish the Regional Seas Programme for the Sargasso Sea within the UNEP framework. As noted above, OSPAR exists essentially outside the UNEP framework. Although there may be a number of reasons why the OSPAR Contracting Parties made this choice, one might have been their belief that they would enjoy greater control over the direction and activities of OSPAR if they created it outside the UN system. The nations concerned with the Sargasso Sea would also need to consider this question carefully.

A second fundamental question would be whether to include marine areas of the Sargasso Sea under national jurisdiction within the geographic scope of the new organization. To do so would be to adopt the approach of OSPAR. But there may be political sensitivities entailed that would need to be taken into account, not the least of which may be the fact that the current Hamilton Declaration has Government signatories, such as the Principality of Monaco, that do not have maritime zones abutting the Sargasso Sea.

13 Advantages of Pursuing the OSPAR Approach

If the governments concerned with the Sargasso Sea chose to create a Regional Seas Programme for that region modeled on OSPAR, the Sargasso Sea programme and OSPAR would have similar mandates for adjacent areas of the Atlantic Ocean. This would likely mean that a close working relationship between the two organizations could be expected to arise, which would be a significant advantage. In such a situation, some additional OSPAR Contracting Parties might also consider it a natural step to join a regional convention for the Sargasso Sea, further strengthening the new organization.

14 Disadvantages of Pursuing the OSPAR Approach

The primary disadvantage of using OSPAR as a model may have to do with a mismatch between the main focus of OSPAR—controlling marine pollution—and the primary threats to the Sargasso Sea, of which marine pollution is only one of many. Indeed, the UN estimates that 80 percent of marine pollution originates on land,[89] and given that the Sargasso Sea has very little land area within it, controlling land-based marine pollution may not be a particularly high priority for an enhanced Sargasso Sea Commission.

15 Considering a Hybrid Model—or Even a Completely New Model

The foregoing sections suggest that, while both have attractive attributes, neither the CCAMLR model nor the OSPAR model may be a perfect fit for the circumstances facing the Sargasso Sea. CCAMLR, which prides itself—with some justification—as having engaged in "ecosystem-based management" even before that term became well-known, nevertheless devotes most of its attention to developing and implementing relatively routine fisheries conservation and management measures, particularly to combat overfishing and IUU fishing. In other words, CCAMLR in reality performs functions similar to most RFMOs, despite having a mandate wider than most RFMOs. Two existing RFMOs—ICCAT and NAFO—already have responsibility for managing certain fishing activities over some or all of the Sargasso Sea. Creating another organization that focused primarily on fisheries management would not address the full spectrum of threats to the Sargasso Sea, some of which are arguably more pressing than overfishing and IUU fishing.

OSPAR, though perhaps the most effective Regional Seas Programme in existence, lacks two features that may be quite important elements of a comprehensive regime for the Sargasso Sea. First, OSPAR has no express mandate to manage fisheries. Within the OSPAR area, those functions are instead the responsibility of several RFMOs, principally the North-East Atlantic Fisheries Commission. The Sargasso Sea, by contrast, faces a fisheries management "gap," as described above, insofar as there is no effective RFMO managing fisheries other than for tuna and tuna-like species in much of its area, i.e., the portion of the Sargasso Sea south of the NAFO Convention Area.[90] Second, OSPAR has no real mandate to provide technical or other assistance to developing States,

89 http://www.unesco.org/new/en/natural-sciences/ioc-oceans/focus-areas/rio-20-ocean/blueprint-for-the-future-we-want/marine-pollution/facts-and-figures-on-marine-pollution/.

90 Note, however, that the Western Central Atlantic Fisheries Commission (WECAFC), which was set up in 1973 as an Advisory Body under Article VI of the FAO Constitution, has an area of competence that covers the Sargasso Sea. There are also discussions ongoing regarding WECAFC's possible transformation into a Regional Fisheries Management Body (under Art XIV). *See* Western Central Atlantic Fishery Commission Scientific Advisory Group, *Summary report of the First preparatory meeting of the Western Central Atlantic Fishery Commission (WECAFC) for the transformation into a Regional Fisheries*

none of whom are members of OSPAR. States with significant interests in the Sargasso Sea include both developed and developing States, which suggests that an enhanced Sargasso Sea Commission might need, as part of its mandate, some way to assist its developing State members in carrying out agreed commitments.

16 What a Hybrid or New Model Might Entail

Governments concerned with strengthening stewardship of the Sargasso Sea could consider a hybrid model, borrowing elements of both the CCAMLR approach and the OSPAR approach, to meet the specific needs of the Sargasso Sea. It may also be possible to add to this hybrid model certain elements that are not formally part of either the CCAMLR or OSPAR approach, thus creating a truly new model.

For example, a strengthened Sargasso Sea Commission could have a mandate to fill the fisheries management "gap" mentioned above—i.e., to manage fisheries in the Sargasso Sea that are not under the purview of any existing RFMO. A decision to create such a mandate for the Commission would not be novel. The North Pacific Fisheries Commission, established in 2015, filled a similar "gap" in fisheries management in that part of the ocean, having responsibility only for managing fisheries for marine species that are not "covered by pre-existing international fisheries management instruments within the area of competence of such instruments."[91] For the Sargasso Sea Commission, such a mandate would presumably cover fisheries other than for tuna and tuna-like species and for species that occur south of the NAFO Convention Area.

A strengthened Sargasso Sea Commission could also perform some, and possibly most, of the functions of OSPAR. More precisely, it could serve as the forum in which its members agree on steps to prevent and eliminate marine pollution, both land-based and ship-based, as well as to protect the Sargasso Sea against the adverse effects of human activities writ large, in partnership perhaps with organizations such as the International Maritime Organization (IMO) and the International Seabed Authority (ISA). The Commission would presumably be given the authority to adopt binding decisions on such matters,

Management Organization WECAFC/SAG/X/2019/2, (Jun. 2019), http://www.fao.org/fi/static-media/MeetingDocuments/WECAFC/SAG2019/2.pdf.

91 Convention on the Conservation and Management of High Seas Fisheries Resources in the North Pacific Ocean art. 1(h)(iv), Feb. 24, 2012, S. Treaty Doc. No. 113-2.

as well as non-binding decisions where its members felt those to be more appropriate.

In addition, the strengthened Sargasso Sea Commission could retain certain of its existing functions. Like both CCAMLR and OSPAR, it could commission scientific research relating to the Sargasso Sea and disseminate the results of such research. It could also continue to develop and present proposals for consideration and adoption by other regional and sectoral bodies, such as NAFO, ICCAT, the IMO and the ISA.

As noted above, the Sargasso Sea Commission will continue to have both developed and developing members, perhaps more of each in the future. A strengthened Commission—one that was capable of adopting measures binding on its members—might also include among its functions some type of capacity-building program to assist its developing State members in implementing their commitments.

If the governments concerned launch the process to strengthen the Sargasso Sea Commission in these suggested ways, the effort could also create possible synergies with the negotiation and expected entry into force of a new BBNJ Agreement. For example, the Sargasso Sea could become a model with which to demonstrate how governments can, in respect of a given area beyond national jurisdiction, develop and implement area-based management tools, conduct environmental impact assessments, and improve knowledge related to marine genetic resources. Moreover, the future BBNJ Agreement seems likely to have to rely to some extent on regional bodies to implement at least some aspects of its provisions once it enters into force. The strengthened Commission could serve as such a body for the Sargasso Sea.

17 Implementing the Hybrid or New Model

A binding international agreement would be necessary to reestablish the Sargasso Sea Commission to play the kind of roles described above. Many of the elements of such an agreement would be similar to the agreement outlined above, with necessary adjustments to the provisions dealing with the Commission's purpose and mandate.

The governments concerned would also face some of the same choices noted above in connection with implementing the OSPAR model. Those include whether to place the new Commission within the UNEP framework and whether to include any marine areas within national jurisdiction as part of the geographic scope of the new Commission.

In considering a hybrid or new model, governments concerned with the Sargasso Sea may benefit from experiences of Large Marine Ecosystem (LME) initiatives that have been undertaken in other parts of the world. These initiatives have been supported through the Global Environment Facility (GEF) in areas such as the Caribbean Sea, the Benguela Current (in the Southeast Atlantic Ocean), and the Canary Current (in the Eastern Central Atlantic), to name just a few.

Typically, the GEF provides initial funds for a "diagnostic analysis" of a given LME to determine the challenges it faces and possible means to meet those challenges. Based on the outcome of that analysis, the GEF then seeks both political support and co-financing from relevant governments to implement measures to improve stewardship of the LME. In some cases, such as the Benguela Current, this has resulted in the establishment of an intergovernmental commission with features similar in some respects to the strengthened Sargasso Sea Commission contemplated in this paper.[92] As discussed above, the recently approved GEF project for the Sargasso Sea has adapted the Transboundary Diagnostic Analysis tool developed for transboundary coastal ecosystems to an Ecosystem Diagnostic Analysis (EDA) more suited to a high seas ecosystem. That EDA will inform the development of a Strategic Action Programme that will propose a future framework for the sustainable conservation and governance of the Sargasso Sea.

18 Relationship between a Hybrid/New Model and Other International Bodies and Regimes

Another key question in considering a hybrid or new model for the Sargasso Sea would be how precisely to articulate the relationship of the new regime with other international bodies and regimes. As currently configured, the limited mandate and authority of the Sargasso Sea Commission give it only limited influence over such other bodies and regimes. The Commission has used its influence to good effect to date, but might be able to secure greater cooperation if it worked on a level playing field with other entities—i.e., as a full-fledged international organization with a clearly defined mandate, legal personality and a reasonable budget. Among other things, these new attributes

92 David Freestone, "The Role of the World Bank and the Global Environment Facility in the Implementation of the Regime of the Law of the Sea Convention" in David Freestone, *The World Bank and Sustainable Development—Legal Essays*, (Leiden & Boston: Martinus Nijhoff, 2012) 143–162.

would likely give the Commission greater standing to make its voice heard in other international fora, including the United Nations.

In negotiating the international agreement that would reestablish the Commission in this way, the governments concerned would need to give careful attention to a number of questions that will likely arise in this regard. For example, how would the measures that the Commission might adopt regarding fisheries south of the NAFO Convention relate to measures adopted by NAFO itself? An examination of the ways in which other RFMOs in neighboring ocean areas relate to one another, such as NAFO and NEAFC and the two tuna RFMOs that cover the Pacific (the Inter-American Tropical Tuna Commission and the Western and Central Pacific Fisheries Commission) might provide answers to this question. Similarly, if the Sargasso Sea Commission had the authority to establish marine protected areas, how would such a decision affect, or relate to, the mandates of sectoral bodies such as the IMO and ISA? While the experiences of other ocean governance organizations, such as OSPAR, might suggest answers to this question, guidance on the issue might ultimately depend on the provisions of a new BBNJ Agreement.

19 Advantages of Pursuing This Approach

The chief advantage of pursuing a hybrid or new approach would be that it would give the governments concerned the greatest ability to tailor the strengthened Sargasso Sea Commission to the needs of the Sargasso Sea. As noted above, the unique ecosystem of the Sargasso Sea faces challenges from a wide array of human activities. A new international agreement for the Sargasso Sea could help address each of these challenges, either directly through a strengthened Sargasso Sea Commission or through the enhanced influence that a strengthened Commission would have with other international bodies and regimes.

20 Disadvantages of Pursuing This Approach

Perhaps the greatest disadvantage of the hybrid or new approach is simply that it contemplates something new and somewhat ambitious. Cautious governments may resist this approach, at least at first. The hybrid or new model suggested also raises some novel questions about the precise scope of the mandate to be given to the reestablished Sargasso Sea Commission and the manner in which it might interact with existing regional and sectoral regimes.

21 Conclusion

Governments concerned with the Sargasso Sea face a choice. They can continue to interact with each other through the mechanism of the Sargasso Sea Commission as currently configured—a known and flexible entity with a growing, if limited, presence on the international stage. Or they can take the next step to build a regime to safeguard the Sargasso Sea in a more robust fashion by re-establishing the Commission on the basis of an international agreement. This paper has laid out several options for doing this, although other options may also exist.

The new GEF-financed Sargasso Sea project will provide an ideal opportunity for all those involved in the current Sargasso Sea initiative as well as a wider group of stakeholders to consider models for a sustainable future. If nothing else, the selected model should provide a consistent financing source for the work of the Commission and its Secretariat. Moreover, by the time the four-year GEF project is complete it seems likely that the BBNJ Treaty negotiations will have been completed and the challenges of implementing its new regime will have begun. These challenges may well spur the development of a new class of Regional Ocean Governance Organizations that will be able to take advantage of the opportunities presented by the new treaty and to undertake the implementation of its provisions at a regional level.[93] The Sargasso Sea seems likely to be well positioned to provide a viable model for this new species of regional organizations.

93 See further David Freestone, "The Sargasso Sea Commission: An Evolving New Paradigm for High Seas Ecosystem Governance?" in "Challenges and Opportunities in Regional Governance of Ocean Ecosystems," *Frontiers in Marine Science* (2021) 8:668253. doi: 10.3389/fmars.2021.668253 1-10.

CHAPTER 8

Equity Must Anchor the BBNJ Treaty

Autumn Bordner

1 Introduction

The United Nations Convention on the Law of the Sea (UNCLOS) is often described as setting forth a comprehensive regime for governance of the ocean and its resources. Yet UNCLOS does not directly address marine biodiversity in the 64% of the ocean that lies beyond national jurisdiction.[1] Limited governance frameworks apply to specific activities (e.g., shipping),[2] resources (e.g, tuna stocks),[3] and locations (e.g., the Arctic)[4] beyond national jurisdiction, but there is no comprehensive legal regime addressing conservation or management of marine biodiversity outside sovereign waters. This patchwork approach leaves governance gaps, and is a poor fit for the interconnected ocean ecosystem.

The lack of a comprehensive regime for marine biodiversity is significant. Areas beyond national jurisdiction (ABNJ), including the water column and seabed beyond States' 200 nautical mile exclusive economic zones contain 90% of the ocean's biomass, 95% of the Earth's total habitat by volume, and a vast array of rare and unique species.[5] This rich biodiversity provides crucial ecosystem services, including regulation of the global climate and production of oxygen.[6] The biodiversity in ABNJ also provides an important source of food, income, and employment for millions, and the largely unexplored pool of

1 Harriet Harden-Davies & Paul Snelgrove, "Science Collaboration for Capacity Building: Advancing Technology Transfer Through a Treaty for Biodiversity Beyond National Jurisdiction," *Frontiers in Marine Policy* 7: (2020): 1.

2 International Maritime Organization, "IMO and Its Role in Protecting the World's Oceans," https://www.imo.org/en/MediaCentre/HotTopics/Pages/oceans-default.aspx.

3 North Atlantic Salmon Conservation Organization, "North-East Atlantic Commission," http://www.nasco.int/neac.html.

4 Commission for the Conservation of Antarctic Marine Living Resources, "About CCAMLR," https://www.ccamlr.org/en/organisation.

5 International Union for Conservation of Nature, "Governing Areas Beyond National Jurisdiction," https://www.iucn.org/resources/issues-briefs/governing-areas-beyond-national-jurisdiction.

6 Ibid.

 | DOI:10.1163/9789004514218_010

marine genetic resources in ABNJ is anticipated to provide medical and pharmaceutical breakthroughs that could have a transformative impact on human health and well-being.[7]

This biodiversity beyond national jurisdiction (BBNJ) is also a "quintessential common,"[8] making these life-sustaining resources vulnerable to overexploitation, with potentially dire consequences. Indeed, biodiversity beyond national jurisdiction is already in peril. Human impacts including overfishing, climate change, and pollution have seriously degraded most of the ocean's ecosystems.[9] And the rate of degradation is only increasing.[10]

Moreover, while decline of the ocean threatens all humankind, the benefits of marine biodiversity are primarily enjoyed by a small number of wealthy and powerful countries and actors, while the negative impacts of marine degradation are disproportionately felt by the poorest and most vulnerable.[11] For example, profits from fishing and other maritime industries on the high seas,[12] patents from marine genetic resources,[13] and the technology and resources to engage in marine scientific research[14] are largely consolidated in a few wealthy nations. Meanwhile, the adverse impacts of ocean degradation, including sea-level rise, marine pollution, and species loss disproportionately impact communities in economically-disadvantaged countries, especially island and coastal communities who depend on the ocean for subsistence and cultural practices.[15] The unsustainable exploitation of marine biodiversity also

7 Ibid.

8 "Conservation and sustainable use of marine biological diversity beyond areas of national jurisdiction—BBNJ," *International Institute for Sustainable Development: Earth Negotiations Bulletin*, https://enb.iisd.org/negotiations/conservation-and-sustainable-use-marine-biological-diversity-beyond-areas-national.

9 United Nations, *The First Global Integrated Marine Assessment* (2016), available at: https://www.un.org/regularprocess/content/first-world-ocean-assessment.

10 Benjamin S. Halpern et al., "Recent Pace of Change in Human Impacts on the World's Ocean," *Scientific Reports* 9 (2019): 11609.

11 Henrik Osterblum et al., *Towards Ocean Equity*, World Resources Institute (2020), available at: https://www.oceanpanel.org/sites/default/files/2020-04/towards-ocean-equity.pdf.

12 As of 2018, five high-income countries were responsible for 82% of global fishing effort. McCauley et al., "Wealthy Countries Dominate Industrial Fishing." *Science Advances* 4 (2018).

13 As of October 2017, actors located in 10 countries held 98% of patents for marine genetic resources. Robert R. Blasiak et al., "Corporate Control and Global Governance of Marine Genetic Resources," *Science Advances* 4 (2018).

14 Harriet Harden-Davies & Paul Snelgrove, "Science Collaboration for Capacity Building."

15 Osterblum et al., *Towards Ocean Equity*; Nathan J. Bennett et al. "Towards a Sustainable and Equitable Blue Economy," *Nature Sustainability* 2 (2019): 991.

threatens the ability of future generations to access essential ocean resources and services.[16]

In recent years, the international community has recognized the centrality of the ocean and its resources to human well-being and sustainable development. In July 2015, after years of planning and discussion, a global consensus around the need to sustainably manage BBNJ led the U.N. General Assembly to pass a resolution committing to development of "an international legally binding instrument under [UNCLOS] on the conservation and sustainable use of marine biological diversity of areas beyond national jurisdiction."[17] Since then, States have been working to "elaborate the text" of a new BBNJ Treaty, with "a view to developing the instrument as soon as possible."[18] The last of four formal negotiation sessions, known as intergovernmental conferences (IGC) was held from 8 to 17 March 2022.[19] While the objective was to produce a finalized treaty text by the close of this session, States were unable to achieve consensus.[20]

States remain fundamentally divided on a number of key issues. Perhaps the most contentious—and most fundamental—is the question of what governance principle should guide the treaty. A numerically small but powerful group of developed countries asserts the primacy of the "freedom of the seas" principle.[21] In contrast, the majority of countries—comprising virtually the entire developing world along with China—take the position that the "common heritage of mankind" (CHM) principle should govern.[22] These oppositional positions have, if anything, calcified over the course of the BBNJ process, leaving some to wonder whether resolution is possible.[23]

---

16 Ibid.

17 G.A. Res. 69/292 (July 6, 2015), available at: https://undocs.org/A/RES/69/292.

18 G.A. Res. 72/249 (Jan. 19, 2018), available at: https://undocs.org/en/A/RES/72/249.

19 United Nations, "Intergovernmental Conference on Marine Biodiversity of Areas Beyond National Jurisdiction," https://www.un.org/bbnj/.

20 Elizabeth M. De Santo et al., "Stuck in the Middle with You (and Not Much Time Left): The Third Intergovernmental Conference on Biodiversity Beyond National Jurisdiction," *Marine Policy* 117 (2020): 1; Karen McVeigh, "UN Treaty Summit Collapses as States Accused of Dragging Out Talks," *The Guardian* (Mar. 28, 2022).

21 A.B.M. Vadrot et al., "Who Owns Marine Biodiversity? Contesting the World Order Through the 'Common Heritage of Humankind' Principle," *Environmental Politics* (2021), DOI: 10.1080/09644016.2021.1911442.

22 Ibid.

23 Vito De Lucia, "The Question of the Common Heritage of Mankind and the Negotiations Towards a Global Treaty on Marine Biodiversity in Areas Beyond National Jurisdiction: No End in Sight?," *McGill International Journal of Sustainable Development Law & Policy* 16 (2020): 139; De Santo et al., "Stuck in the Middle," 8.

This ideological schism between developed and developing States hearkens back to the initial negotiation of UNCLOS in the 1960s and 1970s.[24] Then, as now, states hotly contested which principle should govern the seabed and its resources beyond national jurisdiction (the Area), with developed nations advocating for adherence to the traditional freedom of the seas regime and developing nations pushing for application of the then-novel concept of the common heritage of mankind.[25] Ultimately, although CHM was incorporated into UNCLOS as the governance regime for the Area, implementation has fallen short of the developing world's hopes, with the inequality between developed and developing states vis a vis the ocean largely unchanged since UNCLOS entered into force nearly 30 years ago.[26]

Against this historical backdrop, this chapter examines the continuation of the debate between freedom of the seas and CHM in the BBNJ Treaty negotiations. The debate is, at its core, about global equity. For developing nations, the BBNJ Treaty presents an opportunity to reanimate the CHM principle and take meaningful steps toward the long-held goal of replacing the status quo with a more equitable world order. Meanwhile, although expressing commitment to principles of equity and sustainable development,[27] the developed world remains resistant to changing a system that works in its favor.

The chapter concludes that in order to achieve successful "conservation and sustainable use of marine biodiversity," the BBNJ treaty must be driven by considerations of equity—whether under the label of the common heritage of mankind or not. Moreover, as governance of the Area demonstrates, codifying

---

24 The "developed" and "developing" dichotomy is a widely accepted euphemism standing in for a number of interrelated attributes including "colonizer" and "colonized," "rich" and "poor," and "dominant" and "marginalized." The terms have been criticized as reinforcing outdated hierarchical notions of developing nations as inferior, and developed nations as the ideal. Epeli Hau'ofa, "Our Sea of Islands," *The Contemporary Pacific* 6 (1994): 147. These terms also tend to obscure the reality that the wealth and power concentrated in developed nations is at least partially the product of their historical (and in some cases, ongoing) exploitation of developing nations. Ibid; Walter Rodney, *How Europe Underdeveloped Africa* (Washington, D.C.: Howard University Press, 1972); David Williams, "Aid and Sovereignty: Quasi-states and International Financial Institutions," *Review of International Studies* 26 (2000): 557. Acknowledging these problems with the "developed" and "developing" dichotomy, this article nevertheless employs these terms because they are standard in discussing ideological disagreements in the context of BBNJ negotiations.

25 Marie Bourrel et al., "The Common Heritage of Mankind as a Means to Assess and Advance Equity in Deep Sea Mining," *Marine Policy* 95 (2018): 311.

26 Bourrel et al., "The Common Heritage of Mankind as a Means to Assess and Advance Equity."

27 United Nations, "The Sustainable Development Agenda," https://www.un.org/sustainable development/development-agenda/.

equitable principles in the instrument is not enough; states must meaningfully commit to and implement those principles.

2 Debating Principles during UNCLOS Negotiations

Tensions between the principles of freedom of the seas and CHM have been present since the inception of UNCLOS. When negotiations for UNCLOS began in the mid-Twentieth Century, the freedom of the high seas had been a dominant principle in the law of the sea for three centuries.[28] This principle, which was ideologically connected with laissez-faire economic theory, provided that the ocean is free to all and belongs to none.[29] In other words, while States enjoyed sovereignty over a narrow band of water near their coasts, beyond that zone anyone could freely use ocean space and resources.[30]

Up until UNCLOS' negotiation, the central tension in the law of the sea concerned where state sovereignty ended and the freedom of the seas regime began.[31] It came to a head in the mid-Twentieth Century, as technology rapidly advanced and States' ability to explore and exploit the sea increased dramatically. Maritime powers asserted *de facto* control beyond their borders, and States began making expansive claims to jurisdiction off their coasts.[32] At the same time, it was becoming clear that ocean resources were not—as previously believed—inexhaustible. New maritime technologies enabled an unprecedented expansion in maritime activity and resource extraction, depleting resource stocks and significantly increasing marine pollution in waters that were "free to all." It became clear that a regime of unlimited freedom was no longer tenable. The desire to ameliorate these conflicts was the driving force

28 Dutch jurist Hugo Grotius wrote the foundational treatise on the freedom of the high seas doctrine, "Mare Liberum," in 1609. The freedom of the seas gained dominance at the beginning of the 18th Century. *See* Tullio Treves, "High Seas," *Oxford Public International Law* (Jan. 2009), https://opil.ouplaw.com/view/10.1093/law:epil/9780199231690/law-9780199231690-e1174.

29 Edward H. Buehrig, "Freedom of the Seas: 1917, 1941," *Journal of Politics* 6 (1944): 3; United Nations Division for Ocean Affairs and the Law of the Sea, "The United Nations Convention on the Law of the Sea (a Historical Perspective)" (1998), https://www.un.org/Depts/los/convention_agreements/convention_historical_perspective.htm#Historical%20Perspective.

30 "UNCLOS (a Historical Perspective)."

31 Mónica Brito, "Mare Liberum vs. Mare Clausum: Grotius, Freitas, and Selden's Debate on Dominion over the Seas," *Journal of the History of Ideas* 74 (2003): 361.

32 "UNCLOS (a Historical Perspective)."

behind the international effort to codify a comprehensive law of a sea, ultimately leading to the negotiation of UNCLOS.[33]

UNCLOS was negotiated from 1958 to 1982.[34] Negotiators struck a balance between the principles of state sovereignty and freedom of the seas through the concept of maritime zones. Under the maritime zone regime, sovereignty weakens with distance from shore until, beyond 200 nautical miles, no State can assert jurisdiction. But the appropriate governance regime for this "commons" area beyond national jurisdiction proved more difficult to settle. Indeed, governance of the ocean commons proved to be the most fraught issue throughout the treaty's negotiation, reflecting the divergent goals of developed and developing states.

Developed states, especially traditional maritime empires, wished to maintain a strong freedom of the seas doctrine beyond national jurisdiction. This regime would enable them to leverage cutting-edge technologies to project maritime power, conduct marine scientific research, and exploit ocean resources. Of particular interest was the possibility of exploiting deep seabed minerals, which were seen as virtually inexhaustible and highly profitable.[35]

In the past, the preference of these nations might have gone unchallenged. But as UNCLOS' negotiations commenced, the political organization of the world was undergoing a radical change that brought new, dissenting voices to the table. In 1945, the newly drafted United Nations' Charter codified the right of all peoples to self-determination. And in 1960, the U.N. General Assembly adopted the "Declaration on the Granting of Independence to Colonial Countries and Peoples," which called for "colonialism in all its forms and manifestations" to come to a "speedy and unconditional end."[36] In the following years, more than 80 colonies gained independence and joined the family of nations.[37] These former colonies (now considered developing nations) were thus emancipated to engage in international politics along with their former colonizers (now considered developed nations).

Outside the law-of-the-sea context, these newly-minted States advanced the notion of a new international economic order (NIEO)—a series of "reforms

33 Ibid.

34 Ibid.

35 Julie Hunter et al., "Broadening Common Heritage: Addressing Gaps in the Deep Sea Mining Regulatory Regime," *Harvard Environmental Law Review Online* (2018), https://harvardelr.com/2018/04/16/broadening-common-heritage/; John D. Lewis, "The Deep Sea Resources," *Naval War College Review* 21 (1969): 130.

36 G.A. Res. 1514 (XV) (Dec. 14, 1960).

37 Surabhi Ranganathan, "Decolonization and International Law: Putting the Ocean on the Map," *Journal of the History of International Law* 23 (2020): 161, 162.

to the structure, governance, and norms of the global economy" designed to "correct inequalities and redress injustices" caused by colonization in order to achieve a world in which all states were truly equal.[38] Among other things, the NIEO called for equitable redistribution of wealth, technology transfer and capacity building, sovereign equality, and global solidarity in addressing matters of common interest.[39] These principles were adopted by the U.N. General Assembly in 1974 in the "Declaration on the Establishment of a New Economic Order."[40]

Developing nations wished to inject the same equitable principles into the law of the sea. They opposed a freedom of the seas approach because only developed states had the resources and capacity to take advantage of resources in areas beyond national jurisdiction and feared that a freedom of the seas regime would only deepen global inequity.[41] Given the heightened interest in deep sea mining at the time, this concern was particularly acute with respect to governance of the deep seabed.

Guided by the NIEO, Malta's Ambassador to the United Nations, Arvid Pardo, put forth an alternative to the freedom of the seas regime for the deep seabed. In a now-famous speech, he called upon all nations to recognize the seabed and its resources as the "common heritage of mankind."[42] "The time has come," he asserted, "to recognise as a basic principle of international law the overriding common interest of mankind in the preservation of the quality of the marine environment and in the rational and equitable development of resources lying beyond national jurisdiction."[43] These resources, Pardo explained, should not be subject to private appropriation or exploitation, but held in trust and managed for the benefit of all mankind, including future generations. Further, all countries should participate equally in the management of these resources, and their benefits should be equitably redistributed, with the aim of achieving economic parity between decolonizing countries and traditional powers.[44] This principle was initially envisaged as applying to the

38 Nils Gilman, "The New International Economic Order: A Reintroduction" *Humanity Journal* 6 (2016), available at: http://humanityjournal.org/issue6-1/the-new-international-economic-order-a-reintroduction/; G.A. Res. 3201 (S-VI) (May 1, 1974).

39 G.A. Res. 3201 (S-VI) (May 1, 1974).

40 Ibid.

41 De Santo et al., "Stuck in the Middle," 8; De Lucia, "The Question of the Common Heritage," 156–57.

42 Summary Records of the 1515th Meeting, U.N. Doc. A/C.1/PV.1515 (1977).

43 Ibid.

44 Ibid.

entirety of the ocean and its resources,[45] but—perhaps because such a broad application was too contentious[46]—Pardo confined his focus to the seabed.

Developing States rallied around CHM, which they saw as essential to economic justice. Developed States, meanwhile, adamantly opposed the principle, which was adverse to their economic interests in the deep seabed. They argued that the freedom of the high seas regime already governed areas beyond national jurisdiction and that "deep seabed resources could not belong to the world community" under that regime.[47]

Ultimately, developing states were successful in inserting CHM into UNCLOS as the governance regime for "the Area and its resources."[48] UNCLOS sets out the fundamental principles of the CHM regime as articulated by Pardo: The Area and its resources shall not be subject to appropriation or to the exercise of sovereignty or sovereign rights; they shall only be used for peaceful purposes; and resource exploration and exploitation shall be carried out for the benefit of mankind, "giving particular consideration to the interests and needs of the developing countries."[49] UNCLOS also established the International Seabed Authority (ISA) as an independent international entity charged with implementing the CHM regime.[50] The inclusion of the CHM principle in UNCLOS was seen as a considerable victory for developing countries in their quest for a more equitable future.[51]

But this victory was short-lived. Even after CHM was inserted into UNCLOS as the legal principle governing the Area, several powerful countries remained strongly opposed. Spearheaded by the United States, these nations refused to ratify UNCLOS unless changes were made.[52] This opposition led to the 1994 Implementing Agreement on Part IX of UNCLOS.[53] While nominally affirming commitment to CHM, the 1994 Agreement undermined the principle. It

45 Prue Taylor, "The Common Heritage of Mankind: Expanding the Oceanic Circle," in International Ocean Institute—Canada (ed.), *The Future of Ocean Governance and Capacity Development: Essays in Honor of Elisabeth Mann Borgese* (Lieden: Brill, 2018).

46 Ibid.

47 Ibid.; Marie Bourrel, "The Common Heritage of Mankind as a Means to Assess and Advance Equity," 312; Edward Guntrip, "The Common Heritage of Mankind: An Adequate Regime for Managing the Seabed?," *Melbourne Journal of International Law* 4 (2003): 376.

48 UNCLOS, art. 136.

49 Ibid., art. 137, 140, 141, 148.

50 Ibid., art. 152.

51 Ranganathan, "Decolonization and International Law," 168.

52 Marjorie Ann Browne, *The Law of the Sea Convention and U.S. Policy*, Congressional Research Service Issue Brief for Congress (2006).

53 Waseem Ahmad Qureshi, "Protecting the Common Heritage of Mankind Beyond National Jurisdiction," *Arizona Journal of International & Comparative Law* 36 (2019): 81.

specifically provided for resource exploitation by private industry and accrual of private benefits, thereby undercutting the principle of non-appropriation.[54] It created a decision-making process that effectively gives developed nations veto power, thereby undercutting the CHM principle of equal participation.[55] And it made transfer of technology voluntary, reduced the financial obligations of developed States, and left specification of benefit sharing to a later time, thereby undercutting the principle of equitable redistribution.[56] Interest in seabed mining subsequently faded as it became clear that the industry was not economically viable.

In recent years, as technological advancement has reawakened the possibility of profitable exploitation of the deep seabed, the ISA has begun drafting a mining code setting forth the resource exploration and exploitation regime in more detail. The draft code does not strongly express the equity-focused wealth redistribution and benefit sharing envisioned by developing nations at the time of UNCLOS' drafting. The code focuses instead on fostering competitive markets among those who already possess the technology and resources to undertake mining, and makes no explicit provision for economic benefit sharing, despite the fact that Article 140(2) of UNCLOS specifically calls for "the equitable sharing of financial and other economic benefits."[57] To date, twenty-nine contracts for resource exploitation in the Area have been issued—all to corporations from developed nations.[58] Moreover, while the mining code contains provisions requiring environmental protection, the current lack of understanding about the deep-sea environment and the environmental consequences of seabed mining make deep sea mineral extraction an unavoidably risky venture.[59] The environmental harms of experimental deep sea mining within national jurisdiction have already had an adverse impact on Indigenous islanders and other vulnerable groups in the vicinity, and it is likely that the

54 Agreement Related to the Implementation of Part IX of the Convention (1994), pt. 2, pt. 6, pt. 8 [1994 Agreement].

55 Ibid., pt. 3.

56 Ibid., pt. 5.; Isabel Feichtner, "Sharing the Riches of the Sea: The Redistributive and Fiscal Dimension of Deep Seabed Exploitation," *European Journal of International Law* 30 (2019): 601; Aline Jaeckel, "Benefitting from the Common Heritage of Humankind: From Expectation to Reality," *International Journal of Marine & Coastal Law* 35 (2020): 660; Qureshi, "Protecting the Common Heritage," 106.

57 International Seabed Authority, *Draft Regulations on the Exploitation of Mineral Resources in the Area*, ISA Doc. ISBA/25/C/WP.1 (Mar. 22, 2019).

58 International Union for Conservation of Nature, "Deep Sea Mining," https://www.iucn.org/resources/issues-briefs/deep-sea-mining.

59 Hunter et al., "Broadening Common Heritage."

environmental harms caused by mining beyond national jurisdiction will likewise be inequitably distributed.[60]

Moreover, application of the CHM to the Area does not "affect the legal status of the waters superjacent to the Area."[61] Instead, the water column outside national jurisdiction remains governed by the freedom of the seas regime—"open to all states, whether coastal or landlocked."[62] Under UNCLOS, this principle is not absolute. It instead comprises several enumerated "freedoms," namely, the freedom of navigation and overflight, freedom to lay submarine cables and pipelines, freedom to construct artificial islands and other installations, freedom to fish, and freedom to conduct marine scientific research.[63] These enumerated freedoms may only be "exercised under the conditions laid down by this Convention and by other rules of international law."[64] States also have an affirmative duty to act cooperatively to ensure the conservation of living resources on the high seas.[65]

The ideals of the NIEO were included in other aspects of UNCLOS as well. The preamble states that one of the objectives of the treaty is to promote a "just and equitable international economic order which takes into account the interests and needs of mankind as a whole and, in particular, the special interests and needs of developing countries." In addition, State-parties have a general duty to promote capacity development and transfer of marine technology "on an equitable basis" to "accelerate the social and economic development of the developing states."[66] But despite the non-discretionary nature of these commitments, meaningful implementation has never been achieved.[67]

In short, while developing states arguably won the theoretical debate during negotiation of UNCLOS, injecting the treaty with robust equity-focused language and ideologies such as CHM, implementation has fallen far short of realizing the "more just and equitable" economic world order these States hoped for. Instead, the laissez-faire freedom of the seas approach favored by developed nations continues to dominate practical implementation of the law of the sea in areas beyond national jurisdiction.

60 Julian Aguon & Julie Hunter, "Second Wave Due Diligence: The Case for Incorporating the Norm of Free, Prior, and Informed Consent into the Deep Sea Mining Regulatory Regime," *Stanford Environmental Law Journal* 38 (2018): 3.

61 UNCLOS, art. 135.

62 Ibid., art. 87.

63 Ibid.

64 Ibid.

65 Ibid., art. 116–120.

66 Ibid., pt. XIV, art. 266.

67 Harden-Davies & Snelgrove, "Science Collaboration for Capacity Building," 2.

3 Debating Principles during BBNJ Negotiations

UNCLOS sets forth governance regimes for the *spatial* extent of the ABNJ—the Area and the high seas. But UNCLOS does not expressly govern marine biodiversity *within* ABNJ. Some States, such as Algeria, have suggested the topic of marine biodiversity beyond national jurisdiction was not included in UNCLOS because, by contrast to the heightened global interest in deep sea minerals at the time, the abundance or importance of living resources in ABNJ remained largely unknown.[68] Others, such as Japan, have disagreed.[69]

Whatever the reason for the omission, recent scientific advancements have made plain both the critical importance of marine biodiversity and the alarming rate of marine environmental decline. These factors have prompted the ongoing global effort to draft a legally-binding treaty on the conservation and sustainable use of BBNJ. Negotiations have, in turn, ignited old debates between developed and developing States about what legal regime should apply: freedom of the high seas or CHM. As one commentator has noted, "[i]n essence, the [BBNJ] dispute mirrors UNCLOS negotiations in the 1970s and 1980s," with developed States advocating for maintenance of traditional freedoms and developing States advocating for change to promote equity.[70]

The vast majority of States support CHM as the guiding principle of the BBNJ Treaty. Virtually all developing States, including the 143 nations that comprise the G77 plus China, the African Group, the Pacific Island Forum, the Association of Small Island States, the Land-Locked Developing Nations, and the Caribbean Community, have voiced support for CHM. Meanwhile, a numerically small but highly influential group of developed nations, including the United States, the European Union, Australia, Japan, and the Republic of Korea, as well as the Russian Federation wholly reject any reference to the CHM principle in the treaty and instead assert that freedom of the seas controls. As during the drafting of UNCLOS, this tension—especially with respect to marine genetic resources (MGRs)—has been the source of the "deepest disagreements" and has dominated negotiations on the BBNJ Treaty.[71]

68 De Lucia, "The Question of the Common Heritage," 149.

69 Ibid.

70 Vadrot et al., "Who Owns Marine Biodiversity?".

71 David Leary, "Agreeing to Disagree on What We Have or Have Not Agreed On: The Current State of Play of the BBNJ Negotiations on the Status of Marine Genetic Resources in Areas Beyond National Jurisdiction," *Marine Policy* 99 (2019): 21.

4 History of the BBNJ Negotiations

The concept of a BBNJ treaty has been under discussion since at least 2004, when the U.N. General Assembly established an Informal Working Group to study issues relating to the conservation and sustainable use of BBNJ. In 2011, the Working Group agreed upon a "package" of four issues to be addressed by the treaty: (1) marine protected areas and other area-based management tools; (2) MGRs, including access and benefit sharing; (3) environmental impact assessments; and (4) capacity building and transfer of technology.[72]

At the 2012 U.N. Sustainable Development Conference, States formally committed to addressing "on an urgent basis ... the issue of the conservation and sustainable use of marine biological diversity of [ABNJ], including by taking a decision on the development of an international instrument under [UNCLOS]."[73] In July 2015, the U.N. General Assembly passed a resolution formally committing to drafting a BBNJ Treaty to focus on the four "package" items identified in 2011.[74] Formal negotiating sessions (IGCs) were held in September 2018, March-April 2019, and August 2019. The final IGC, which was postponed due to the COVID-19 pandemic, was held in March 2022, with the objective of producing a finalized treaty text.[75] This objective was not achieved, however, and further negotiations will be required to reach an agreement.

Tensions between proponents of CHM and proponents of the freedom of the seas have suffused the BBNJ Treaty process from the start. At the pre-negotiation stage, discussions about these principles focused purely on what regime should govern exploitation of MGRs.[76] But by IGC-2 many developing nations were asserting that CHM should be the "key principle" underpinning the entire treaty.[77] Developed nations flatly disagreed, leading to deadlock. In what was likely an effort to circumvent this disagreement, the IGC President wholly omitted the CHM concept from the draft treaty text after IGC-2, though CHM principles remained scattered throughout.[78] This omission led

72 Fran Humphries & Harriet Harden-Davies, "Practical Policy Solutions for the Final Stage of the BBNJ Treaty Negotiations," *Marine Policy* 122 (2020): 104214. Capacity-building was likely included in the package in recognition of States' historic failure to implement UNCLOS' capacity building and transfer of marine technology provisions. Harden-Davies & Snelgrove, "Science Collaboration for Capacity Building," 2.

73 Lisa M. Campbell et al., "Oceans at Rio +20," *Conservation Letters* 6 (2020): 439.

74 G.A. Res. 69/292 (July 6, 2015).

75 G.A. Res. 75/570 (June 25, 2021), https://www.undocs.org/en/A/75/L.96.

76 Vadrot et al., "Who Owns Marine Biodiversity?".

77 Ibid.

78 Vito de Lucia, "A Very Quick Look at the Revised Draft Text of the New Agreement on Marine Biodiversity in Areas Beyond National Jurisdiction," *EJIL: Talk!* (Jan. 23, 2020),

to considerable discontent among developing States. At IGC-3, delegates from developing States voiced concerns about a preference in the process for more politically powerful developed States and made impassioned statements regarding the importance of including the CHM principle in the treaty text.[79] For example, Algeria on behalf of the African Group stated that omission of the principle would be "like giving life to a treaty of this importance without a soul."[80] Developed States, in turn, doubled down, indicating that any mention of CHM in the treaty—whether express or implied—would be unacceptable.[81]

In response to the rigorous advocacy of developing states, references to CHM were reinserted into the draft text following IGC-3, though entirely bracketed to indicate no convergence of views.[82] No resolution on these issues was achieved at IGC-4 despite the goal of finalizing the treaty test. Deep divisions persist with no signs of resolution. Both sides have put forth a variety of arguments in favor of their position. These arguments primarily take two forms: legal arguments, grounded in UNCLOS and other relevant legal regimes; and normative arguments, advancing reasons why one principle or the other *should* govern.

5 Legal Arguments

Both developed and developing nations advance legal arguments in support of their positions. Developed nations argue that, under the plain language of UNCLOS, only the Area and its mineral resources are governed by CHM.[83] Article 136 provides that the "Area and its resources" are the CHM. Article 133 defines the Area's resources as "all solid, liquid or gaseous mineral resources in situ in the Area at or beneath the seabed, including polymetallic nodules." Thus, developed States argue, living resources in the Area were intentionally

https://www.ejiltalk.org/a-very-quick-look-at-the-revised-draft-text-of-the-new-agreement-on-marine-biodiversity-in-areas-beyond-national-jurisdiction/.

79 Vadrot et al., "Who Owns Marine Biodiversity?"

80 Mohammed Bessedik, "Statement on Behalf of the African Group" (Aug. 19, 2019), statements.unmeetings.org/media2/21996848/algeria-obo-african-group.pdf.

81 De Lucia, "The Question of the Common Heritage," 151.

82 "Revised Draft Text of an Agreement Under the United Nations Convention on the Law of the Sea on the Conservation and Sustainable Use of Marine Biological Diversity of Areas Beyond National Jurisdiction," United Nations (Nov. 27, 2019), https://www.un.org/bbnj/sites/www.un.org.bbnj/files/revised_draft_text_a.conf_.232.2020.11_advance_unedited_version.pdf.

83 Vadrot et al., "Who Owns Marine Biodiversity?"

excluded from the regime. Likewise, they point to Article 135, which expressly states that CHM does not apply to the water column above the Area. It follows that UNCLOS also excludes living resources in that water column from the CHM regime.[84] Further, developed countries assert that marine biodiversity is explicitly covered by enumerated freedoms, including freedom to fish and freedom to conduct marine scientific research.[85] Finally, they argue that application of the CHM regime to MGRs, in particular, would upset existing international intellectual property rights regimes, thereby violating the U.N. General Assembly's mandate that the BBNJ Treaty not undermine existing instruments, frameworks, and bodies.[86]

Developing States also find legal support for their position in UNCLOS. The G77, African Group, and Pacific Islands Forum, among others, have taken the position that living resources in the Area are already encompassed by the CHM regime.[87] They argue that UNCLOS' lack of explicit reference to living organisms in the Area was not meant to exclude these resources from the CHM, but merely reflects the lack of economic interest in them at the time.[88] Nevertheless, developing States assert, the spirit of UNCLOS and U.N. Resolution 2749 (the resolution formally recognizing CHM as applicable to the Area) make it clear that the Area and *all* of its resources—both living and non-living—are the common heritage of mankind.[89] Similarly, they argue that UNCLOS' lack of explicit reference to biodiversity in the high seas does not mean that these organisms are governed by the freedom of the seas regime. Rather, the CHM principle governs because it has become a principle of customary international law applicable to common resources, including marine biodiversity. Some argue further that Article 311(6) of UNCLOS, which permits no derogation from the CHM principle, supports this view.[90]

Finally, some developing states have pointed to the Convention on Biological Diversity (CBD) and Nagoya Protocol, which employ the CHM principle to

---

84 Tullio Scovazzi, "The Right to Genetic Resources Beyond National Jurisdiction: Challenges for the Ongoing Negotiations at the United Nations," in Catherine Banet (ed.), *The Law of the Seabed* (Lieden: Brill 2020).

85 De Lucia, "The Question of the Common Heritage," 144.

86 G.A. Res. 72/249 (Jan. 19, 2018), https://undocs.org/en/A/RES/72/249.

87 "Statement on Behalf of the G77 and China on Agenda Item 6: Marine Genetic Resources" (Mar. 27, 2017), https://www.g77.org/statement/getstatement.php?id=170327.

88 Rachel Tiller et al., "The Once and Future Treaty: Towards a New Regime for Biodiversity in Areas Beyond National Jurisdiction," *Marine Policy* 99 (2019): 239.

89 Ibid.

90 De Lucia, "The Question of the Common Heritage," 148; Qureshi, "Protecting the Common Heritage," 99.

govern biodiversity within national jurisdiction.[91] Paralleling developed nations' arguments about undermining intellectual property regimes, developing nations argue that failure to apply the CHM principle to biodiversity beyond national jurisdiction would conflict with the governance regime for biodiversity within national jurisdiction, especially with respect to the numerous marine species that traverse jurisdictional boundaries.[92]

Because UNCLOS is silent on the governance of biodiversity in ABNJ, neither of these positions is indisputably correct. An equally plausible read—especially accounting for the limited understanding of marine biodiversity beyond national jurisdiction at the time of UNCLOS' drafting—is that the treaty simply fails to address this issue, leaving a governance gap which either principle could legitimately fill. Further, as many commentators have stated, UNCLOS may be properly considered a "living treaty"—capable of adapting to new scientific understandings as well as evolving international norms and values.[93] Given UNCLOS' ambiguity and flexibility, pure legal arguments do not resolve the issue. Rather, which principle should guide the BBNJ Treaty is a normative question.

6 Normative Arguments

Normative arguments have also been raised on both sides of the debate, reflecting the persistence of fundamental ideological differences between developed and developing States. Developed States advocate for adherence to traditional governance principles, including freedom of the seas, which "ensure their continued ability to exploit ocean spaces and resources."[94] They reject any expansion of the CHM principle as an unacceptable "renegotiation of UNCLOS."[95] The United States, for example, maintains that considerations of economic equity fall outside the mandate of the BBNJ Treaty, which should merely implement UNCLOS provisions on the conservation and use of marine

91 De Lucia, "The Question of the Common Heritage," 154.

92 Ibid. It is interesting to note that in the case of the CBD, developed States advocated for CHM to apply to biodiversity within national jurisdiction, to allow outside scientists and industry to access natural resources that would otherwise be under the absolute control of sovereign states. Similarly, advocates on both sides of the BBNJ debate rely on the compatibility requirement but are selective in the existing regimes they cite.

93 *See, e.g.*, Jill Barrett & Richard Barnes (eds.), *Law of the Sea: UNCLOS as a Living Treaty* (London: British Institute of International and Comparative Law, 2016).

94 De Santo et al., "Stuck in the Middle with You," 3.

95 De Lucia, "The Question of the Common Heritage," 144.

biodiversity, not create mechanisms for redistributing global wealth or restructuring the global economic order.[96]

As during UNCLOS negotiations, developed nations advocate for freedom of the seas in order to promote capitalist values, including free, open, and competitive markets.[97] They raise concerns that application of the CHM principle, especially to MGRs, would stymie scientific advancement and innovation. Shifting from a regime that allows privatized study and exploitation of living resources to one that requires open and equal sharing of information and benefits, they argue, would disincentivize investment in scientific technologies, infrastructure, and research.[98] And, pointing to problems with implementation of the CHM principle to MGRs within national jurisdiction under the CBD and Nagoya Protocol, developed nations argue that the bureaucracy required to manage MGRs as CHM would further inhibit scientific research.[99] Fundamentally, developed nations are concerned with preserving the existing legal, political, and economic orders, under which they enjoy a dominant position.[100]

The normative values advanced by developing nations are the inverse of those put forth by their developed counterparts. Whereas developed nations advocate for adherence to preexisting norms, developing nations express discontent with a status quo that has left them perpetually subordinate. The dream of an alternative global order built around the values of equity, solidarity, and common interests persists. Developing States see this change as not only compatible with UNCLOS, but necessary to fulfill the Convention's promise of a more "just and equitable" future. As they did during negotiation of UNCLOS, developing States see CHM as a path to overdue change.[101]

Specifically, proponents of CHM point out that only a few States enjoy the scientific and technological resources needed to access and benefit from biodiversity in international waters, allowing those few to effectively monopolize a common good. For example, as one commentator points out, "98% of all patent sequences from MGRs are registered in 10 countries, leaving 165 countries underrepresented."[102] Without a mechanism to remedy

96 Vadrot et al., "Who Owns Marine Biodiversity?," table 1.

97 Ranganathan, "Decolonization and International Law," 178.

98 Vadrot et al., "Who Owns Marine Biodiversity?".

99 Ibid.

100 Ibid.; Philip E. Steinberg, *The Social Construction of the Ocean* (Cambridge: Cambridge Univ. Press, 2001).

101 Vadrot et al., "Who Owns Marine Biodiversity?".

102 Elizabeth M. De Santo et al, "Protecting Biodiversity in Areas Beyond National Jurisdiction: An Earth Systems Governance Perspective," *Earth Systems Governance*

this inequality, the gap between developed and developing states will only increase. In addition, developing States argue that persistent imbalances in resources and capacity prevents developing nations from engaging equally in conservation research and decision-making.[103] Put differently, unless the scientific and technological gap between developed and developing States is closed, not all countries will be able to fulfill their rights and obligations under the treaty.

Many developing States take the position that only strong implementation of the CHM principle can overcome these challenges. Perhaps mindful of the weak implementation of CHM under UNCLOS, the G77 and China advocate for specific means of implementing the principle. For example, with respect to MGRs, the G77 and China have stressed that benefit sharing must be mandatory, benefits must be equitably shared among all States, and both monetary and non-monetary benefits must be shared.[104]

Developing States also argue that CHM is essential to advance the conservation and sustainability goals of the BBNJ Treaty. For example, at IGC-3, the representative of Tuvalu on behalf of the Pacific Islands Forum stated that the Treaty should go beyond the status quo, to be more "ambitious and practical than existing frameworks." Likewise, the representative of the Philippines explained that the CHM principle was a necessary "anchor" to preserve and protect biodiversity as a common resource for the benefit of all. Calling on all nations to support the principle, he explained "[w]e must remember that, at the end of the day, we live in a common world and sail within a single sea."[105] Numerous other delegates also emphasized the fundamental importance of the ocean and its biodiversity to all humanity, and argued that CHM is the principle best suited to sustainably manage this common resource for the benefit of current and future generations.[106]

2 (2019): 1; Robert Blasiak et al., "Corporate Control and Global Governance of Marine Genetic Resources," *Science Advances* 4 (2018): 1.

103 S. Partelow, et al., "Tropical Marine Sciences: Knowledge Production in a Web of Path Dependencies," *PLOS One* 15(2) (2020): e0228613, https://doi.org/10.1371/journal.pone.0228613.

104 Marine Genetic Resources, Including Questions on the Sharing of Benefits, UN Doc CRP A/ CONF.232/2019/MGR/CRP.4 (2019).

105 United Nations, "New Oceans Treaty Must Be Robust, Practical in Application, Delegates Stress, Closing Third Round of Marine Biodiversity Negotiations," (Aug. 30, 2019), https://www.un.org/press/en/2019/sea2118.doc.html.

106 Ibid.; Vadrot et al., "Who Owns Marine Biodiversity?"

7 Moving Forward: Conservation and Sustainable Use Require Equity

The polarization between developed and developing states is grounded in a fundamental disagreement about the global status quo. Developed nations are largely comfortable with the current distribution of resources and power and resist addressing economic equity in the BBNJ Treaty. In contrast, developing nations are discontented, believing that UNCLOS promised a more "just and equitable" world that has yet to be achieved. They see the BBNJ Treaty as a mechanism to move closer to that ideal. As one commentator has put it, the dispute "stands for deeply rooted inequalities between traditional maritime powers and the developing world."[107] Yet in order to produce a legally binding treaty, some consensus must be reached.

One path to consensus could run through the Treaty's stated objectives, which point toward the values that must guide its implementation. The BBNJ Treaty is intended to facilitate "conservation" and "sustainable use" of marine biodiversity beyond national jurisdiction. The Treaty, moreover, is not being negotiated in a vacuum, but is intended to help achieve the sustainable development goals (SDGs), particularly SDG 14, Life Below Water. Indeed, it was at the 2012 U.N. Sustainable Development Conference that states first committed to drafting the BBNJ Treaty.[108] Put another way, the Treaty serves the global community's overarching goal to "promote sustainable development."[109]

That cannot be done without equity.[110] This reality is reflected in the U.N. Sustainable Development Agenda, which seek to achieve "peace and prosperity for people and the planet, now and into the future."[111] The SDGs aim to eradicate poverty, reduce inequality in and among countries, promote economic prosperity for all, and steward the environment for the well-being of current and future generations. SDG 14, which focuses particularly on oceans, contains equity targets including increasing economic benefits from sustainable use of

107 Vadrot et al., "Who Owns Marine Biodiversity?"

108 International Union for Conservation of Nature, "Marine Biodiversity of Areas Beyond National Jurisdiction (BBNJ)," https://www.iucn.org/theme/environmental-law/our-work/oceans-and-coasts/marine-biodiversity-areas-beyond-national-jurisdiction-bbnj.

109 United Nations, "The 17 Goals," https://sdgs.un.org/goals.

110 Osterblum et al., *Towards Ocean Equity*; Mark Fleurbaey et al., "Sustainable Development and Equity," in O. Edenhofer et al. (eds.) *Climate Change 2014: Mitigation of Climate Change; Contribution of Working Group III to the Fifth Assessment Report of the Intergovernmental Panel on Climate Change* (Cambridge: Cambridge Univ. Press, 2014); Sharon Beder, "Costing the Earth: Equity, Sustainable Development and Environmental Economics," *New Zealand Journal of Environmental Law* 4 (2000): 227.

111 United Nations, "The 17 Goals."

marine resources for small island developing States and least developed countries, increasing capacity development and transfer of marine technology, and "enhanc[ing] the contribution of marine biodiversity to the development of developing countries." Because historic injustices and entrenched inequities are the source of most sustainability challenges, equity is "integral" to achieving these goals.[112]

The desire to promote equality and economic prosperity is not new, nor is the recognition that achieving this goal requires redressing systemic injustice. This was, in fact, the platform that decolonizing States put forth in the 1970s with the NIEO. After the U.N. General Assembly adopted the "Declaration on the Granting of Independence to Colonial Countries and Peoples," much of the global South gained independence. But the dynamics of colonialism persisted. After decades, if not centuries, subject to political domination and economic exploitation, the nations that soon came to be known as "developing countries" lacked the political, economic, and institutional power of their "developed" counterparts.

The NIEO aimed to eradicate "inequities and injustices in the international system, eliminate the gap between developed and developing countries, ensure accelerating economic and social development, and secure peace and justice." This effort was to be based on principles of "equity, sovereign equality, interdependence, common interest, cooperation and solidarity among all States."[113] In other words, the NIEO aimed to achieve sustainable development.[114]

The U.N. General Assembly endorsed the NIEO in the 1970s, adopting the "Declaration on the Establishment of a New International Economic Order." But the "political leadership of the major powers of the north was unified in its disdain" for the ideology.[115] Absent support from developed nations, the NIEO faded away into obscurity, as neoliberalism—an ideology that rejects the notion of (and therefore entrenches) structural injustice—gained dominance in the 1980s.[116]

In the law of the sea context, this history played out through the strong expression of the CHM principle in UNCLOS, followed by its neutered

---

112 Osterblum et al., *Towards Ocean Equity*, 2; Mark Fleurbaey et al., "Sustainable Development and Equity," 287–88.

113 G.A. Res. 3201 (S-VI) (May 1, 1974).

114 Vinod K. Aggarwal & Steve Weber, "The New New International Economic Order," *Harvard Business Review* (Apr. 18, 2012), https://hbr.org/2012/04/the-new-new-international-econ.

115 Gilman, "The New International Economic Order: A Reintroduction."

116 Maurizio Lazzarato, "Neoliberalism in Action: Inequality, Insecurity and the Reconstitution of the Social," *Theory, Culture, & Society* 26 (2009): 109.

implementation. Likewise, UNCLOS' provisions for building equity, including through capacity development and transfer of marine technology, remain underdeveloped. And far from the justice and equity promised in UNCLOS' preamble, today inequity remains a "systemic feature" of the ocean economy and ocean governance.[117]

With the rise of the sustainable development paradigm, and especially the SDGs, the equity platform of the NIEO appears to be experiencing a rebirth—but with important differences. In contrast to the "disdain" developed nations felt for the NIEO, the U.N. Sustainable Development Agenda has been universally accepted; in fact, developed countries self-identify as champions of sustainable development.[118] Moreover, the problems of historic and structural injustice are increasingly acknowledged, and "[t]he international community increasingly recognises equity as central to achieving the SDGs."[119] While the SDG framework has been criticized by some as privileging the neoliberal paradigm rather than supporting the transformative shifts required for true sustainable development,[120] it is nevertheless true that the framework legitimizes the call for global equity.

To the extent that the global community—and developed nations in particular—are committed to sustainable development, they should make good on that commitment by instilling principles of equity into the BBNJ Treaty. This includes not only commitments to equity between developed and developing States and between current and future generations, but also consideration of non-State actors including Indigenous peoples, coastal communities, and non-self-governing territories.[121]

Moreover, as the weak implementation of the CHM principle in the Area shows, textual commitments to equity are not enough. They must be accompanied by mechanisms that will ensure meaningful implementation. This means designing systems that enable equal engagement among all nations in undertaking BBNJ activities and associated decision-making, provide fair

---

117 Osterblum et al., *Towards Ocean Equity*, 24.

118 OECD, "OECD and the Sustainable Development Goals: Delivering on Universal Goals and Targets," https://www.oecd.org/dac/sustainable-development-goals.htm; Anthony F. Pipa et al., "American Leadership in Advancing the SDGs to Achieve Equity and Sustainability," Brookings (Nov. 12, 2020), https://www.brookings.edu/blog/up-front/2020/11/12/american-leadership-in-advancing-the-sdgs-to-achieve-equity-and-sustainability/.

119 Osterblum et al., *Towards Ocean Equity*, 11.

120 Heloise Weber, "Politics of 'Leaving No One Behind': Contesting the 2030 Sustainable Development Goals Agenda," *Globalizations* 14 (2017): 399.

121 Clement Yow Mulalap et al., "Traditional Knowledge and the BBNJ Instrument," *Marine Policy* 122 (2020): 104103.

distribution of wealth and benefits, and ensure stewardship that protects the interests of future generations.[122]

8 Conclusion

Despite their express commitment to the sustainable development agenda, developed States have voiced fierce opposition to any inclusion of the CHM and the equitable principles it entails in the BBNJ Treaty. Developing states, meanwhile, insist that the CHM must govern. Although the CHM principle remains contentious, the concept of sustainable development is universally accepted. Reframing the conversation in terms of sustainability could lend legitimacy to developing States' position. While anchoring the BBNJ Treaty to CHM could have the benefit of clarifying and strengthening that principle in the Area, it may be driving developed State resistance.

Regardless of the framing ultimately employed, all States should remember their goal of sustainable development and, to that end, meaningfully commit to equity in the BBNJ Treaty. Human well-being depends upon the sustainable management of the ocean and its resources, and sustainable management requires equity. The BBNJ Treaty—if implemented with this goal in mind—could, at last, help create the "more just and equitable" world promised by UNCLOS.[123]

---

122 It should be noted that procedural equity is also important. This means recognizing the sovereign equality of all nations through equal voice and participatory power. At IGC-3, several delegations referenced this issue, requesting, for example, that parallel sessions be minimized to enable smaller delegations to participate as much as possible and that developed states make contributions to the voluntary fund to support participation of delegations from least developed countries.

123 UNCLOS, Preamble.

Index

www.ingramcontent.com/pod-product-compliance
Lightning Source LLC
Chambersburg PA
CBHW070248260926
51849CB00001BA/37
9789004514201